I0138873

A HOUSE IN THE HOMELAND

✳ WORLDING THE MIDDLE EAST

A House in the Homeland

ARMENIAN PILGRIMAGES TO PLACES OF ANCESTRAL MEMORY

Carel Bertram

STANFORD UNIVERSITY PRESS

STANFORD, CALIFORNIA

STANFORD UNIVERSITY PRESS
Stanford, California

©2022 by Carel Bertram. All rights reserved.

No part of this book may be reproduced or transmitted in any form or by any means, electronic or mechanical, including photocopying and recording, or in any information storage or retrieval system without the prior written permission of Stanford University Press.

Printed in the United States of America on acid-free, archival-quality paper

MAP © Carel Bertram. Excerpt from "What I Can Tell You" is reproduced with the permission of Gregory Djanikian and Carnegie Mellon University Press.

Library of Congress Cataloging-in-Publication Data

Names: Bertram, Carel, 1943– author.
Title: A house in the homeland : Armenian pilgrimages to places of ancestral memory / Carel Bertram.
Other titles: Worlding the Middle East.
Description: Stanford, California : Stanford University Press, [2022] | Series: Worlding the Middle East | Includes bibliographical references and index.
Identifiers: LCCN 2021045116 (print) | LCCN 2021045117 (ebook) | ISBN 9781503630208 (cloth) | ISBN 9781503631649 (paperback) | ISBN 9781503631656 (ebook)
Subjects: LCSH: Armenians—Travel—Turkey. | Pilgrims and pilgrimages—Turkey. | Armenian Genocide, 1915–1923. | Armenian diaspora. | Collective memory.
Classification: LCC DS172.2 .B47 2022 (print) | LCC DS172.2 (ebook) | DDC 956.6/20154—dc23/eng/20211012
LC record available at https://lccn.loc.gov/2021045116
LC ebook record available at https://lccn.loc.gov/2021045117

Cover design: Angela Moody

Cover image: The town of Yozgat by Vahan Berberian, painted from memory in 1911. Used with permission from his great niece Mary Ann Arakelian Kazanjian.

Typeset by Newgen in Arno Pro 11/14

To Denise Spellberg:

For her mentoring, supported by a dialogue of the mind—and framed by her heart.

To the memory of my mother, Manya Bertram:

For her life's work of Tikkun Olam based on her authentic, energetic, selfless love for people.

And to Armen Aroyan:

For the power of his pilgrimages, and for accepting me.

Contents

Note on Language, Transliteration, and Place-Names

TURKISH LANGUAGE AND TRANSLITERATIONS[1]

Those ancestors and elders of the Western Armenian pilgrims who spoke and read Turkish used Arabic orthography. This was replaced by the Roman alphabet according to the language reforms of the early Turkish Republic. This book uses only this romanized Turkish alphabet, whether referring to the Ottoman or the Republican period. Here is a guide to the pronunciation of letters not used in the English alphabet, or used differently than in English:

C "j" as in "journey"

Ç "ch" as in "cherry"

Ğ (soft g) lengthens the sound of the vowel preceding it; silent when between two vowels

I (dotless i [ɪ]) "i" as in "girl" or "thinner"

İ (dotted i, also dotted as a capital letter) "ee" as in "tree." Note the difference between the two "I"s in the Turkish spelling of "Diyarbakır"

Ö "u" as in "turn" or "eu" in French "feu"

Ş "sh" as in "shallow"

Ü "u" as in "cube" or "u" as in French "aigu"

EASTERN AND WESTERN ARMENIAN LANGUAGE AND TRANSLITERATIONS

Many of my print sources are in Armenian—as were many of my oral sources. When a source uses the Armenian alphabet and orthography, I have tried to supply a pronounceable Roman alphabet transliteration of the Western Armenian spelling, as Western Armenian is the language spoken by the people who appear in this book. However, I preserve Eastern Armenian spelling when it appears in the title of a book or in a WorldCat entry. And when the name of an author or other individual is typically given in Eastern spelling, I use that spelling or I give both the Eastern and Western spellings.

GEOGRAPHICAL PLACE-NAMES

Similarly, I have used the Western Armenian spellings of geographical place-names, as used by the pilgrims or known by their elders and ancestors. When possible, I include known variants. Providing place-names is further complicated by people's frequent use of the name of a larger town (e.g., Van) to stand in for the name of a small village (e.g., Ankugh) in the larger town's orbit.[2] I have also included current Turkish (T:) place-names, where applicable, to help readers find or research their hometowns. These Turkish names appear with the first substantive reference to a place.

Only a hundred or so of the thousands of Historical Armenia's villages [and towns] are visited or referenced in this book. Nonetheless, this is still too many to represent on our map. Moreover, those that do appear are given only approximate locations. For exact locations of any places mentioned in this book, readers may enter the current Turkish (T:) place-name here: https://nisanyanmap.com/.

HISTORICAL ARMENIA

Պոլիս BOLIS
CONSTANTINOPLE
ISTANBUL

Samsun

Ordu

Trabzon

Merzifon

Amasya

Shabinkarahisar

Yozgat

Tokat

Sis-
Çataloluk

Govdun
Sivas

Erzincan

Agn

Dzak
Arapgir

Aghen

Munjusun

Gesi

Kayseri

Kharpert
Husenig
Elazig Mezre

Tomarza

Chunkush

Malatya

Zeytun

Marash

Jibin

Viranshehir
Urfa

Mersin

Sis

Antep

Hasanbeyli

Adana

Kilis

The
MEDITERRANEAN

Aleppo

Երկիր
HOMELAND
YERGIR

Musa Dagh

Carel Bertram
2021

EUPHRATES R.

The BLACK SEA

Kars ○

Ani ○

ARAXES R.

Erzurum ○ ○ Dzitogh

Mt. Ararat

Keghi ○

○ Bingöl

MURAT R.

Aghtamar

Van ○
○ Ankugh
Lake Van

○ Moush
○ Sasun
○ Bitlis

Lidje ○

Diyarbakir ○

AND I CAN TELL YOU
  THAT THE DREAM I HAVE
IS TO WALK BACK TO THIS VILLAGE
AND STAND IN THE SQUARE
  FOR A MOMENT,
FEELING THE HISTORY OF IT
  ON MY SKIN,
A HISTORY OF DEPARTURES,
VANISHINGS.
                    Gregory Djanikian

TIGRIS R.

THINNING THE VEIL

ENCOUNTERING JESUS CHRIST IN THE BOOK OF REVELATION

SHANE J. WOOD

ivp
Academic

An imprint of InterVarsity Press
Downers Grove, Illinois

InterVarsity Press
P.O. Box 1400 | Downers Grove, IL 60515-1426
ivpress.com | email@ivpress.com

©2025 by Shane Joseph Wood

All rights reserved. No part of this book may be reproduced in any form without written permission from InterVarsity Press.

InterVarsity Press® is the publishing division of InterVarsity Christian Fellowship/USA®. For more information, visit intervarsity.org.

All Scripture quotations, unless otherwise indicated, are translated by the author.

While any stories in this book are true, some names and identifying information may have been changed to protect the privacy of individuals.

The publisher cannot verify the accuracy or functionality of website URLs used in this book beyond the date of publication.

Cover design: Faceout Studio, Tim Green
Interior design: Jeanna Wiggins
Images: © duncan1890 / DigitalVision Vectors via Getty Images

ISBN 978-1-5140-0922-2 (print) | ISBN 978-1-5140-0923-9 (digital)

Printed in the United States of America ♾

Library of Congress Cataloging-in-Publication Data
A catalog record for this book is available from the Library of Congress.

32   31   30   29   28   27   26   25 | 13   12   11   10   9   8   7   6   5   4

"What an exciting and engaging exploration of the book of Revelation! Shane Wood reminds us what this book is all about: a revelation of Jesus Christ. He doesn't give you all the answers—but he ensures you are asking the right questions."

Ian Paul, author of *Revelation: An Introduction and Commentary* (Tyndale New Testament Commentaries)

"Shane Wood's *Thinning the Veil* offers a thick exposition of the book of Revelation. The book is historically informed and exegetically rich yet offers an accessible explanation to one of the most mystifying books in the Bible. Wood's approach combines textual analysis with takeaways and practical tips for reading that will enrich readers of the New Testament."

Michael F. Bird, deputy principal at Ridley College in Melbourne, Australia

"This book preaches! Nothing like a traditional commentary, *Thinning the Veil* speaks to the heart, opening up the book of Revelation as it is meant to be done—one eye on the text, the other on our lives. Deeply aware that the last book of the Bible does not offer fortune telling cartography but aims to soften our hearts to the intimacy of a crucified and risen King, Shane Wood opens our eyes to just how tantalizingly thin the veil between heaven and earth has become in our incarnate Lord. Meditate on this book; it models a combination of scholarly depth and spiritual direction."

Hans Boersma, professor at Nashotah House Theological Seminary in Wisconsin and author of *Pierced by Love*

"It truly is difficult to overstate how poetic, prophetic, and breathtaking this accessible journey through John's Apocalypse is. Not only did it help me read the revelation of Jesus Christ better historically, theologically, and exegetically, but I walked away with a deeper love for God. Shane Wood has written a masterful book that deserves a wide reading."

A.J. Swoboda, associate professor of Bible and theology at Bushnell University and author of *The Gift of Thorns*

"Too often, focus on finding a 'road map' for the end times misses the truth that Revelation is about Jesus Christ! Shane Wood does a marvelous job unveiling Jesus in this challenging Bible book. His moving illustrations and strong applications draw the reader into the heart of Revelation and, indeed, into the very heart of God. Accompanying tools (including videos) present practical ways to enter Revelation's text in a transforming way. Well-researched and compellingly written, this book offers insights for those new to Revelation and those who already love its revelation of Jesus."

Dana M. Harris, professor and chair of the New Testament department at Trinity Evangelical Divinity School

TO MY CHILDREN:

ZION, PAIGE, MADDOX, AND ROBERT

You are my compass

Ever guiding me to God

Ever teaching me his grace

Ever challenging me to be a

better father today than I was before

When I look at you

I know who I am

And who I want to become

CONTENTS

LIST OF ILLUSTRATIONS

ACKNOWLEDGMENTS

THIS BOOK WAS WRITTEN OVER SEVERAL MONTHS in various locations in seven different cities, ranging from my home in Joplin, Missouri, to museums in Bentonville, Arkansas, to libraries in Houston and Boston and coffee shops in New York and San Antonio. To this balcony here in Athens, Greece, overlooking the bustlings of life, love, and worry.

Each environment added different textures to the content herein, different challenges and perspectives, ever expanding my understanding and my capacity to receive more. More of God's creation. More of the Spirit's transformation. More of the Revelation of Jesus Christ.

Right now, I'm thankful. For the journey. For the failures. For more than what words can contain.

I'm grateful for Rachel Hastings and the entire team at InterVarsity Press. Rachel was excited about this project within the first few moments of our conversation at the Society of Biblical Literature conference in Denver, and her passion for this book hasn't waned to date. Even in moments of my own doubt, she counseled with unwavering confidence. What's before you simply isn't what it would've been without her care and expertise.

I'm grateful for the kindness and hospitality of the staff at the Hephzibah House (NYC) and the Lanier Theological Library (Houston). The excellent accommodations were only exceeded by their warmth and grace, even when I set off the alarm at the library early on a Sunday morning. In particular, Drew Davis and David Capes deserve unique thanks. Drew's relentless support and David's tender care will not be quickly forgotten.

Others showed their support through countless conversations, edits, texts, and encouraging words. Thanks to Rebecca Gill, Murphy Alvis, my guys in

the Josey Wales club, and my students in both undergrad and grad courses on the book of Revelation.

Chris Breuer, research assistant par excellence: thank you for your patience and persistence. Regardless of the request or challenge, you never wavered in your drive for excellence.

Justin Miller, thank you for your consistent care and encouragement throughout this process even as you were battling your own beasts.

Sergio Rizo, you, my friend, are a constant. In highs and lows, you call me to be more than I am today, reminding me of the power of the elephant. I'm better with you in my life.

Justin Wood, you are an ever-present support. One of the only people I know who reads everything I write, regardless of the drivel I produce. That consistent presence is felt and deeply appreciated. Thank you, brother.

To my parents, my brothers and sisters, nieces and nephews. You are a joy I don't get to swim in as much as I desire, and yet each interaction is a gift I treasure. I love you.

To my children, to whom this book is dedicated: I see God in you. You teach me more about his love and grace, mercy and hope than any degree I possess. My love for you is without end.

To my wife, Sara. Words cannot express my love for you. My gratitude for you. The last few years, we've walked through the fires and floods arm in arm, trusting God will respond. Watching you unfold has been one of my greatest joys to date. Doing life with you is the greatest gift God has given me. As always: I love you. Same. Ditto.

ABBREVIATIONS

Primary sources

Aem.   Plutarch, *Aemilius Paullus*

Ann.   Tacitus, *Annales*

Ant. rom.   Dionysius of Halicarnassus, *Antiquitates romanae*

Dom.   Suetonius, *Domitianus*

Ep. Pont.   Ovid, *Epistulae ex Ponto*

Hist. Rom.   *History of Rome*

J.W.   Josephus, *Jewish War*

LXX   Septuagint

Mith.   Appian, *Mithridatic Wars*

Nat.   Pliny the Elder, *Naturalis historia*

Pun.   Appian, *Punic Wars*

Res gest.   Augustus, *Res gestae divi Augusti*

Verr.   Cicero, *In Verrem*

Secondary sources

ANF   *The Ante-Nicene Fathers*. Edited by Alexander Roberts and James Donaldson. 1885–1887. 10 vols. Repr., Peabody, MA: Hendrickson, 1994

AUSS   *Andrew University Seminary Studies*

LCL   Loeb Classical Library

NIGTC   New International Greek Testament Commentary

PG   Patrologia Graeca [= *Patrologiae Cursus Completus*: Series Graeca]. Edited by Jacques-Paul Migne. 162 vols. Paris, 1857–1886

RIC 1   Sutherland, C. H. V. *31 BC to AD 69, Augustus to Vitellius*. Vol. 1 of *Roman Imperial Coinage*. 2nd ed. London: Spink, 1984

RIC 2   Mattingly, Harold, and Edward Allen Sydenham. *Vespasian–*
              Hadrian (69–138). Volume 2 of *Roman Imperial Coinage.* London:
              Spink, 1986
WBC   Word Biblical Commentary

Introduction

THE REVELATION
OF JESUS CHRIST
(Revelation 1:1)

[The Apocalypse] is a revelation of Jesus Christ. . . . It is a thoroughly
christological mystery, a possibility that arises first through
the incarnation. The Son possesses [this mystery] in its fullness,
one he can share with his believers and gives to John as first in love.

ADRIENNE VON SPEYR

REVELATION DOESN'T START WHERE WE ASSUME. We expect prophetic utterances that predict the future. Maybe our future. Maybe someone
else's. Or maybe just the cataclysmic end of all things.

Yet, Revelation doesn't begin here. It doesn't situate the reader at the table
of a cosmic fortuneteller ready to divine the Christian tea leaves designed to
serve our desire to control and conquer what will be. No, Revelation overlooks our interests and sidesteps our questions, evading our expectations
altogether in search of something greater. Something deeper. Something
more along the lines of healing and transformation than fortunetelling and
code cracking.

Revelation thins the veil separating heaven and earth to provide perspective and a path to overcome what's broken in us, around us, and because

---

From an untranslated spiritual commentary on Revelation by Adrienne von Speyr. The translation is
my own.

of us. Revelation reaches into the recesses of our souls to confront the portions we've entrusted to the darkness instead of the light. Revelation unveils mysteries of healing located only when "in the Spirit" (Rev 1:10) and opposes the deceptions of death imprisoning Christian and non-Christian alike.[1]

Woven into the scenes of beasts, battles, and satanic suffering is a clarion call for all to "come." To drink deep of the streams of living water. To taste the fruit of the tree of life. To join the choir of heaven singing songs of God's redemption and reign. Not just in the future but in the here and now.

More than prediction, Revelation is an invitation. An invocation. An encounter with the Word become flesh, with the conqueror of death, with the crucified King. With the Son of Man seated at the right hand of the Father, who, by God's grace, walks among the lampstands both comforting and confronting a world captivated by conflict.

THE LAST AND THE FIRST

Last words of a loved one are treasures beyond measure. We race overnight to their deathbed, hoping to hear one last word. If, by God's grace, they do speak, we gather each word into the box of our heart and label it "Fragile: Handle with care."

I still cling to the last words my mentor ever said to me. I dust them off, especially on dark days, and recite them to remind me of my anchor. He was diagnosed with terminal cancer, and mere months before he passed, we stood by his car readied to venture home. We embraced, knowing this could be our last goodbye. Then, he stepped back, held my shoulders, and gently repeated three or four times, "Shane, just hold on to Jesus. *Just hold on to Jesus.*" We wiped our tears. Allowed the silence to speak love's three words. And he drove away.

My grandma's last words were more simple, if not more circuitous. Struggling with Alzheimer's, she repeated the same dialogue with me several times, always beginning with, "Well, Shane-daner! When did you get here?" I'd tell her we just arrived. She'd look around the room, point at my daughter, and lean over with hushed tones, "Well, who is that young lady?"

Smiling, I'd respond, "Well, Mamaw, that's my daughter Paige."

---

[1] All translations are my own unless otherwise noted.

Lunging back in her chair, she'd look at me exasperated (with a tinge of confusion), "No! You're not old enough to have a daughter that age?"

I'd nod my head, smiling back (with a tinge of sadness). "Yep, that's my baby girl."

She'd laugh, shake her head, and softly say, "Well, I just can't believe it."

We'd pause for a moment or two. She'd reach for my hand, placing it between hers. With tears welling up, she'd whisper, "I'm really glad you're here."

Shortly thereafter, she'd look around the room, glance up at me, and her eyes would widen, "Well, Shane-daner! When did you get here?" Repeating the dialogue anew. Time and again. Grace upon grace.

Last words are as precious as they are rife with meaning. They capture a piece of our heart if not our curiosity. They direct our paths if not our questions. They are treasured and repeated, and serve as guides for what comes next.

Last words matter. And first words are no different.

I'll never forget when my oldest son, Zion, said my name. It was the same electricity I'd feel when all four of my kids would gibber the same two syllables, "Da-da." For weeks, he'd been jabbering and grunting, without any discernible patterns, but I was still straining and hoping he'd parrot my exaggerated pleas, "Say *da-da*. . . . Say *daaaa-daaaa*."

Finally, it happened. Sitting in his highchair, looking intently at a piece of mashed food, with slobber soaking his onesie, without my prompting, amid his indiscernible gibberish, yet clearly and without question, I heard it: "Da-da."

I jumped up and let out a cry that startled him to tears. But that's okay; I was crying too. Moments later, after he and I both gathered ourselves, he said it again, "Da-da." A name with variations I never tire of hearing. But the first time is simply precious. Because, like last words, first words matter.

Whether the words come in the opening scene or at the final bow, first and last words matter because they communicate *what we value*. What we cherish. Where our heart resides, and where our hope finds its home.

And the book of Revelation is no different.

FIRST WORDS MATTER

John begins Revelation with five words. Five words often forgotten as the revelation unfolds, lost in the chaos of commentaries, prophecy experts, and

rapture debates. Five words that summarize the heart of this book and the blessed Seer on Patmos: "The revelation of Jesus Christ" (Rev 1:1).

John writes this letter in exile on the island of Patmos. In exile for testifying to "the Word of God and the testimony of Jesus" (Rev 1:9). In exile from the seven churches of Asia Minor (Rev 1:4, 11). Seven churches living life in the shadow of the Roman Empire, struggling with conflict and compromise, disorientation and despair. Seven churches desperate for a word from the Lord. Desperate for understanding and explanation. Desperate for a revelation of Jesus Christ.

For many interpreters, though, that simply isn't enough. "Revelation must be more," they implore. Somehow prediction seems far more satisfying than simply Jesus. A chronological road map of the future seems far more intriguing than depictions and declarations of Christ.

Several years ago, I was in Russia teaching Revelation. Over several sessions, I proclaimed the power of the first five words of this book, "The Revelation of Jesus Christ." I emphasized the Word's pervasiveness in the words of Revelation. I explained how whether we're in the seals, the trumpets, or the bowls, or confronted by dragons, beasts, or false prophets, the goal is the same: *reveal Jesus.*

In the final session, however, the paterfamilias of the church unveiled his displeasure. Boris was a quintessential Russian: thick goatee, strong physique, and an oversized furry hat with optional flaps. When he spoke, others listened. His voice boomed with authority.

He began his "question" by pounding his fist on the table, flushing his cheeks with red strain. The interpreter translated the first line or two and then went silent as Boris increased his volume and pace. I quickly realized the interpreter was censoring this eruption for my sake. For three full minutes, everyone sat still as Boris unleashed his frustration with ever-increasing intensity.

And then the room fell silent.

No one moved.

Boris too.

Slowly, the interpreter turned to me and said, "Umm. . . . He says . . . well, ummm . . . if what you are saying is right, then . . . umm . . . then the book of Revelation is no different from any other book of the New Testament."

Immediately, I replied, "Tell him he's right."

"What?!?!" the interpreter fired back.

"Tell him *he's right*," I restated. "That's exactly what I'm saying. I'm saying the book of Revelation is doing the same thing as Matthew, as John, as Acts, as Romans, as 1 Peter: it's revealing *Jesus Christ*."

You see, first words matter. They express value. They guide our steps. They communicate the center of our hearts. Revelation begins not by accident but on purpose with these five words: *the Revelation of Jesus Christ*.

Why? Because in times of struggle, in times of rebellion, in times of spiritual, physical, or emotional conflict, what we need most is a revelation of Jesus Christ. A picture so pristine and crystalline that no guesses are necessary or debates possible or predictions needed. For the Alpha and the Omega, the Beginning and the End, is present, ready to walk with us, come what may.

The first words of the Apocalypse, then, are not to be discarded, overlooked, or ignored. They are our guide. They are the center of what follows. They express what John values, even if we don't.

QUESTIONING OUR ASSUMPTIONS

Regardless of how creative or forceful we become, Revelation is steadfast in its intention. Relentless in its determination to reveal Jesus. We offer blood-red moons predicting the end of all; Revelation offers Jesus. We sleuth presidential candidates for marks of the beast; Revelation offers Jesus. In place of the rapture or seven years of tribulation or the emergence of an antichrist, Revelation emphatically and without reserve unveils Jesus. Simply Jesus. Which creates tension. Why? Because Revelation doesn't start where *we* assume, comply with *our* demands, or find value in our *countless* attempts to apprehend the future.

Consider the tendency to approach Revelation as a *chronological road map of the future*. An approach that *assumes* Revelation sleuthed adequately will reveal the sequence of events leading up to and including the end of the world. Revelation, then, is dissected and parsed for clues to the rise of China or your run-of-the-mill Apache helicopter—clues that, when woven together with the headlines of the latest news feed, can reveal whether we are in the middle of the fourth seal or the third trumpet or the sixth bowl. Clues that reveal *when* the world will end. Or so we assume.

Assumptions influence vision and guide our questions. If Revelation is a chronological road map of the future, then our questions demand the text to answer: "When will the world end? How will we know it's drawing near? What signs signal the coming rapture? Is [fill in the name of a political enemy] the antichrist?" These questions and endless others are understandable if we assume Revelation intends to predict. But what if Revelation doesn't want to answer these questions? What if Revelation simply isn't interested in providing a road map for the future at all? Will we allow the text to speak? Or will we just shout our questions all the more loudly, with hands pressed over our ears like the Sanhedrin storming Stephen with stones (Acts 7:54-60)?

The problem with this chronological-road-map-of-the-future approach is that it simply ignores the text. It overlooks the original readers (Rev 1:4, 11; 2:1–3:20). Treats the first five words like fodder for the fire of the future just waiting to be deciphered by the next prophecy expert to tackle the jigsaw puzzle of the Apocalypse. In fact, it ignores not just the first five words but the entire text. The imagery. The message. The transformation Revelation targets that stretches far beyond a prediction—road map or otherwise.

WRECKING OUR ROAD MAPS

Take, for example, Revelation 6:12, "And I watched as he opened the sixth seal." The pronouns of this sentence summarize the first five and a half chapters of the Apocalypse. "I" is John, and "he" is Jesus. In Revelation 1, John is exiled on the island of Patmos (Rev 1:9) when the cosmic Christ appears before him radiant (Rev 1:16), with a voice as strong and soothing as "the sound of many waters" (Rev 1:15; see Rev 1:10). Jesus commissions John to deliver God's message to the seven churches in Asia Minor (Rev 1:11, 19; 2:1–3:22), a message unfolding in Revelation 2–3 in red letters.

In Revelation 4, John is transported from Patmos to a rhapsodic worship service in the heavenly throne room (Rev 4:1-2), complete with "flashes of lightning and rumblings and peals of thunder" (Rev 4:5). Twenty-four regally arrayed elders surround the throne (Rev 4:4, 10-11) as four living creatures (Rev 4:6-8) cry out day and night without ceasing, "Holy, Holy, Holy is the Lord God, the Almighty one, the one who was and is and is to come" (Rev 4:8).

As the adulation reverberates in the heavenly halls, John's attention is arrested by a scroll secured with seven seals in God's right hand (Rev 5:1).

Tension builds. No one in heaven or on earth, in the sea or on the land, alive or dead, is worthy to break the seals, to receive this word from the Lord, to peer inside this divine scroll (Rev 5:2-3).

And so, John weeps (Rev 5:4). Desperate for a word from the Lord, the Seer sobs in anguish.

Yet, like at the sight of a morning star heralding the dawn of a new day (Rev 2:28; 22:16), the tension and the tears wither away with the pronouncement of the Lion of the tribe of Judah (Rev 5:5). The *one* who is worthy. The *one* who appears, though, not as a proud Lion but as a slain Lamb (Rev 5:6). Sovereignty secured through sacrifice. Sacrifice that purchased for God every tribe, tongue, people, and nation, transforming them into a kingdom and priests (Rev 5:9-10).

In Revelation 6, the Lamb opens the first four seals to reveal four horsemen hell-bent on conquest (Rev 6:2), the violent eviction of peace (Rev 6:4), the grieving of economies (Rev 6:6), and the exaltation of death over life, war over peace, plague over plenty (Rev 6:8). In short, devastation that's vast yet familiar to John and the seven churches living under Rome's reign.

Unfortunately, the fifth seal offers little respite. John sees souls of the martyrs in heaven, who, like the Lamb, were slain for their witness (Rev 6:9). They're crying out a haunting query: "Sovereign Lord, the holy and true one, how long until you judge the earth dwellers and avenge our blood?" (Rev 6:10).

Then comes the sixth seal in Revelation 6:12: "And I [John] watched as he [the slain Lamb] opened the sixth seal." A massive earthquake signals the shaking of the heavens, with the dramatic pronouncement that "the *stars in the sky fell to earth*, as a fig tree casts its unripe figs when shaken by intense wind" (Rev 6:13). This verse presents a significant problem for our chronological road maps of the future. Namely, if just *one* star were to fall from the sky and collide with the earth, the world and life as we know it would be over. No tomorrow. No "and then . . ." No chance for a seventh seal.

And this shouldn't be controversial. The sun at the center of our solar system is an average-sized star. It has a diameter of over 860,000 miles of fire, gas, and mass. The earth's diameter is 7,918 miles. If the earth and the sun collided, the sun would be fine. The earth, on the other hand? Not fine. Incinerated. Destroyed. No more.

And that's just *one* star. Revelation 6:13 says "stars." More than one.

At this point, our chronological road map of the future encounters a serious dilemma: the world appears to end, but we're only in Revelation 6. We still have sixteen more chapters to go. And if we keep on reading, it just gets worse. "The sky peeled off like a scroll being rolled up, and *every* mountain and island was removed from its place" (Rev 6:14). If by some miraculous fluke the massive stars didn't decisively annihilate the globe, removing "*every* mountain and island" would hardly be a welcomed encore. By itself, landmass expulsion of this sort would be so cataclysmic for the earth, its climate, and all creation that it too would be the end of life as we know it. But, once again, we're still only in Revelation 6.

And, once again, continuing to read doesn't alleviate the tension; it strains the road map greater still:

> And the kings of the earth, the important persons, the generals, the rich, the powerful, and everyone, slave and free, concealed themselves in the caves and in the rocks of the mountains. And they cried out to the mountains and the rocks, "Fall on us and hide us from the face of the one sitting on the throne and from the wrath of the Lamb, because *the great day of their wrath has* come, and who can stand?" (Rev 6:15-17)

As creation upheaves, evil cries out and clings to the earth as its salvation. The honesty of their question is rivaled only by their despair. The great day of God's wrath has come, "and who can stand?" Throughout the Old and New Testaments, the "great day of God's wrath" is also known as judgment day. Or the end of everything. The end of rebellion, pain, death, and sin; the beginning of harmony, rest, community, and complete restoration. The end of old creation, and the beginning of everything new.

At this point, I don't know how John could be more clear. The astral shower (Rev 6:13), the earth-mass eradication (Rev 6:14), and the day of judgment (Rev 6:15-17) all point to one event: *the end of the world*. If this is true, the chronological-road-map assumption suffers quite a bit—because we're only in Revelation 6. We still have sixteen more chapters to go. And the world's denouement has already arrived.

And if we keep reading, it only gets worse. Judgment day reappears five chapters later, this time in the seventh trumpet: "And the nations raged with fury but were confronted by your wrath. And *the time has come to judge the*

dead—to reward your servants, the prophets, and the holy ones (both small and great), the ones revering your name, and to destroy those who destroy the earth" (Rev 11:18).

Once again, judgment day. The *end of the world.* The problem is, *once again*, we still have eleven chapters to go. And the world has come to its end twice.

In fact, the book of Revelation comes to the end of the world over and over and over and over again: seven times, by my count (Rev 6; 11; 14; 16; 19; 20; 21). Why? Because Revelation's target is bigger than mere prediction or for-tunetelling cartography. Each time the "end of the world" is invoked, it is in service of a greater aim: thinning the veil. Revealing Jesus Christ. Trans-forming those with ears to hear what the Spirit says to the churches.

Indeed, when our assumptions about the text guide our questions for the text, chaos ensues, climaxing in a confrontation between what we demand and what the text demands from us. The question is, Who will win?

THE REVELATION OF JESUS CHRIST

Revelation doesn't match our expectations for chronological road maps. But that's good news, not something to lament. More than prediction or seven years of tribulation, Revelation was written to reveal Jesus. To unveil Christ. To open our eyes, soften our hearts, entice our ears to hear the message of the crucified King, now risen and reigning. A message typically forgotten in times of trial, in moments of disarray, in worlds caught up in the torrent of tragedy and war. A message the seven churches of Asia Minor desperately needed to hear—and a message we desperately need to overhear today.

What follows in the rest of this book is not a verse-by-verse commentary, although all twenty-two chapters of Revelation are mined deeply. It's not an exhaustive exploration of every theological issue, although theological wres-tlings abound. It is a work of the academy and the church, the classroom and the pew. Exegetical and academic without ignoring application and implica-tions for today. Yes, scholarly citations arise, although not at the rate some may prefer. But this is intentional. For what follows is an exploration of John's Apocalypse governed by the first five words, guided by God's revelation em-bodied in Christ's incarnation, the person of Jesus who housed heaven and earth in one flesh. And the results are striking.

"The Revelation of Jesus Christ" reveals that the veil between heaven and earth is not as thick as we assume (chapter 1), inviting the possibility for an intimacy far more piercing than many understand or prefer (chapter 2). The unveiling of *who God is* and *what God has done* (chapter 3) provides clarity for our worship and our war with the world (chapter 4), revealing a God in desperate pursuit of all, including enemies (chapter 5). Clarifying God's identity clarifies who the true enemy is (chapter 6) and how to fight that enemy effectively (chapter 7). The life and death of Jesus unveil the true nature of evil (chapter 8) and remind us that in Christ we are victorious, despite what the world may say and our sufferings may accept (chapter 9). Through the cross of Christ, union with God is once again possible. A union lost in Genesis 3 yet restored in Revelation 21–22 through God's pursuit of his beloved creation (chapter 10).

However naive it may seem, John believed that Christ's identity, Jesus' story, "the revelation of Jesus Christ" (Rev 1:1), was our guide. Not just in the highs but in the lows, not just in wealth but in poverty, not just in Revelation 1 but in all the words that come thereafter. In Christ, the veil becomes quite thin, revealing heaven's resolute opposition to our brokenness. To our wounds. To the barriers between humanity and divinity that, whether real or perceived, prevent us from receiving God's grace like healing rain reviving a parched land.

Indeed, Revelation begins with Jesus. And deep loneliness.

GOING DEEPER

At the end of each chapter, there are additional exercises and resources to more deeply unearth the text and yourself. These additions are organized under three headings:

> *The tool*—videos/exercises engaging a principle to interpret Scripture
> *The text*—videos/exercises engaging aspects of the chapter's Revelation text
> *The takeaway*—Spiritual practices/questions to invite the Word to penetrate your soul

Each element can be used individually or as a group, discussed aloud or written in a journal for personal study. Each category may build on something in the present chapter or a prior chapter, or set up conversations in

chapters to come. The idea is to partner with the Spirit to engage the text with your mind and more.

For this chapter, explore the following elements:

> **THE TOOL:** Context. If we take the Bible out of context, we can make the Bible say whatever we want. Whether intentional or not, the temptation to transform the Word of God into our image (instead of the opposite) is treacherous. Watch this video on context (www.ivpress.com/wood-intro-a) and wrestle with the following questions:

1. Have you ever had your words taken out of context? If so, explain the situation, how it made you feel, how you responded, and how you wish you would've responded.

2. What are the dangers of taking the Bible out of context? How does this danger apply to Revelation in particular?

3. How could understanding the biblical context help us interpret and apply Scripture more effectively?

> **THE TEXT:** The Revelation of Jesus Christ (Rev 1:1). "The Revelation of Jesus Christ" offers insights into the relationship between God and humanity, heaven and earth. After watching this video (www.ivpress .com/wood-intro-b), answer the following questions:

1. Is Jesus truly enough? Are we more in love with knowing the future or knowing God's face revealed in Christ?

2. Why is prediction so enticing for humanity? What's the relationship between prediction and power?

3. What revelation is Christ challenging you with in this season of life?

> **THE TAKEAWAY:** Praying through God's Word. If Revelation's goal isn't prediction of the future but transformation of the reader, then approaching Scripture to more clearly hear the Spirit is essential. What follows is an ancient Christian prayer practice centered on God's Word called lectio divina. Here's how it works:

First movement: Reading the text

1. Read Revelation 1:1-6 aloud two times slowly.

2. Sit in silence for one to two minutes, asking the Spirit to surface a word or phrase from the text.

3. Write down the word or phrase the Spirit unearthed without any elaboration.

Second movement: Reflecting on God's Word

1. Read Revelation 1:1-6 aloud for a third time.

2. Sit in silence for two to three minutes, reflecting on the question, How does this word/phrase intersect with my life today?

3. Write down how this word or phrase is affecting you in this moment.

Third movement: Responding to God's Word

1. Read Revelation 1:1-6 aloud for the fourth time.

2. Sit in silence for two to three minutes and reflect on the question, How is God calling me to respond?

3. Prayerfully write down your response to God's call.

Fourth movement: Resting in God

1. Read Revelation 1:1-6 aloud for the last time.

2. Sit in silence for two to three minutes, merely resting in God's Word.

3. Close your time with a verbalized prayer thanking God for this encounter with his Spirit.

1

THINNING THE VEIL
(Revelation 1)

The Casualty of Loneliness

How long, LORD? Will you forget me forever? How long will you
hide your face from me? How long must I struggle in my soul
and have sorrow in my heart day after day? How long shall
my enemy triumph over me? Behold and answer me,
LORD my God. Give light to my eyes, or I will sleep in death.

PSALM 13:1-4, A PSALM OF DAVID

WE DON'T HAVE TO LOOK FOR LONELINESS. It finds *us*. All of us.
Regardless of gender, race, creed, or nation, loneliness is universal.

Loneliness is always on the hunt. Undeterred by our bank accounts. Relentless in our times of struggle. Unforgiving even in a crowded room. Loneliness lurks, feasting on the guilty and the holy. The saints of old, like David,
and sinners today, such as me.

6-20-23, 2:39 a.m. (my journal)
I'm trying to hold it all together. But God, I feel betrayed by you. Abandoned
by you. And I've felt that way for a long time. I'm broken. But you won't
freaking put me back together. So, I fade. No hope of resurrection. . . . Do you
care? No manipulation. Genuine question. Do you even freaking care? Then
why won't you show it? Why won't you prove it? Where the hell are you?

Loneliness wafts over the soul like smoke wisping from the end of incense. A foggy shroud unfurling with lies and deceit. Loneliness whispers, "You don't belong." Loneliness mutters, "You aren't worth the effort." Loneliness convinces that God is no longer Immanuel but something closer to perpetually disappointed.

> **6-13-23, 11:49 p.m. (my journal)**
>
> God, are you proud of me? This question seems to hound me relentlessly. . . . I feel like a failure. I feel like I have no faith. . . . I feel like a waste. I feel like I'm a massive disappointment. A spiritual, spoiled brat. To be honest, I don't know if I'm worthy of your investment. There just seems to be so many more cut out for this than me. I just don't feel like I belong anywhere. I feel trapped. Cut off. My life more of a cautionary tale than anything else. Will you meet me here? Will I even be able to see you?

Loneliness woos us to desperation or depression, typically interweaving both into a confluence of confusion and pain. An ever-increasing descent into isolation and anger, numbness and panic, insecurity and frenzied motion. Loneliness blooms in desolation. Demands segregation. Thrives in exile.

> **6-11-23, 4:17 p.m. (my journal)**
>
> God, my heart is remarkably resistant to your love. My body stubbornly resistant to your healing. My mind exhausted. My will retired. Where do I turn, Lord? Have I grown deaf to your Spirit? Have you stopped speaking to my wayward heart—no longer wanting to waste your time on me? Is there hope? My goodness, hope is elusive. It seems so tangible at times, yet scares away so easily. I seem to swim in it as I go to sleep, only to awake to despair as a bedfellow with hope nowhere to be found. . . . Please be with me, God. Truly with me. Do you see me, God? Can you hear me through this soul besmirched with stains of sin? Then cleanse me, Jesus.

Loneliness finds us all. Those forgotten in the slums, those ignored on a corner holding cardboard, those abused, misused, and falsely accused. Regardless of age, time of day, personality, or prosperity, loneliness neglects no one. Includes all in its embrace. Sinners and saints, young and experienced, new converts and even apostles.

AN APOSTLE'S STRUGGLE

In Revelation 1, at the end of the first century CE (ca. 90–96),[1] John was on the island of Patmos *alone* and *lonely*. Exiled by Rome for his testimony to Jesus (Rev 1:9).[2] Away from Asia Minor and the seven churches he pastored. Away from his family. From his friends. Alone on an island as the last living apostle.[3]

An apostle who witnessed the birth of Jesus' ministry (Jn 2:1-12), the final breath of Jesus' body (Jn 19:25-30), and even the empty tomb populated by linen and nothing else (Jn 20:3-8). An apostle who watched Thomas place his hands in Jesus' wounds (Jn 20:24-29), the Holy Spirit's outpouring at Pentecost (Acts 2:1-4), and the gospel exploding from Jerusalem to the ends of the earth (Acts 8:1; 15:1-35). An apostle entrusted with caring for Christ's mother (Jn 19:26-27), with nurturing churches planted by Paul such as Ephesus (Irenaeus, *Against Heresies* 3.1.1; 3.3.4), and with preaching the good news to the powerful, the impoverished, and the broken (1 Jn 1:1-4; Acts of John 38-39).

And yet, here at the beginning of our Revelation, John is condemned to an island of loneliness. Unsure of what's next. Uncertain of his ministry's success. Unclear on whether God is intent on fulfilling his promises, yet quite clear on Rome's appeal to dominance, violence, and the title "the kingdom of heaven reigning on earth."

It's not clear when John arrived on Patmos or how long he was on the island before Revelation 1. We don't know whether John arrived during the

---

[1]For detailed analysis on the date of Revelation, see Shane J. Wood, *The Alter-Imperial Paradigm: Empire Studies and the Book of Revelation* (Leiden: Brill, 2016), 110-31, 132-85.

[2]For more discussion on John's exile as "physical persecution," see Wood, *Alter-Imperial Paradigm*, 140-47.

[3]When I refer to "John" or "the apostle," I'm not suggesting that "John, son of Zebedee" is the author of Revelation. Instead, I'm appealing to the narrative arc regarding the life of John, son of Zebedee, preserved by the Johannine tradition. John Behr argues convincingly that the Gospel of John and Revelation were written by the same author. See Behr, *John the Theologian and His Paschal Gospel: A Prologue to Theology* (Oxford: Oxford University Press, 2019), 43-98. He concludes, however, that the author of both is the enigmatic figure "John the Elder." While I do not find his methodology or conclusion for John the Elder persuasive, the Johannine tradition does indeed reference this *elder* moniker in the introduction of both 2 John and 3 John. As a result, the authorship of the Johannine texts is likely not solved by a single individual but by a Johannine tradition traced back to John, son of Zebedee (possibly responsible for portions of the corpus) also including John the Elder (also possibly responsible for portions of the corpus). Thus, my reference to "John" or "the apostle" and even "the disciple" points to John, son of Zebedee preserved in the Johannine tradition, but not as a means to preclude the legitimacy of John the Elder as a possible author as well.

hot, dry months of May–August. Or the wet, dreary months of December–January, which provide only six to seven hours of sunlight a day. We don't know whether his aged body was riddled with years-old ailments, lingering aches and pains, or battling a fresh cold deeply set in his laboring lungs. We don't know the condition of his heart, soul, mind, or strength (Mk 12:30).

But we do know that John was stretched thin. On the precipice of breaking. At his emotional end. For example, at the sight of a sealed scroll in God's hand, John bursts into tears, virtually inconsolable, desperate for a word from the Lord (Rev 5:4). Still later, erratic and irrational, John twice falls prostrate to worship at the feet of an angel (Rev 19:10; 22:8), both times receiving a stern rebuke and a command to "Worship God!" (Rev 19:10; 22:9). John is not himself. Quite unlike the beloved disciple from the Gospel bearing his name, the steady disciple bold enough to stand at the foot of the cross as the rest scatter out of self-preservation (Jn 19:26-27).

The strain of loneliness tempts even titans to transform into something far less than who they truly are. In Revelation 1, John is *alone* and *lonely*. Alone and wrestling. Alone and agonizing, questioning, clinging. Alone and desperate for a revelation.

Moments like these, however long or short they may be, seem suffocating. The stomach twists as the mind sprints, the chest constricts as the breath quickens, and God's silence thickens with each question unanswered, with each prayer pending:

> God, are you there? Do you hear my cries? Do you see my pain? Why won't you respond? Are you angry with me? Are you listening to me? Why are you withholding? "I cry to you, LORD, for help. In the morning, my prayer comes to meet you. Why, LORD, do you reject me? Why do you hide your face from me? . . . You have taken away my beloved friend and neighbor. Darkness is my closest friend." (Ps 88:13-14, 18)

Such pain plagues the faithful and the far off, the pastor and the prodigal. Without response, the veil between heaven and earth seems impenetrable. A chasm of chaos. Whatever the cause or catalyst for this curse of silence, the result is the same: loneliness.

TRANSFORMED BY LONELINESS

Yet, such a description may just be projection. Saints, so I'm learning, simply don't experience loneliness as I do. Yes, they struggle. Indeed, they languish. But their pain retains meaning. Not through sadistic twists and turns but through a belief that union with God simply doesn't translate to our faculties. That as grace presses deeper into our souls stained with worry and fatigued by wandering, we experience life as a "ray of darkness"; we encounter truth in a "cloud of unknowing."[4]

God's silence is mistaken for indifference when in fact he's speaking in a language foreign to our senses, yet quite familiar to the recesses of our soul. A language more fit for the Spirit than for sin, more attuned to our suffering than we presume. Drawing closer to God's radiant glory, as bright as "the sun shining in all its brilliance" (Rev 1:16 NIV), we are blinded by grace. What worked before no longer works. What helped before no longer helps. All of our idols are awash with a light so bright all now seems dark; God so close all now seems lost.

Yes, John is alone and lonely. But it may not be a loneliness understood by those uninitiated in the divine intimacy found only in the "dark night of the soul."[5]

Consider Mother Teresa. In 2007, the book *Come Be My Light*, a biography compiled from her journal and intimate letters with her spiritual mentors, came with both excitement and scandal. These writings, which Mother Teresa pleaded to have destroyed, revealed the inner world of a saint who, from the outside, appeared closer to Jesus than most. Yet she recounts an enduring silence, an absence of Christ's presence for more than twenty-seven years. A darkness and poverty of soul that rivaled the darkness and poverty she served in every day among the poor and dying in the slums of Calcutta.

> **Undated, ca. 1959 (her journal)**
> In the darkness . . . I call, I cling, I want—and there is no One to answer—no One on Whom I can cling—no, No One.—Alone. The darkness is so dark—and I am alone.—Unwanted, forsaken.—The loneliness of the heart that wants love

---

[4]Pseudo-Dionysius, *De mystica theologia* 1.1 (PG 3:999) writes of a "ray of darkness." The Christian contemplative classic *The Cloud of Unknowing* was penned by an anonymous monk in the fourteenth century.

[5]This phrase was coined by St. John of the Cross, a sixteenth-century Carmelite friar, in his masterpieces, *The Ascent of Mount Carmel* and *The Dark Night*.

is unbearable.—Where is my faith?—Even deep down, right in, there is nothing but emptiness & darkness.—My God—how painful is this unknown pain. It pains without ceasing.—I have no faith. . . . Love—the word—it brings nothing.—I am told God loves me—and yet the reality of darkness & coldness & emptiness is so great that nothing touches my soul.[6]

"How is this possible?" many quipped. "Is she a faux saint, hypocritically speaking of God's love while absorbing wounds from her divine abuser?" Such questions are spoken from a perspective that misunderstands silence and God's presence in the form of loneliness. For even during immense internal agony, Mother Teresa resolves, "I am not alone—I have His darkness."[7]

A mystery here may yet minister to our understanding of the Revelation of Jesus Christ just as much as it may illumine the cavernous longing in our souls that compels us to deconstruct our faith, abandon the bride, lash out at Christian culture, and even more. For silence is a divine strategy, the dark night a gift of grace, the cloud of unknowing evidence of an awakening of intimacy.

Indeed, the pain of the process is real: "[In the dark night,] the longings for God become so intense that it will seem to individuals that their bones are drying up in this thirst [of love]," proffering a suffering "worse than death."[8] But the purpose isn't punishment or divine neglect. It's intimacy. Unity with the infinite. Nearness to the "light of the world," whose gaze is so brilliant that all our senses go mute, blinded by his radiant presence. For in order to draw near to the one beyond all senses, our senses must meet their end, as St. John of the Cross (1542–1591) admits.[9]

Thus, what appears as divine abandonment is actually a divine strategy for ineffable intimacy. So Padre Pio, a twentieth-century Franciscan saint (1887–1968), comforted a child of the faith afflicted with inner loneliness by unveiling heaven's design. "What is producing such desolation in your spirit," he suggests, "is a very special grace."[10] The "alarm and terror" at the inner

---

[6]Mother Teresa, *Come Be My Light: The Private Writings of the "Saint of Calcutta,"* ed. Brian Kolodiej-chuk (New York: Doubleday, 2007), 186-87. The peculiar capitalization and frequent use of em dashes as a multipurpose punctuation mark are unique to Mother Teresa's writing style.

[7]Teresa, *Come Be My Light*, 223.

[8]Teresa, *Come Be My Light*, 187, 59.

[9]John of the Cross, *Selected Writings*, ed. Kieran Kavanaugh (New York: Paulist Press, 1987), 178, 181.

[10]The quotations in this paragraph are from a letter written by Padre Pio to his spiritual daughter Raffaelina Cerase on February 28, 1915, as recorded in *Padre Pio's Spiritual Direction for Every Day*, ed. Gianluigi Pasquale, trans. Marsha Daigle-Williamson (Cincinnati, OH: Franciscan Media, 2011), 153.

loneliness is "the poor soul's reaction to this grace." When the radiant light of God draws near to the soul saturated in death, life "finds the soul unprepared and not well adapted . . . to receive this supernatural light." Ill-equipped and caught off-guard, "the poor soul," Padre Pio explains, "experiences terror and fear in its faculties, memory, intelligence, and will." However, over time, the soul's sight adjusts to the light, and "little by little, it soon begins to feel the healing effects of this new grace." A new grace that feeds the malnourished with an intimacy surpassing all cravings.

With such a cloud of witnesses, loneliness transforms into a conduit of transformation. If seen, if perceived, if welcomed as grace. To embrace loneliness as a gift, even in the face of the great silence, we must harness its despair as the essential spark that ignites faith, that increases longing for God, for his Word, for his presence.

Loneliness, as in the dark night of the soul, will produce intimacy and clarity beyond reason and articulation if it isn't shunned but partnered with. Resiliently embraced. Harnessed with joy in suffering, so that, with Mother Teresa, we can say, "I will smile at Your Hidden Face—always."[11]

And in Revelation 1, this is just how John responds.

ENCOUNTERING THE COSMIC CHRIST

Loneliness wooed John to his knees, pressed him into prayer and pleading "on the Lord's Day" (Rev 1:10). Loneliness situated John on Patmos in a posture of surrender, a disposition of receptivity to encounter God intimately. An ineffable union fit for the mysterious phrase "in the Spirit" (Rev 1:10).

"In the Spirit," John's loneliness is transformed from isolation into a conduit through which God can be received, or maybe, still better, *perceived*. For "in the Spirit," John's senses are no longer dulled by dereliction, but surpassed. Unfettered to hear and see what the Spirit says and unveils.[12]

"In the Spirit," John hears "a sonorous voice like a trumpet" (Rev 1:10), shattering the phantasm of solitude. Alone on Patmos, John turns (Rev 1:12) and sees Christ transfigured: "His face as brilliant as the sun shines" (Rev 1:16;

---

[11]Teresa, *Come Be My Light*, 187.
[12]Revelation is saturated with senses: sight is referenced over 125 times (e.g., Rev 1:12; 7:1-2; 22:8); hearing over 120 times (e.g., Rev 2:7, 11, 17, 29; 3:3, 6, 13, 20, 22; 19:1; 21:3); touch over 20 times (e.g., Rev 1:17; 2:1; 7:9); taste over 12 times (e.g., Rev 8:11; 10:9-10; 17:16); smell 3 times (e.g., Rev 8:3-4; 19:3).

cf. Mt 17:2); "His hair as white as wool, as white as snow" (Rev 1:14; cf. Dan 7:9); "His feet like bronze flamed in a furnace" (Rev 1:15; cf. Rev 10:1); "His eyes as a fiery flame" (Rev 1:14; cf. Dan 7:9).

No, John is not alone. Christ is present. As always, Jesus is here, yet quite unlike the crucified "King of the Jews" (Jn 19:19-22), who cried out from the cross in John's Gospel, "I thirst" (Jn 19:28). Here, in Revelation 1, on the island of Patmos, Christ lacks nothing. For what was finished on the cross (Jn 19:30) is now present without a veil to cover the Lord's glory (2 Cor 3:7-18). Christ's divinity now on full display for those with eyes to see in the dark.

In Revelation 1:13, John identifies "the voice that was speaking to me" (Rev 1:12) with the peculiar phrase "one like a son of man." A designation that conjures a context of ancient exile and prophecy. In Daniel 7, living in the shadow of Babylon, the prophet receives a vision fit for the book of Revelation: beasts are coming out of the sea (Dan 7:2-7; cf. Rev 13:1-8) resembling a lion, a bear, and a leopard (Dan 7:4-6; cf. Rev 13:2), some with ten horns (Dan 7:7; cf. Rev 13:1) and others with the power to crush any who oppose their authority (Dan 7:7; cf. Rev 13:7-8). Daniel is enamored and astonished (Dan 7:8; cf. Rev 17:6), but his vision is interrupted by divine presence. Entering the heavenly throne room, the Ancient of Days (Dan 7:9) is seated in sovereignty, wearing "a robe as white as snow" with "the hair of his head as white as wool" (Dan 7:9 LXX). The throne itself was "flaming with fire," with chariot-like wheels "as a fiery flame" (Dan 7:9 LXX). A great multitude stood before the throne in anticipation of what was to come (Dan 7:10). Or, better still, *who* was to come: "In my vision at night I watched, and look! Coming with the clouds of heaven was *one like a son of man*" (Dan 7:13).

The parallel language is not incidental but intentional. Yet the parallel is anything but a one-to-one correlation. John, as elsewhere in Revelation, invokes the Old Testament to bring greater clarity to the Revelation of Jesus Christ.[13] Or to demonstrate how Jesus brings greater clarity to the sacred Scriptures.

The initial parallel is clear: "one like a son of man" (Rev 1:13; Dan 7:13) who is "coming with the clouds" (Rev 1:7; Dan 7:13) and rightfully celebrated as supremely sovereign (Rev 1:5-6; Dan 7:14). But John moves beyond what the Old Testament affirms, blending the imagery of the "Ancient of Days" with

---

[13]By my count, there are over 516 allusions to the Old Testament in the 404 verses of Revelation.

the "one like a son of man." In Daniel 7:9, the Ancient of Days has clothing "white as snow" and hair "white as wool," whereas in Revelation 1:14, Jesus' hair is "white as wool, as white as snow." The throne of the Ancient of Days is aflame with fire, wheels ablaze (Dan 7:9), whereas John identifies the feet of Christ "like bronze flamed in a furnace" (Rev 1:15) and "his eyes as a fiery flame" (Rev 1:14). Daniel's vision, then, matures in Revelation to depict the "one like a son of man" with imagery more fit for the Ancient of Days himself.

This high Christology unfolds further as the Revelation unfurls. In Revelation 5, the heavenly elder comforts the weeping prophet (Rev 5:4-5) by redirecting his attention to the triumphant Lamb "appearing as if it had been slaughtered" (Rev 5:6). Yet it's the location of the slain Lamb that startles: "[The Lamb is] standing in the middle of the throne, surrounded by the four living creatures and the elders" (Rev 5:6)—the same cast who encircled God's "throne in heaven" (Rev 4:2, 4, 6) with songs of praise and postures of worship. If such an infringement on the Shekinah could be excused, the chapter's concluding hymn would surely cause concern: "To the one sitting on the throne *and* to the Lamb be praise and honor and glory and power, for ever and ever!" (Rev 5:13; cf. Rev 7:17; 22:3).[14]

Revelation modifies Daniel's vision not by mere happenstance but strategically, Christocentrically. Daniel discerned through the revelation and narrative of Jesus Christ. A narrative invoked in Jesus' trifold appellation in Revelation 1:5:

"the faithful witness": an allusion to Christ's death on the cross[15]

"the firstborn from the dead": an allusion to Christ's resurrection[16]

---

[14]Cf. Babylonian Talmud Sanhedrin 38b. For analysis of early Christian worship/hymns and Jesus' divine status, see Larry Hurtado, *Lord Jesus Christ: Devotion to Jesus in Earliest Christianity* (Grand Rapids, MI: Eerdmans, 2003), 605-19.

[15]The word μάρτυς (here translated "witness," and from which the English word *martyr* is derived) is used five times in Revelation (Rev 1:5; 2:13; 3:14; 11:3; 17:6). Each time it refers to the death of Christ or one of his followers. Significantly, the moniker "faithful witness" is used only three times: for Jesus (Rev 1:5; cf. Rev 3:14, ὁ μάρτυς ὁ πιστὸς καὶ ἀληθινός) and for Antipas (ὁ μάρτυς μου ὁ πιστός μου), who was put to death in the city of Pergamum (Rev 2:13).

[16]Oddly, the word *resurrection* (ἀνάστασις) is used only twice, in Rev 20:5 and Rev 20:6, neither in reference to Jesus. Nevertheless, Christ's resurrection saturates the Apocalypse in a variety of creative expressions that resist a simple word study: "I am the Living One. I was dead, but look! I am alive for ever and ever!" (Rev 1:18); "who became dead yet lived" (Rev 2:8); and describing the two witnesses, whose ministry reflects Christ, "after the three and half days, the spirit of life from God entered them, and they stood on their feet" (Rev 11:11). The resurrection of Jesus is even parodied by the "beast from the sea" when it "appeared to have been slaughtered in death, but the fatal wound was healed" (Rev 13:3).

"the ruler of the kings of the earth": an allusion to Christ's ascension
to heaven[17]

The story of Christ, retold in Revelation time and again, unveils the divinity
and sovereignty of Christ. So, in Revelation 1:17-18, Jesus can claim the divine
identifier "I am the First and the Last" (Rev 1:17; cf. Rev 2:8) because of his
death on the cross ("I was dead," Rev 1:18) and his triumphant resurrection
("I'm alive for ever and ever," Rev 1:18), which secure universal dominion in
his ascension to God's right hand ("And I possess the keys of Death and
Hades," Rev 1:18).[18]

Such a revelation of Jesus Christ changes not just our understanding of
Old Testament texts such as Daniel 7 but even our understanding of loneliness, the veil between heaven and earth, and grace itself.

THINNING THE VEIL

Grace is a movement of God toward humanity. Toward the fallen and the
forlorn. Toward the forsaken and the crestfallen. Toward us. Grace is a divine
movement impossible to reproduce or fabricate or coerce, yet a movement
unmistakable to those on the receiving end. For grace does more than just
"get us out of hell"; it unveils. Transforms. Creates all things new. Even "in
the beginning."

God's first movement toward humanity, his first grace, didn't occur on the
cross or in the virgin birth or with the law on Sinai or with the exodus from
Egypt. God's first grace occurs in the first five words of sacred Scripture: "In
the beginning God created" (Gen 1:1). Not from a sense of loss or a payment
for an overdue debt but from a divine desire. As the twenty-four elders of
Revelation 4:11 melodically instruct, God "created all things, and *through your
will* they came to being and were created."

---

[17]Throughout Scripture, depictions of the ascension are always in the context of kingdom, sovereignty,
or reigning (cf. Acts 1:3-9; Dan 7:13-14). This kingdom context is why the ascension is at times invoked with the shorthand "sat down at the right hand of God," a position of sovereignty (Mk 14:62;
Acts 2:32-36; 5:31; Rom 8:34; Eph 1:20-21; Col 3:1; Heb 1:3; 8:1; 10:12-13; 12:2; 1 Pet 3:22; Rev 3:21; cf.
Mk 16:19; Acts 7:55-56).

[18]In Rev 1:8, God the Father invokes the parallel sobriquet, "I am the Alpha and the Omega," which
he reintroduces in Rev 21:6, adding "the Beginning and the End." Incredibly, Rev 22:13 combines all
three parallel monikers in red letters: "I am the Alpha and the Omega, the First and the Last, the
Beginning and the End."

God birthed creation by his choice; he sustains creation by his desire. He pours himself out anew each day and each moment, so that breath continues to fill life's lungs, so that gravity continues to secure love's attraction, so that the heavens, day after day, "pour out speech" (Ps 19:2) testifying to God's glory, goodness, and grace.

Nevertheless, creation, both space and time, is a gift of grace often misconstrued. Space is warred over, while time maligned—never enough of either to satisfy the avaricious heart of humanity originally fashioned in the image of a God (Gen 1:26-27) who, ironically, withholds nothing. Sacrifices all for everyone. Pours himself out on evil and his own indiscriminately.

As in the Garden of Eden, though, humanity still longs to live with no boundaries, no limits, no restrictions. Humanity crafts anything and everything to transcend space and time, re-envisioning creation as not a movement of grace but something more akin to incarceration. A flaming sword preventing us from going back to Eden while compelling us toward our inevitable appointment with death, the ultimate end of our space and our time. Humanity imagines a body-like prison fettered to creation.[19] Manacled by space and time.

Yet, in the beginning, God created both space and time as an act of grace. An ineffable context through which the boundaried and the boundless can commune, the finite and the eternal can interact, God and humanity can walk together "in the cool of the day" (Gen 3:8). Yes, God is beyond all, yet in creation, *because* of space and time, humanity can encounter him. The boundaries of creation make possible interaction with the boundless Creator. In other words, creation is grace, a movement of God toward us.

Humanity, though, deceived by the "ancient serpent called the devil and Satan" (Rev 12:9), chose to conjoin creation with death (Gen 3:6-7), converting the pure into the perverted and reinterpreting the cosmos as an impenetrable barrier between God and his beloved. Creation, then, became the thorn in the flesh of divine intimacy—cosmological bars imprisoning us from ourselves, from others, and from heaven's gaze. As expected, space and time were imbued with loneliness, a movement of death toward humanity.

However, our reinvention of creation in the image of death didn't pause God's pursuit or prevent God from drawing near. Regardless of what our

---

[19]See Philo, *De specialibus legibus* 3.1-6; *Legum allegoriae* 3.72-74.

senses say, creation doesn't limit God's presence but engenders the possibility of divine intimacy. Alone on Patmos, John still encounters the cosmic Christ (Rev 1:10-21), unveiling a truth that echoes throughout the entirety of Revelation: the veil between heaven and earth is not as thick as we assume.

All throughout the Apocalypse space and time intermingle with eternity and the abode of God in a way that is as seamless as Christ's clothes bartered at the foot of the cross (Jn 19:23-24). For, in Revelation, cosmology collapses under the weight of God's pursuit. So, Jesus visits earth in Revelation 1, even as John graces the heavenly throne room in Revelation 4–5. In Revelation 7, John sees the multitude of Christ-followers *on earth* (Rev 7:1-8), and with a glance he sees the "great multitude that no one could count from every nation, tribe, people, and tongue, *standing before the throne* and before the Lamb" (Rev 7:9).[20] All throughout Revelation, this theme plays on repeat, so that what happens in heaven affects earth, and so too the reverse.

Consider the seven seals. The Lamb enthroned in heaven (Rev 5:6) opens the first four seals (Rev 6:1, 3, 5, 7), each resulting in an earthly consequence, because what happens in heaven affects the earth. In the seventh seal, though, it's the prayers of the saints on earth that render heaven silent "for about half an hour" (Rev 8:1, 3), because what happens on earth touches heaven. Why? Because in spite of what loneliness promises, in Revelation, space doesn't separate. And time is no different. In Christ, time is no longer a barrier or even linear. In Revelation, time moves uninterrupted from the beginning of eternity (Rev 6:12-17; 11:15-19; 16:17-21) to the very creation of the earth. So, the death of Jesus under Pontius Pilate pervades not just first-century Palestine but the entire timeline, for, according to Revelation, "the Lamb was slain from the foundation of the world" (Rev 13:8).

The Revelation of Jesus Christ, then, reveals that the veil between humanity and divinity is actually quite porous, easily penetrated, rendering heaven and earth, time and eternity, at times almost indistinguishable (Rev 14:1-20). The veil is so thin that in Revelation the abode of God and the abode of humanity interact without hindrance, a wedding of the divine and

---

[20]Revelation 7:1-3 painstakingly locates the 144,000 on earth, with the angels standing at "the four corners of the earth," obstructing the "four winds of the earth" from moving about "the earth or on the sea or on any tree" (Rev 7:1), before receiving the command to "not harm the earth or the sea or the trees until we might seal the servants of our God on their foreheads" (Rev 7:3).

the human found only in the incarnation itself. In the person of Jesus Christ. Fully human yet fully God. A union that foreshadows the promise to come in Revelation 21, where heaven and earth are indeed new because they are, once again, *one*—as it was "in the beginning."

In the Revelation of Jesus Christ, the veil between God and humanity is "torn in two from top to bottom" (Mt 27:51). Cosmology collapses, not whimsically but strategically. Purposefully. Revelation thins the veil to consume our loneliness, to transform our quarantine into the conduit through which heaven draws near to earth to respond to the cavernous void created by the tyranny of death. Revelation confronts the satanic deception that in creation, we are alone, exiled on an island of misery and isolation. Instead, Revelation reveals the startling truth that heaven is closer than we assume. That even in our loneliness, God is nearer than we surmise or at times can endure.

GRACED BY LONELINESS

In Revelation 1:17-18, cosmology collapses under the weight of God's pursuit. In these two verses, an image of intimacy unfolds, a depiction of death's undoing, a divine movement of grace that summarizes the point of this chapter, the message of Revelation, and the heart of the gospel as a whole.

In Revelation 1:12-16, Jesus draws near (grace), and John is overwhelmed. Undone. "And when I saw him," John recounts, "I fell to his feet as though dead" (Rev 1:17).[21] A posture mirroring his lonely heart. But John doesn't cling to Christ's feet like Mary in the garden (Jn 20:11-17) or pepper Jesus with questions like the two on the road to Emmaus (Lk 24:13-29). John buries his

---

[21]Most commentators spend little space on the first part of Rev 1:17. For example, in G. K. Beale's 1,245-page tome, about ninety words are used on this text. See Beale, *The Book of Revelation*, NIGTC (Grand Rapids, MI: Eerdmans, 1999), 213. Perhaps scholars relegate this text because the action is seen as a typical feature or "stereotyped behavior" of the prophetic genre. See James Moffatt, "The Revelation of St. John the Divine," in *The Expositor's Greek Testament* (Grand Rapids, MI: Eerdmans, 1951), 5:345. See also David E. Aune, *Revelation*, WBC 52A-52C (Nashville: Thomas Nelson, 1997–1998), 1:99; G. R. Beasley-Murray, *The Book of Revelation*, New Century Bible (Grand Rapids, MI: Eerdmans, 1974), 67; Christopher C. Rowland, "The Book of Revelation: Introduction, Commentary, and Reflections," in *The New Interpreter's Bible* (Nashville: Abingdon, 1998), 12:567. Nevertheless, Rev 1:17 adds a unique detail absent from other prophetic theophanies. Whereas elements such as "falling to the ground" (Dan 8:17; Ezek 1:28; 43:3; 44:4), a "loud voice" guiding the vision (Dan 8:16; Ezek 1:28; 43:2), and the comforting command "Do not fear" (Dan 10:12) are all found elsewhere, John's addition "as though dead" seems to describe more than just his reaction to the divine appearance—it appears to extend to the plight of the Christian communities navigating the tension of Domitian's reign (for more, see chapter two below).

face in the rocky soil of Patmos, breathes in the dust of the earth that seeks to reclaim his body in death.

John falls at the feet of Christ. His King. His absent friend. That is, until now. For now, Life approaches with brilliant light dispelling all isolation, rending darkness with his presence. Now, Truth appears with a piercing gaze, dissolving all mystery and doubt. Now, Resurrection draws near to confront the death enshrouding his beloved.

Jesus arrives; John falls down as though dead. And silence fills the scene.

The silence of an empty tomb.

The silence of despair defied by hope.

John doesn't move because the dead don't move. John doesn't speak because the dead are mute. John doesn't assert control because the dead are lost in an abyss of surrender. A cosmological collapse crafted in the image of death and separation.

But then: grace.

A movement of God.

Toward us. For us.

"And when I saw him, I fell to his feet as though dead. But he lay his right hand on me saying, 'Do not fear. I am the First and the Last. The Living One. I was dead, but look! I am alive—for ever and ever. And I possess the keys of Death and of Hades'" (Rev 1:17-18).

In response to John's deadness, Jesus makes the first move. A move toward John, drowning in death. Jesus reaches across the chasm and touches him, refusing to allow the story of creation to end in tragedy, refusing to allow cosmology to dictate intimacy. In Christ Jesus, separation is spanned by grace. Christ crosses the canyon of fallen creation, the cavern separating life and death, with a nail-scarred hand, tenderly soothing the wounds of humanity with a divine touch and a profound exhortation, "Do not fear."

Do not fear the loneliness. Do not fear the daunting horizon before you. Do not fear the illusion of divine distance. For perfect love casts out all fear. Exiles fear. Dismisses fear as far as the east is from the west, so as to embolden creation to see beyond the veil that death uses to shroud us from grace, from the movements of God toward his creation. With his touch, Christ whispers words of peace stretching far beyond what language can contain: "Do not fear, dear child. Let the scales fall from your eyes; let life displace death in you,

transform loneliness in you from a barrier into a birth canal. Breathe once again, O my creation, for the Spirit is filling your lungs anew, transforming dust into a divine home, a temple fit for the triune God. Do not fear, for resurrection has come."

THE GOOD NEWS OF THE REVELATION OF JESUS CHRIST

Revelation 1:17-18 is the gospel in short. The book of Revelation in brief. The Revelation of Jesus Christ in toto. Death is touched by life in a movement of grace that casts out all fear and dispels any doubt: the veil between humanity and divinity is quite thin. Our brokenness hasn't gone unnoticed, our rebellion hasn't gone unperceived, our resilience won't go unrewarded. Because God is near; he is moving. He is breaking every barrier, traversing any boundary, not just to be by you but to transform you. All of you. Through the Revelation of Jesus Christ.

Without question, Revelation's target is not prediction but transformation. Of you. Of me. Of all that is broken.

Revelation comes to us and finds us wallowing in loneliness. Finds us face down as though dead. Unable to move or respond or to do much more than weep and make things worse. Revelation responds by spanning the chasm of death with the touch of life. Revelation responds with a message of intimacy beyond imagination, of God's movement beyond perception, of healing far beyond what we can procure through our own efforts and strain. Revelation responds with grace: God's movement toward his broken creation.

To those east of Eden, Revelation sings songs of transformation, conducts hymns of liberation, and marches to the rhythm of the divine heartbeat found in all creation, embedded in the image of God shrouded with garments of skin. Revelation, by God's grace, thins the veil between heaven and earth, revealing, among other things, a God who is near. Intimately so.

GOING DEEPER

> **THE TOOL:** Context, part 2. Assumptions can be blinding, obscuring our ability to see others or even Scripture clearly. Watch this video on challenging assumptions (www.ivpress.com/wood-la) and wrestle with the following questions:

1. What assumptions have people made about you? How did they make you feel?

2. What assumptions have you made about other people (be as specific as you can)? How did they affect your interaction with them?

3. Before this study, what assumptions did you have about Revelation? How did that affect the questions you asked about the text?

THE TEXT: Encountering Christ (Rev 1:1-21). Loneliness threatens our ability to see God clearly. Yet God confronts our loneliness with divine presence. After watching this video (www.ivpress.com/wood-1b), answer the following questions:

1. When you are lonely or struggling to see God move, what questions saturate your prayers? What thoughts pervade your heart and mind?

2. Recount a time when you saw God move or answer your prayer. What prayers did you offer in response? What thoughts filled your soul?

3. If Christ were sitting next to you right now, what questions would you ask him? What words would you offer him?

THE TAKEAWAY: Encountering the voice of God. Revelation 1:3 says, "Blessed is the one who *reads aloud* the words of this prophecy." Since the majority of the first-century world was illiterate, most Christians experienced the New Testament letters by hearing the Word of God. Not reading them. Thus, the ancient Christian prayer practice of auditio divina centers on the transforming power of hearing God's Word. Here's how it works:

1. Go to www.biblica.com/resources/niv-audio-bible-listen-online-for -free/ and navigate to Revelation 1.

2. Click the audio link at the top of the passage so the narrator reads the passage out loud.

3. Close your eyes and allow God's Word to wash over you.

4. Reflect on the following:

> What word or phrase stuck out to you? What do you think the Lord is saying to you through that word or phrase?

> What image or symbol stuck out to you? What do you think the first-century Christian would have experienced hearing that same symbol?

> Compare and contrast hearing the Word of God with reading the Word of God.

2

THE MYSTERY OF INTIMACY
(Revelation 2–3)

Tension, Terror, and
Seven Golden Lampstands

—————

And when I turned I saw seven golden lampstands,
and in the middle of the lampstands was one like a son of man.

REVELATION 1:12-13

IN REVELATION 1, imagery saturates Christ's visit to Patmos—"a so-norous voice like a trumpet" (Rev 1:10), "eyes like fiery flame" (Rev 1:14), "a sharp, double-edged sword" protruding from the cosmic King's mouth (Rev 1:16). Each image interlaced into the narrative of Christ's coming, the story of Jesus drawing near to John to dispel all loneliness with divine presence.

Strangely, Revelation 1 ends in verse 20 with a seemingly trivial detail, a hinge verse that highlights two images with two definitions. "The mystery of the seven stars that you saw in my right hand," Jesus clarifies, "and the seven golden lampstands is this: the seven stars are the angels of the seven churches, and the seven lampstands are the seven churches."

This explanation seems odd at best. Almost out of place altogether. Of all the symbols seamlessly woven throughout Revelation 1, the seven stars and the seven lampstands hardly stick out as candidates for special treatment. Yet, far from a throwaway comment, Revelation 1:20 disrupts the narrative's flow deliberately. Purposefully. Ending the chapter intentionally with imagery fit

to pastor the prophet and his people. Symbols celebrating the central theme of Revelation 2–3: *intimacy.*

SURPRISED BY INTIMACY

Intimacy is often misunderstood, fabricated with a definition somewhere between obligation and luxury. Yet intimacy resists reduction and refuses mere replicas, for it understands its worth, the value it offers to those brazen enough to approach it and, by God's grace, apprehend it. Wield it. Surrender to it, fully and unconfused. Understanding simultaneously the risk and the treasure present therein.

In Revelation 1:12, John turns to see the voice penetrating his loneliness. But before he's enraptured by the cosmic Christ, he's transfixed by "seven golden lampstands" (Rev 1:12). Furniture not seen on Patmos moments earlier, yet now potently present. Furniture more fit for the temple in Jerusalem (Zech 4:1-6), yet now decorating the island of exile on the "Lord's Day" (Rev 1:10). The full import of the imagery, however, is delayed until Revelation 1:20, where the "seven lampstands" are identified as "the seven churches," surfacing an oft-overlooked interpretive key for the rest of the Apocalypse: Revelation was written to real people at a real time going through real issues.

Revelation is not fantasy or history written in advance. It's the letter of a pastor to his people, a message from John the minister to the seven churches in Asia Minor (Rev 1:4, 11). Churches filled with life, love, heartache, happiness. Churches filled with *real* people who had families they adored, stress at their jobs, finances to manage, dreams to navigate, worries to address. Real people who, each day, cooked meals, washed laundry, and fixed broken items around the house. Real people who struggled with resentment, rebellious children, and the Roman Empire.

Revelation was written to a weary group of churches clinging to hope that seemed to be quickly fading. A vulnerable group of Christians targeted at the end of the first century CE (ca. 90–96) by Roman society and the emperor Domitian. A confused group of Christ-followers struggling to see God, stumbling into complacency and compromise, and languishing in loneliness miles away from their minister.

You see, loneliness wasn't confined to John on Patmos but present also in the pews of every church stretching from Ephesus to Laodicea. When John

was exiled, the seven churches of Asia Minor lost their pastor. Lost their friend. With each passing day, "What's going to happen to our brother in Christ?" matured into "What's going to happen to us?" before it congealed into "God, where are you?" A downward descent into the abyss of loneliness.

However, the veil between heaven and earth is not as thick as we assume. For Revelation 1:20 unveils more than just the definition of an image; it unveils a profound mystery mentioned in Revelation 1:13 and repeated in Revelation 2:1: "and in the middle of the lampstands was one like a son of man" (Rev 1:13).

Jesus is walking among the churches. Walking in the midst of the lampstands. Beyond what eyes can see and minds perceive, Christ is present with each Christian in every congregation in all seven cities. Intimately so.

THE MYSTERY OF INTIMACY

I know my wife intimately. Not just sexually. In fact, to reduce our union to sex adulterates the depths of what it actually is. The beauty of what it contains. For intimacy, at its core, is knowing another and being fully known. Without reservation or withholding. With a recklessness that shuns secrets, a vulnerability that knows not how to feign feelings. Intimacy—*true* intimacy—strains toward one end: to be fully known and to fully know another.

And I know my wife. *Intimately.*

I know the smell of her breath before a kiss after a long cry. I know how she curls the end of her hair between her two fingers when she's deep in thought, pressing them gently and unconsciously to her lips. I know the pain of her black and white dress, and I know the joy in her voice when the first colors emerge in autumn. I know the sound of her sigh after her first drink of coconut LaCroix; the sound of her sneeze, which is never just one—the second always interrupting the first. I know the feeling of her fingers as they interlace mine and the difference in how we hold hands in the car versus walking down a city street or as we fall asleep. I know her lotion's smell, her favorite episode of *Friends*, and why the cactus ignites her heart. I know, without question, that after the waiter serves our food, she'll ask for a bite of mine (regardless of what I get) and offer me some of hers (even though she knows I'll always refuse). I'm not surprised when her head hurts forty-five minutes into the day without coffee or when she creates something beautiful out of something others saw as mere scraps. I know for her there is light in the mourning that others simply cannot see. I know how

the distant sound of an owl stirs something deep in her soul; how the sun, moon, and stars soothe and disturb her tender heart. I know the rhythm and the pattern with which she rubbed my back as I wept in our room, I know how breaking the rules in any card game infuriates her without end, and I know that as she reads this paragraph, tears are disrupting her vision. Not out of choice but because she overwhelms easy when she feels seen. *Truly* seen.

I know my wife. *Intimately.* Her patterns, her fears, her longings, her joy. I know her. But this didn't happen in a moment, for intimacy isn't incidental. It must be nurtured. Persistently. Without end. Even over distance, real or perceived.

I'm writing this chapter in the Utopia Diner in downtown New York City on West Seventy-Second and Amsterdam, near Broadway. It was the only place Google suggested that could accommodate my cumbersome dietary restrictions and my irrational craving for an omelet. As I paused to take a bite, the conversation two tables over arrested my attention. A young woman sat across from a weathered woman tethered to an oxygen tank.

"Oh, please don't cry," the young woman pleaded. "It's gonna be okay. I promise."

Sniffles. Short breaths. Long pauses.

A slight nod. "No, it won't."

"*Yes*, it will," the young woman exclaimed. "We're gonna get you a phone and set up a time each week to talk."

She paused, ever so briefly. Looking for hope to surface on her friend's face.

"I'll be back in August, but right now, I have to go. I don't have a choice."

The weathered woman's breathing deepened. Her arms began to tremble. No words emerged even as her mouth partially opened and closed with each attempt, her lip quivering just under the plastic tube draped around her face and under her nose.

"Listen," the young woman said, grabbing her friend's hand, "it's going to be okay. *We know each other*. We've built this relationship to last. We're going to be in each other's lives till the end. We can do this."

The weathered woman nodded her head once again. This time, though, in agreement. With a subtle resolve. Smiling for the first time, she wiped away a few tears, squeezed her young friend's hand, and whispered, exaggerating each word, "We. Know. Each. Other."

Intimacy withers without consistency, but it can reach a depth of union where time and space aren't able to disrupt the connection. Intimacy of this sort is typically forged in a fire, infused with steel-like endurance through tragedy or suffering. Your companions in catastrophe know you in a way that others simply don't. They've seen the contours of pain in the depths of your soul that even you didn't know existed, and if you did, you wouldn't allow them to surface or be seen by you or by others anyhow. That is, if the pain could be controlled. But unexpected pain disrupts our personas and false selves, not allowing pretense. We are exposed. Completely. No time to conceal or place to hide. We are seen. Fully.

Which is why intimacy is appropriately labeled terrifying.

INTIMATE LETTERS

Jesus knows the churches of Revelation 2–3. *Intimately.* He knows their struggles, their perseverance, their compromise, their triumphs, their hopes, their names, their stories. He knows the last time they laughed, the first time they cried, the superstitions they irrationally hold, and the faith that emboldens them to stare down even death as it draws near. He knows them. Not out of obligation or luxury but with an intimacy forged in the fire of his suffering and theirs. An intimacy infused with love in the shape of a cross.

Written in red letters, Revelation 2–3 is birthed from Christ's lips and blood. Words that bring balm to severe burns ("I know your affliction and your poverty, but you are rich!" [Rev 2:9]), words that shatter illusory living ("Wake up! And strengthen what remains that is about to die" [Rev 3:2]), words that tenderly call the Christ-follower to deeper layers of devotion ("I know you have little strength . . . [yet] hold on to what you have, so that no one might take your crown" [Rev 3:8, 11]). Words in red letters that reveal not only the character of God but the intimacy with which this God, walking among the lampstands, knows and understands each of the seven churches of Revelation.

Each letter has a similar structure and form, but without formality or sterility. To begin each letter, Jesus speaks to the angel of each church (Rev 2:1, 8, 12, 18; 3:1, 7, 14), an angel responsible for more than just delivering the message, entrusted also with the vitality of each congregation.[1] Following

---

[1] The word ἄγγελος can be translated either "angel" or "messenger," prompting some to interpret the referent in Rev 2–3 as a human messenger or congregant leader. See William Hendriksen, *More than Conquerors: An Interpretation of the Book of Revelation* (Grand Rapids, MI: Baker Books, 1982), 58;

Jesus' angelic address, each letter celebrates an image of the "one like a son of man" from Revelation 1, tethering the message to God's identity, reminding each church of who he is and, as his followers, who they are to be. These letters, then, are more than just words from heaven afar to churches abandoned on earth. Each message is accompanied with a heavenly attendant, with heaven's presence, reminding each church and every Christian that the veil between heaven and earth is not as thick as we assume.

The symmetry of structure extends to each letter's end as well. Each epistle concludes with a promise to those who "overcome" (νικάω), who triumph in the spiritual war that's raging in and around them (Rev 2:7, 11, 17, 26; 3:5, 12, 21). Each letter also ends with a call to arms, an appeal to senses beyond what senses can obtain: "Whoever has an ear, let them hear what the Spirit says to the churches" (Rev 2:7, 11, 17, 29; 3:6, 13, 22).[2] All seven letters maintain a

---

John F. Walvoord, *The Revelation of Jesus Christ: A Commentary* (Chicago: Moody, 1966), 53. Nevertheless, given the essential function of "otherworldly beings" in apocalyptic texts (e.g., 1 Enoch 1:2; 2 Baruch 55:3), translating ἄγγελος as "angel" seems most favorable. The idea of angels in charge of territories (Deut 32:8 LXX; Dan 10:13, 20) or even directly connected to individuals (Acts 12:15) was not foreign to first-century Jewish/Christian thinking. Additionally, angels play a significant role throughout the rest of Revelation (Rev 1:1; 5:2, 11; 7:1-2, 11; 8:2-5, 6-13; 9:1, 11-15; 10:1-11; 11:15; 12:7; 14:6-12, 15-19; 15:1, 6-8; 16:1-17; 17:1-7; 18:1-3, 21-24; 19:17-18; 20:1-3; 21:9-10, 17; 22:6-11, 16).

[2]Each letter to the churches also includes an assessment of their status—commendation, condemnation, or both—with two churches receiving no condemnation (Smyrna and Philadelphia) and two receiving no commendation (Sardis and Laodicea). Additionally, the seven letters have a chiastic structure, with Thyatira in the middle:

  A. *Ephesus*—spiritual depravity threatens their status as a church (Rev 2:5)

    B. *Smyrna*—steadfast in their faith, they receive no condemnation from Christ but are promised persecution and a crown (Rev 2:10)

      C. *Pergamum*—compromising with culture: idolatry and sexual immorality (Rev 2:14)

        D. *Thyatira*—struggling with compromise, but they have improved over time (Rev 2:19)

      C'. *Sardis*—compromising with culture: lack of integrity (Rev 3:1)

    B'. *Philadelphia*—steadfast in their faith, they receive no condemnation from Christ but are promised persecution and a crown (Rev 3:11)

  A'. *Laodicea*—spiritual depravity threatens their status as a church (Rev 3:16)

The structure of the seven letters also parallels ancient Near Eastern suzerain-vassal covenantal treaties, typically containing these key elements: preamble, prologue, stipulation, curse, blessing, and witness. For more discussion, see William H. Shea, "The Covenantal Form of the Letters to the Seven Churches," *AUSS* 21, no. 1 (Spring 1983): 71-84; Kenneth A. Strand, "A Further Note on the Covenantal Form in the Book of Revelation," *AUSS* 21, no. 3 (Autumn 1983): 251-64; Willem Altink, "Theological Motives for the Use of 1 Chronicles 16:8-36 as Background for Revelation 14:6-7," *AUSS* 24, no. 3 (Autumn 1986): 211-21.

beautifully predictable structure that contains powerfully piercing intimacy. A fully knowing of the other even if the other pretends to hide from grace.

Each church in each letter is reminded of Christ's pervasive presence with the same repeated phrase: "I know" (οἶδα). "I know your deeds," Jesus reveals, both good and evil (Rev 2:2); "I know your affliction" (Rev 2:9), your persistence (Rev 2:13), your growth (Rev 2:19), your reputation (Rev 3:1), your victories (Rev 3:8), your rebellion (Rev 3:15). "I know" (οἶδα) is pronounced to all seven churches, and all in red letters. All from Christ's mouth. Any illusion, then, of divine abandonment or Christian camouflage is dissolved with "I know," exposing the allure and the alarm of intimacy.

Jesus *knows* them. Sees them. All of them. All the thoughts and deeds they longed to conceal or reveal are unveiled with precision and perception, producing both comfort and confrontation.

Consider Ephesus, the first church addressed in Revelation 2:1-7. Jesus identifies himself to the angel of the church with images of intimacy from the end of Revelation 1: "These are the words of the one holding the seven stars in his right hand and the one walking among the seven golden lampstands" (Rev 2:1). Such proximity produces insight. Jesus is aware of their difficult plight and affirms their "toil and patient endurance" in the presence of false teachers and nameless "hardships" (Rev 2:2-3). He knows the struggle and the strain braved for his name. And he's proud of their resilience, for he knows the pressure to compromise in Ephesus wasn't superficial or slight.

By the end of the first century CE, the Ephesian renown in the Roman world was multifaceted. Ephesus received the honorific appellation Neokoros in 89/90 CE, indicating a unique cultic center for Roman worship.[3] An honor envied by others hungry to demonstrate Roman allegiance. Similarly, the city housed the illustrious Temple of Domitian, located at a key intersection of city life, featuring thirty-five to forty Attic deities lining the topmost ridge, a larger-than-life statue of the emperor Domitian, and an open-air altar

---

[3]The city of Ephesus was awarded the title Neokoros in the first half of the second century CE as well, further distinguishing it from other cities in Asia Minor with imperial cult temples (especially Pergamum). In Acts 19:35, the title Neokoros (νεωκόρον) is invoked by the city official to remind them of their exalted status. For more discussion, see Steven J. Friesen, *Twice Neokoros: Ephesus, Asia and the Cult of the Flavian Imperial Family*, Religions in the Graeco-Roman World (Leiden: Brill, 1993).

adorned with triumphal procession imagery.[4] Thus, the daily trip to the agora would assault the senses of the Ephesian commoner with sights, sounds, and smells of Roman worship interlaced with claims to imperial dominance.

Still further, Ephesus was home to the temple of Artemis, one of the seven wonders of the ancient world and another locus of cultic honor for the city. This twin daughter of Zeus was born by an olive tree, rendering her temple a "tree shrine" that provided temporary asylum for accused criminals until proper justice could be adjudicated.[5] Or, in other words, a type of tree of life that provided temporary "salvation" for the accused.[6] The deity's legacy and presence supplied the city with singular honor, which explains riotous outbursts of "Great is Artemis of the Ephesians!" when her reputation was threatened or at stake (Acts 19:23-41). Altogether, the honor of Ephesus centered on the collective worship of deities quite at odds with Christ's claims to sovereignty (Rev 1:18) and quite humiliated by his offer to the church to eat from the true tree of life, which doesn't offer transitory refuge but eternal residence "in the paradise of God" (Rev 2:7).

Without question, local pressure for Christians in Ephesus was quite real, and what was at stake was not small. As the city of Pergamum understood all too well, sometimes local tension put the very life of a loved one at stake (Rev 2:13). And Christ knows this *intimately*, for, among other reasons, the cross was a result of local tension and petty politics. Local tensions increase when national tensions boil, which was precisely the problem at the end of the first century CE. Indeed, if Revelation 2–3 can be summarized with the word *intimacy*, the Roman world under the reign of Domitian (81–96 CE) could be summarized with the word *tension*.

---

[4]Traditionally, the temple in Ephesus is known as the Temple of Domitian. However, Friesen argues that the Ephesian temple should be relabeled the "temple of the Sebastoi," since the temple honored the "Augustuses" and not just Domitian himself (*Twice Neokoros*, 35-38). For discussion on the Roman imperial cult and Revelation, see Steven J. Friesen, *Imperial Cults and the Apocalypse of John: Reading Revelation in the Ruins* (Oxford: Oxford University Press, 2001). Friesen also argues for the emperor Titus as the true identity of the enormous statue instead of Domitian (50), as suggested by Georg Daltrop, Ulrich Hausmann, and Max Wegner, *Die Flavier: Vespasian, Titus, Domitian, Nerva, Julia Titi, Domitilla, Domitia* (Berlin: Mann, 1966).

[5]For discussion on the Temple of Artemis's "tree shrine" connection with the cross of Christ as tree of life, see Colin Hemer, *The Letters to the Seven Churches of Asia in Their Local Setting* (repr., Grand Rapids, MI: Eerdmans, 2001), 41-52; cf. Grant R. Osborne, *Revelation*, Baker Exegetical Commentary on the New Testament (Grand Rapids, MI: Baker Books, 2002), 122-24.

[6]Hemer, *Letters*, 51; see also Tacitus, *Ann.* 3.60-63.

Figure 2.1.
Two out of the thirty-five
to forty Attic deities atop
the Temple of Domitian
in Ephesus

Figure 2.2.
Statue of Domitian from
the Temple of Domitian
in Ephesus

Figure 2.3.
Open-air altar from
the Temple of
Domitian in Ephesus

THE REIGN OF TENSION

Domitian's reign began with suspicion and insecurity. The death of his brother Titus, emperor from 79–81 CE, was abrupt and irregular. Rumors of sedition spread as stories of Domitian's jealousy were cited as murderous motivation. Titus was beloved by the masses, heralded as a military hero who, alongside his father, Vespasian, brought stability to the empire by suppressing the Jewish Revolt of 66–73 CE, in the process reducing the city of Jerusalem and its coveted temple to rubble. Domitian, however, was too young to participate in the Jewish wars, and when he came to power, he had no military or political accomplishments of note. Just his brother's mysterious death.

To assuage questions of foul play and to distract from his feeble resume, Domitian began his emperorship with a campaign of benevolence and luxury. The two targets of Domitian's benefaction were the army and the populace, both of which held unique imperial power. Domitian couldn't lure legions to loyalty with shared military experience, so he increased the army's pay to secure their allegiance. Similarly, Domitian seduced the populace with pleasure, offering entertainment and feasts that at times lasted for days on end.[7] Domitian's tactics worked—that is, until the revolt of Saturninus in 89 CE.

Saturninus was a trusted general in charge of Roman military expeditions in Upper Germany. He used his military exploits to unite multiple Roman legions against the emperor Domitian. With rapid intent, Saturninus began marching toward Rome to seize the throne, leaving little opportunity for anyone to react. Yet, an ill-timed thawing of the River Rhine slowed the rogue Roman armies, providing just enough delay for other Roman legions to respond.[8] The coup was suppressed, Saturninus was smashed, but the damage had been done. Domitian's delusions of popularity and pomp were shattered and replaced with terror and vengeance. And no one was safe.

In late 89 CE, Domitian invited the noble elite to a banquet, one unlike any other. "Alone at night without their attendants," the senators and knights entered the banquet hall ominously decorated "pitch black on every

---

[7]Suetonius, *Dom.* 7.3; 4.1-5.
[8]Suetonius, *Dom.* 6.2.

side, ceiling, walls and floor." Adding to the grim affair, beside each guest was "a slab shaped like a gravestone, bearing the guest's name and also a small lamp, such as hang in tombs." Without warning, young boys, "painted black, entered like phantoms," dancing around the guests before sitting at their feet as "sacrifices to departed spirits" were placed on black dishes and set before each guest. Silence filled the room, "as if they were already in the realms of the dead." Fear and trembling filled the hall, unsure of what sinister end was about to come, many expecting to have "his throat cut the next moment."[9]

Without warning, Domitian dismissed everyone from the black banquet. Confused yet relieved, the guests arrived home only to receive word "that a messenger from the Augustus had come." Many expected "to perish this time," but instead the various elements of the banquet were merely delivered, including the tombstone engraved with their name.[10] The message was sent to the noble and all those they represented: from here forward, no one was safe. Not senators, not slaves. No one.

The last half of Domitian's reign followed suit. Fear seized all, and his fierceness seemed to know no end. Senators and those of noble birth were discarded with little recourse to justice. Poets and the populace strained to retain dignity as they strived to prove loyalty. Old enemies were attacked with a renewed vigor. Especially the Jews of the Roman Empire.[11]

CAUGHT IN THE CROSSFIRE

When Domitian's father, Vespasian, took power in 69 CE, the Flavian dynasty had no claim to the throne. They were not of noble birth, unable to trace their lineage to the Julio-Claudian line that populated the emperorship ever since Julius Caesar.[12] Vespasian could point only to a civil war, Romans killing

---

[9]Dio Cassius, *Hist. Rom.* 67.9.3. Unless otherwise noted, all quotations of Dio Cassius follow Dio Cassius, *Roman History*, trans. Earnest Cary, 9 vols., LCL (Cambridge, MA: Harvard University Press, 1914–1927).

[10]Dio Cassius, *Hist. Rom.* 67.9.4-5.

[11]For discussion on the nature of Domitian's reign (as a tyrant leader or a maligned, good ruler), see Shane J. Wood, *The Alter-Imperial Paradigm: Empire Studies and the Book of Revelation* (Leiden: Brill, 2016), 13-16, 132-85.

[12]The Julio-Claudian line began with Julius Caesar (d. March 15, 44 BCE) and continued through the next eight emperors: Augustus (31 BCE–14 CE), Tiberius (14–37 CE), Caligula (37–41 CE), Claudius (41–54 CE), Nero (54–68 CE), Galba (June 8, 68 CE–January 15, 69 CE), Otho (January 15–April 16, 69 CE), and Vitellius (April 19–December 20, 69 CE).

Romans, as justification for his ascendancy.[13] Hardly a narrative worthy of Roman allegiance.

So Vespasian harnessed the suppression of the Jewish Revolt for his propaganda, recasting the event as the subjugation of a foreign enemy who threatened the empire's existence. Images of Jewish subjugation were emblazoned on coins, cemented in architecture, and reenacted in the Flavian triumphal procession of 71 CE.

Figure 2.4.
Vespasian:
RIC 2.1 (69/70 CE).
In celebration of
Jewish subjugation

Thus, the Roman Empire at the end of the first century CE was flooded with anti-Jewish sentiment, resulting in a toxic environment antagonistic toward the Jewish people *and* Christian communities.[14]

After the destruction of the temple in 70 CE, it was more difficult to distinguish between Jews and Christians in the Roman Empire. Geography no longer factored into the Jewish identity, rendering them a *shadow civitas* spread throughout the empire, comparable to the Christians, who didn't worship a God contained in temples "made by the hands of men" (Acts 7:48). Behavior didn't delineate one group from the other, with both known for Sabbath practices, dietary peculiarities, and even the alien act of circumcision.[15] And with both Jews and Christians claiming to be the people of Yahweh and appealing to the same sacred Scriptures, the Roman elite, understandably, didn't discern much, if any, difference between the two. So any anti-Jewish sentiment in the Roman Empire naturally extended to both Jews

---

[13]Octavian was in a similar situation after his victory over Marc Antony at the Battle of Actium in 31 BCE. His ascent to power was through civil war, but his propaganda transformed the struggle into a conquest over a foreign ruler. For more discussion, see Wood, *Alter-Imperial Paradigm*, 83-91, 150-59.

[14]Wood, *Alter-Imperial Paradigm*, 150-75.

[15]Wood, *Alter-Imperial Paradigm*, 176-84.

and Christians alike, leading to a context of tension, infighting, and the temptation to compromise.

At the end of Domitian's reign, tension reigned supreme. His insecurity had
matured into paranoia with murderous consequences. The Roman elite were
uniquely targeted, even as the anti-Jewish sentiment of his father was inten-
sified. Under Domitian, anti-Jewish images were coupled with humiliating
acts that disregarded the dignity of the young and the old, all of which fostered
an environment where a noble couple could be executed for "Jewish living,"
killed for practices popular in Jewish and Christian communities alike.[16]

Understandably, then, Christians were on high alert, some managing
better than others. Revelation 2–3 reveals that Jesus knows each struggle
intimately. He knows the conflict with local Jewish synagogues (Smyrna,
Rev 2:9; Philadelphia, Rev 3:9); he knows the false prophets populating their
pews (Pergamum, Rev 2:14-15; Thyatira, Rev 2:20-25); he knows the names
of those "put to death in your city—where Satan lives" ("Antipas," Rev 2:13).
He knows what the churches wish he knew (their faithfulness) and what they
seek to keep from him (their disobedience).

Jesus knows them *intimately*, because he's walking among the lampstands.
He sees that some stand firm, even to the point of death (Rev 2:8-11, 13; 3:7-13),
and yet, the pervasive imperial tension imperils the allegiance of others
(Rev 3:1-6, 14-22), resulting in varying degrees of cultural compromise and
confusion. Jesus knows *all* of it. In response, he calls all Christians, all seven
churches, to "overcome," to faithfulness in the presence of their enemies, to
mercy in response to injustice, to love as the path to victory. A command
Christ is unwilling to compromise, even for those doing some things
quite well.

---

[16]Suetonius, *Dom.* 12.2: "I recall being present in my youth when the person of a man ninety years
old was examined before the procurator and a very crowded court, to see whether he was circum-
cised." J. C. Rolfe, trans., *Suetonius*, 2 vols., LCL (Cambridge, MA: Harvard University Press, 1913).
Dio Cassius, *Hist. Rom.* 67.14.1-3: "And the same year Domitian slew, along with many others,
Flavius Clemens the consul, although he was a cousin and had to wife Flavia Domitilla, who was
also a relative of the emperor's. The charge brought against them both was that of atheism, a charge
on which many others who drifted into Jewish ways were condemned. Some of these were put to
death, and the rest were at least deprived of their property. Domitilla was merely banished to
Pandateria."

FIGHTING FOR TRUTH IN LOVE

In response to the chaos at the end of the first century CE, the church of Ephesus hardened. Sacrificed tenderness for truth, compassion for correct doctrine, love for being right. Indeed, national and local tension demanded unique resolve, a hardened and resolute determination to pursue Christ at all cost. Jesus understood this. Intimately so. Which is why he commends their zeal for truth, uprooting "wicked people" and "false teaching" (Rev 2:2, 6).

But God's truth void of Christ's love is not obedience but betrayal to the Revelation of Jesus Christ. And something Jesus doesn't tolerate. "You may be good at truth and correct doctrine," Christ quips, "but I hold this against you: You have forsaken the love you had at first . . . and I am *this close* to removing your lampstand" (Rev 2:4-5).[17]

It's easy to forget in a world militant toward Christianity that *how* we say God's truth is just as important as *what* we say. Tension mounts as truth is attacked and zeal consigns love to the sidelines, attacking the enemy with a ferocity more fit for a beast than a lamb. "I just speak the truth," we elide. "It's not my problem if they don't like it."

Yet Christians were never called to sacrifice people on the altar of truth. Christians were never given permission to respond to enemy attacks with attacks of their own so long as it was true. For God's truth spoken without Christ's love ceases to be the truth of God. The content and the form must match, otherwise it's something different altogether. As the apostle Paul pleaded with the church of Corinth almost half a century prior, "And if I have the gift of prophecy and know all mysteries and all knowledge [truth] . . . but not love, I am nothing" (1 Cor 13:2).

Wielding truth as a weapon, regardless of whether we are right, betrays our ignorance of God's truth altogether. For Scripture is quite clear: *Jesus* is the truth (Jn 14:6), the content of our doctrine and our beliefs; the *cross* is the form, God's undying love offered to even his enemies (Lk 23:34). God is unwilling to compromise this combination. This truth discipled in love.

> "Remember the heights from where you've fallen" (Rev 2:5), Christ counsels. "Remember how I found you at your beginning. How I tenderly wooed you into moments of transformation, honoring the depths of your pain, refusing to

---

[17]My paraphrastic translation of the text.

break a bruised reed, but gently guiding you to the truth found in the mystery of a crucified king. *Do the same to others.* Treat them as I have treated you. And if you don't, I will remove your lampstand."[18]

Tension and terror, whatever the source or level, doesn't dismiss the Christian's call to love. It intensifies it. God will accept nothing less from his own.

Cultural compromise and abandoning Christ altogether were more appealing than ever for Christians caught in the imperial crossfire. What they needed, though, wasn't more resolve or teaching, more guilt or prediction, more sermons or legislation. What they needed was a revelation of Jesus Christ so compelling that, by the Spirit's power, they would become more than conquerors. They would become the body of Christ.

I WILL FIGHT YOU FOR YOU

Intimacy is terrifying. The potency unnerving. Although we crave it, we can hardly behold it, exchanging it instead for cheap imitations, hoping they will suffice. But they deceive and disappoint. Intimacy resists fabrication and phoniness. And the counterfeits can't bear the weight of intimacy. So, they crumble. Disintegrate. Leaving us lonelier still and longing for what only intimacy can provide: a reciprocal vulnerability. Fully knowing another and being fully known. A common move *toward*, even if that means at times *against*.

For years, every single Sunday, my family and I had a ritual. Church in the morning, nap in the afternoon, and an Aldi run in the evening to buy groceries for the week.

The Aldi process was pristine and predictable. We'd park the van, two kiddos would gather the bags from the backseat, and one would grab a quarter. Why? Because at Aldi, you bring your own bags for groceries, and you rent a cart for twenty-five cents. My job was to push the cart, entertaining our youngest and monitoring the others for any unapproved items magically appearing in the basket. My wife would masterfully weave us through each aisle, gathering every item for both snacks and meals, all without a list.

The ritual was crisp. Precise. But on this particular night, my daughter disrupted the routine.

---

[18]My paraphrastic elaboration of Revelation 2:4-5.

I honestly don't remember what was said. I don't remember what was done. I just know that on this Sunday, at this Aldi, a sassy pattern of behavior building for several days and weeks developed into a tension that finally crossed the line. So, I broke the Aldi ritual with an invitation: "Hey, baby girl, why don't we take a walk."

We made our way through the parking lot, up the hill, past the urgent care, and toward Academy, the sporting-goods store. As we walked, I asked my beautiful daughter, "Hey, how's your heart?"

I know. That's quite a big question to place on the delicate shoulders of an eleven-year-old. But sometimes asking big questions in safe spaces trains us for greater moments to come.

She answered as best she could, but with an attitude. I gave her space to explore this newfound sass, until finally, standing in the exercise section in Academy, I pointed to the bench press and said, "Sweetheart, why don't you have a seat."

She sat down, swinging her legs off the ledge. I bent down, bowed my head, and silently prayed for wisdom. Why? Because, contrary to popular belief, most parents are just making it up as they go. I didn't know what to say. I didn't know what to do. What I did know was I loved her. Deeply.

"Baby girl," I said as we locked eyes, "I love you more than anything in the world. But your attitude over the last couple of weeks is simply unacceptable. It's not who we are as a family, and it's not how we treat other people."

I paused for a moment or two, unsure where this was going. Then softened my gaze and tone, and continued.

"Here's the truth: Here soon, you'll be a teenager. And a lot will happen over the next few years—some things we can change and some things we can't. But there are two things that will *definitely* happen over the next couple of years, and no one can stop them."

She squirmed a bit, both listening and pretending not to as I pressed forward. "First, you will get older. No one can stop that. That *will* happen. It's nonnegotiable."

"And second," I smiled, voice just above a whisper, "I will fight for you. I will be *with* you because I love you. And *no one* can stop that. That's nonnegotiable."

She turned her head to the side, both loving and struggling with that last truth. Then we caught eyes once again. A subtle movement of intimacy toward each other. So I resumed.

"But *how* these next few years go is up to *you*."

She furrowed her brow, struck by the idea of choice. *Her* choice.

"Either," I continued, "we partner together as you grow older, trying to figure out how to deal with the good and the bad, *as a team*. Or, if this attitude of yours continues, then I love you so much that I will fight you for you. Because, Paigey, you are worth fighting for."

We hugged. We cried. And we resumed our Aldi ritual.

Yet I couldn't help but wonder whether Jesus was saying the same to me. To us. To the church of today. Tenderly yet fiercely, whispering the whole truth but in the shape of love's cross, "You, my beloved, are worth fighting for."

In today's church as in the seven churches of Revelation, every situation is different in each city. Different tensions, struggles, successes, and triumphs. Jesus knows them all. Intimately so. More so than we know or care to admit.

He sees us. Every one of us. Without a veil. He sees those persevering, those struggling, those overcoming, and those abandoning the faith altogether. In response to both extremes and everything in between, Jesus' love and pursuit is fierce yet tender, approaching each of us with two options: we can partner together, *or* I will fight you for you.

This is not a threat birthed out of frustration but a promise begotten by love. Forged in intimacy. Unearthed by death on a cross that offers new life to those bold enough to be fully known. Fully seen. Fully exposed to the one who searches hearts not with accusation but with the gentle touch of a loving Father who longs to give his children life to the full (Jn 10:10).

But the mystery of intimacy isn't solved by our willingness to be fully known, for the depths of intimacy also require fully knowing the other. The question, therefore, at the end of Revelation 2–3 is no longer "Does Christ know me?" Indeed, he does. Without any veil. The question now is, "Do I know him?"

GOING DEEPER

THE TOOL: Definitions. In studying God's Word, the Bible should define biblical words. Not us. Watch this video on the biblical definitions of last days and prophecy (www.ivpress.com/wood-2a) and wrestle with the following:

1. When so-called prophecy experts predict Jesus' coming and fail, what thoughts go through your mind?

   ➤ Does prediction advance the church's witness? Or does it distract from our mission?

2. Google the word *prophecy*. Read three to five sites looking for their definition of *prophecy*.

   ➤ How does this compare with the video's definition of prophecy?

   ➤ How does this compare with the definition of prophecy from your church growing up?

   ➤ What do these comparisons surface in you?

> **THE TEXT:** The closeness of Christ (Rev 2:1–3:22). Jesus knows us. Intimately so. He knows our struggles and our successes, our secrets and our desires. After watching this video (www.ivpress.com/wood-2b), answer the following:

1. To five out of the seven churches in Revelation 2–3, Jesus announces, "I know your deeds." Reflect on this level of intimacy.

   ➤ What comes to mind?

   ➤ What feelings well up?

   ➤ If you truly believed this, what would change about your life?

   ➤ How would it affect us as a church?

2. What is one thing you wish Jesus knew right now? Say it aloud as an offering to God and see how he responds.

> **THE TAKEAWAY:** A letter to the church. In Revelation 2–3, Jesus challenges the seven churches of Asia Minor to wrestle with their responsibility as lampstands for the light of the gospel. What follows is an exercise to position you closer to the voice of Christ in your own life and community.

Write a letter from Jesus to you or a church close to you, including the following elements:

1. Opening: Follow the formula beginning each letter in Revelation 2–3: "To the angel of the church of [name of the church or individual], write:"

2. Identification of Jesus: As with each letter in Revelation 2–3, choose an image of Jesus from Revelation 1 to summarize the letter's message.

3. "I know your deeds": Use this phrase and a description of the deeds— whether positive or negative.

4. Assessment of status: Ascribe a positive or negative assessment of the church/individual based on their deeds described above.

5. Exhortation/encouragement: Include a charge for the areas where the church/individual is struggling and an encouragement for the areas where the church/individual is thriving.

6. Promise for the overcomers: Include a promise for those who are victorious.

7. Call to hear the Spirit: End the letter with the same formula found in Revelation 2–3: "Those with ears to hear, let them hear what the Spirit says to the churches."

NOTE: The goal of this letter is not to accuse or disparage anyone or any community but to wrestle with God's voice in your world.

3

THE POWER IN HEAVEN'S HALLS
(Revelation 4–5)

Identity, Action, and Who God Is

The more you tell someone who they are, the
less you have to tell them what to do.

STUART BRISCOE

ACTION FLOWS FROM IDENTITY. My mom taught me this. Although I'm not sure she remembers.

You see, I was born in a pew. Not literally but essentially. Always in church whenever the doors were open—Sunday morning, Sunday night, Wednesday night. Always saturated in Scripture—memorizing the names of every Bible book and countless memory verses sprinkled throughout. The church was my second home. My world. My friend.

While other kiddos were playing superheroes, I'd get my Bible out, stand on the family couch, and preach hellfire and brimstone to any family member within earshot, believing every one of them desperately needed to repent.

I honestly don't remember a time when I didn't believe or profess I was a Christian, when I wasn't captivated or impressed with Christ.

Nevertheless, as many stories unfold, somewhere along the way I lost my way. My actions betrayed a competing allegiance. A different identity. A new story rivaling the old.

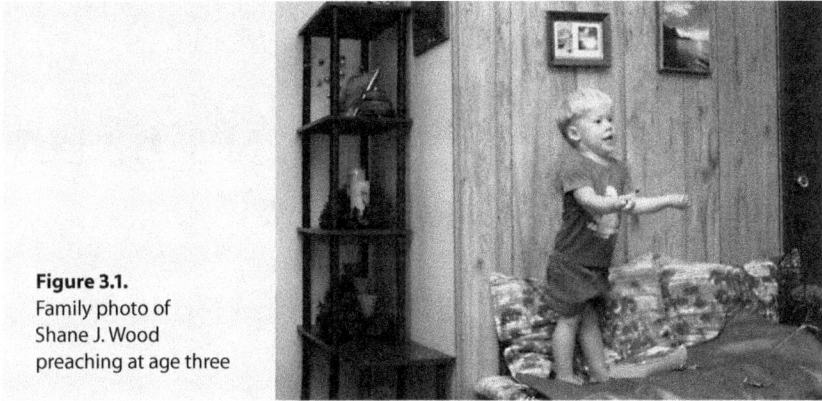

Figure 3.1.
Family photo of
Shane J. Wood
preaching at age three

It was my junior year of high school. I'd been dating a girl for about a year and a half. She wasn't a Christian, and at the time I didn't care. But tension began to build. She was frustrated our relationship hadn't advanced to the stage of sex, and she was quite vocal about it. I was in inner turmoil; I simply didn't know what to do. Maybe confused or conflicted or just run-of-the-mill scared. I'm not sure, to be honest.

I do remember, though, one day coming up from my room in the basement into the living room. My mom was sitting in the green fabric recliner adjacent to the front door and just opposite the out-of-tune upright piano where I'd empty my pockets after coming home. She turned off whatever was on TV with an unfamiliar, "Hey . . . Shane?"

It was something in her voice. Maybe a quiver or a concern. Maybe a memory from her past simmering just below the surface. I wasn't sure, but I knew it was something new. Something that announced the supreme significance of this moment in just two words: *Hey. Shane.*

"Yeah," I groaned with teenage angst.

"I, uh . . . ," she glanced over to my stuff on the ledge of the piano, ". . . the note from your girlfriend was laying open."

My breath tightened as a mix of emotions flushed my face, a cocktail of anger, fear, shame, and betrayal. She noticed.

"I didn't *mean* to read it, but Shane . . ."

She paused. Uncomfortably long.

"Shane—I just want you to remember who you are. Who we are as a family. Christians."

Without another word, she stood up and briskly walked down the hallway to her room, lightly shutting the door.

I was statued. Unsure how to respond. Frozen by embarrassment and disbelief. Shocked by the simple statement: *remember who you are.*

That night, a lot unfolded. Yes, I broke up with my girlfriend, but thanks to my mom, my life was profoundly altered by uncommon wisdom. By a truth subtle yet essential: that action flows from identity. *What I do* is birthed from *who I am.*

An insight that shapes my family to this day.

With each of my four kids, the kindergarten morning routine was exactly the same. We'd pile in the van, lunchbox and backpacks in tow, and as we approached the school, I'd start the family chant:

"Who are we?"

"The Wood family," the little voice intoned.

I'd antiphonally respond, "And who is the Wood family?"

"Christians!"

"And what do Christians do?"

Each kid, over the years, would answer with their own litany of Christian behaviors, something to the effect of, "Christians love, don't hurt people with their hands or feet or words, always tell the truth, and smile a lot."

But the routine was incomplete without these final words: "That's right," I'd smile. "So *remember who you are.*"

As time unfolds and each child grows, the routine is still consistently invoked, just in short. When one of them leaves for a football game or is dropped off at Sunday school or is off to prom or another shift at work, I recite my mother's words: *remember who you are.*

Four words that over the years have been repeated time and again, becoming a sort of family slogan or battle cry: *remember who you are.*

Why? Because action flows from identity.

And that's easy to miss. To obscure. To misunderstand and misinterpret their interplay, their relationship, their power, their unmatched revelation that *what you do* (action) flows from *who you are* (identity).

BEHAVIOR MODIFICATION VERSUS
IDENTITY FORMATION

Too often in the church and as parents, our goal is to change behavior. Sometimes our own but especially that of others. We implore those in our care or
in our sphere to stop acting one way and start acting another. To stop doing
certain things and start doing other things. From clothes to cursing to
drinking to smoking to voting, the list is endless while the goal the same:
replace deviant acts with right living. We preach and seek to modify behavior,
yet neglect to query and pursue the preceding question: What gives birth to
such behavior in the first place?

Reading Revelation 2–3, Jesus appears to make the same mistake. He confronts the seven churches and seems to berate them into new behavior. Actions are assessed, deeds measured, at times affirmed and at others challenged, and what they do or don't do fills the red letters to all seven churches.
Yet, each congregation's conversation is rooted in the context of identity.
His identity.

Each letter, remember, begins with Jesus reminding the rebellious and the
resilient of who he is, harnessing images from his majestic appearance in
Revelation 1:12-20. As the behaviors of the believers surface in each carefully
crafted letter, identity is the fount from which all flows.

To each church, Jesus asks a question that includes behavior while
stretching far beyond it: Do your actions match your identity? Or better still,
do your actions match *my* identity? As Christ-followers, our identity and
therefore our actions must derive from Christ. Or as 1 John 2:6 explains,
"Whoever says, 'I abide in Jesus' must live as Jesus lived."

If action flows from identity, then behavior modification proffers short-
term solutions that produce long-term tragedies. Simply put: a change of
behavior can't persist if a new identity isn't embraced. This is why Paul pleads
in Colossians 2:20-23 to reject the world's wisdom that espouses the legalistic
lines, "Do not handle! Do not taste! Do not touch!" Such mantras tout transformation, but Paul argues that these rules, and others like them, are something sinister masquerading as holy, something more along the lines of "self-
willed religion" and "false humility" dressed in the garb of "severe treatment
of the body." The truth is "[such regulations] lack any value in restraining
indulgence of the flesh" (Col 2:23) and therefore can't produce transformation

of any sort. Such rules are like putting Band-Aids on wounds that need surgery. Sure, action is employed to address the issue, but the action embraced can't fix the problem. The behavior may change for a time, but under the surface the undercurrents still churn, awaiting to sweep the unaware perilously out to sea.

Preaching behavior modification sans identity formation is a practice as foolish as it is pervasive. Why? Because our behavior betrays the identity embraced, for action flows from who we are, and who we are flows from *whose* we are. Whom we claim to follow. Whom we serve as our master. Whom we worship, for better or worse.

In Revelation 2–3, Jesus contrasts the behavior of Christ-followers with his identity. To the church of Pergamum, Jesus is the one who wields "the sharp, double-edged sword" (Rev 2:12; cf. Rev 1:16) even as they permit the preaching of Balaam, who entices believers to wander astray (Rev 2:14-16). To the church of Thyatira, Jesus is the sovereign "Son of God" with eyes "like a fiery flame" (Rev 2:18; cf. Rev 1:14) even as they revel in impurity and sexual immorality (Rev 2:20-23). To the church of Laodicea, Jesus is "the faithful and true witness" who secured sovereignty through the poverty of the cross (Rev 3:14; cf. Rev 1:5, 18) even as they arrogantly boast to heaven, "I am rich, and I have accumulated wealth, and I need nothing" (Rev 3:17). The message in each contrast is quite clear: your actions don't match your claims to Christ.

And to each church—indeed, to each Christian (past, present, and for posterity)—Christ's plea is the same: *remember who you are*. Remember who you are by remembering *whose* you are, because as Christians, our identity is determined by his. Which raises the question, Who is God?

WHO IS GOD?

The purpose of all prophetic works, Old or New Testament, is to reveal who God is to a wayward people. A revelation of God's identity can correct *their* identity, and their behavior will follow accordingly. Far beyond mere prediction, then, prophecy intends to prosecute and persuade a rebellious people to change.[1] To transform. To encounter the God they call their own even as

---

[1] D. Brent Sandy, *Ploughshares and Pruning Hooks: Rethinking the Language of Biblical Prophecy and Apocalyptic* (Downers Grove, IL: InterVarsity Press, 2002), 130-31.

they betray him with a kiss. Prophecy reveals God and expects a response, repentance or continued resilience.

Consider Isaiah 1. God demands Israel's attention—"Hear the word of the LORD, rulers of Sodom"—with an intensity unfamiliar to most Scripture—"Listen to the teaching of our God, people of Gomorrah!" (Is 1:10). Without pretense or pleasantries, God critiques their worship with undertones of identity: "The multitude of your sacrifices, what are they to me?" Does God need to be fed like other deities? With animals he created? Is that who he is? "No!" he reminds them. "I have had enough burnt offerings of rams and the fat of fattened animals. I do not delight in the blood of bulls and lambs and goats" (Is 1:11).

The critique swells as the text unfolds with Israel's incense, Sabbaths, feasts, and festivals, classified by God as "detestable," "worthless," and a "burden" (Is 1:13-14). In postures of prayer and in settings of worship, they stretch out their hands stained with the blood of the "oppressed," the "fatherless," and the "widow" (Is 1:15-17) to honor a God who fights for the forgotten, the vulnerable, and even those enslaved in Egypt (see Ex 22:25-27; 23:6-12; Lev 19:9-10; Deut 10:17-19; 15:7-15; etc.). In response, God withholds none of his disgust:

> You must stop bringing worthless offerings! Your incense is detestable to me. . . . I cannot endure your worthless assemblies. Your New Moons feast and your festivals, I hate with all of my being. They have become a burden to me. I am tired of bearing them. At the stretching out of your hands in prayer, I will hide my eyes from you. Even though you make many prayers, I will not be listening. (Is 1:13-15)

God ends the tirade with a staccato of imperatives targeting Israel's actions: "Remove your evil deeds from before my eyes. Stop doing evil. Learn to do good. Seek justice. Reprove the oppressor. Defend the fatherless. Plead the case of the widow" (Is 1:16-17).

Yet God isn't agitated by mere behavior but by what the behavior unveils: they do not know him. "I reared children and brought them up," God laments at the outset of Isaiah 1, "but they have rebelled against me. An ox knows its owner, a donkey its owner's manger, but Israel does not know [me]. My people do not understand [me]" (Is 1:2-3).

God has gone to great lengths and not with a little strain to reveal who he is to creation, fashioning humanity with his own hands (Gen 2:7), emblazoning his divine image on each (Gen 1:26-27), and walking with them in the cool of the day under Eden's delight and demise (Gen 3:8). In response to their rebellion, he crafted garments of skin to protect them (Gen 3:21); in reply to their cries, he called Moses to liberate them (Ex 3:1-22); in response to their grumbling, he fed them manna in the morning and meat at twilight (Ex 16:1-35); in exchange for their wandering, he crafted ten commandments on stone tablets, revealing himself by declaring, "I am the LORD your God, who brought you from the land of Egypt, from the house of slavery" (Ex 20:2). Consistently and without pause, God pierced the veil between heaven and earth to reveal himself to all creation and to his own.

To counter confusion, he taught Israel the great Shema, "The LORD our God, the Lord is one" (Deut 6:4); to combat corruption, he appointed Israel a new ruler, "a man after my own heart" (1 Sam 13:14); to confront loneliness, he curated a tabernacle (Ex 26:1-37) so he could "dwell in their midst," everpresent with his people (Ex 25:8). With creativity and concern, God reached out to his own and others to reveal his identity to all, whether in the consuming fire on Mount Carmel (1 Kings 18:16-46), in the sling and stones of a small shepherd boy (1 Sam 17:40-51), or in the still small voice to a cowering prophet (1 Kings 19:1-12). All inspired Scripture is a movement of God *toward* us to reveal himself *to* us.

Regardless, though, of how often and in what variety God unveiled his identity, Israel's actions revealed they still did not know him. In Exodus 32, at the foot of Mount Sinai, they fashioned a golden calf and worshiped the graven image because they didn't know him. In Deuteronomy 1, at the precipice of the Promised Land, they refused to enter—"Because the LORD hates us, he brought us out of the land of Egypt . . . to destroy us" (Deut 1:27)—because they did not know him. In 1 Samuel 8, at the end of Samuel's life, the elders of Israel rejected God as their king and instead asked for a king "like all the other nations" (1 Sam 8:5) because they did not know him. And here in Isaiah 1, to the God of the least of these, they stretch out their hands, palms smeared with the blood of orphans and widows before the God who would one day shed his blood for them, because they did not know him.

Action flows from identity. The identity of God's own is determined by who God is. This is precisely why Isaiah 1 gives way to the next sixty-five chapters filled with vivid depictions of who God is, from the branch of the Lord in Isaiah 4 to the suffering servant in Isaiah 53 to the heavenly throne room of Isaiah 6—a scene filled with smoke, chanting seraphim, and God enthroned. A scene, incidentally, like Revelation 4–5.

LIMITING THE LIMITLESS

The collapse of cosmology in Revelation 1 is transposed into a different key in Revelation 4–5. In Revelation 1, God doesn't sit idle as his creation languishes in loneliness and isolation. He makes the first move. He pierces the veil, leaving heaven to visit John on earth. In Revelation 4, however, God invites John to leave earth to visit heaven, to pass through the veil separating the abode of humanity and the abode of God to view earth's struggle from a divine perspective, to hear hope sung by heaven's choir. This heavenly vantage anchors earth's battle and our response in God's identity, not by answering the question "What should we do?" but by unveiling "Who is God?"

Revelation 4–5, though, is not a digression from Revelation 2–3 but a natural outworking. Similar to Isaiah 1, the rebellion and resilience of the seven churches uncover not just wavering or wayward conduct but distortion or disregard for who God is and, as a result, who they are as his people. Action flows from identity, and if they don't know who he is, then they won't know who they are, and they definitely won't know what to do. To correct the actions of the churches, then, the revelation must begin with a reintroduction to the identity of God. Revelation 4–5 is indeed just that— albeit with a Jesus-infused twist.

Upon John's heavenly arrival, language is stretched to its breaking point, revealing God through symbols, songs, and poetic advances. View of the one sitting on the throne is shrouded by brilliant glory. Like "jasper and carnelian" (Rev 4:3), God's presence emits radiant light, emerald emanating like an emblazoned bow around the throne (Rev 4:3). Twenty-four other thrones add to God's grandeur, with each elder dressed in triumphant white robes and crowned with gold (Rev 4:4). Creation quakes with "flashes of lightning and rumblings and peals of thunder" (Rev 4:5), even as a crystal-clear sea sits before the throne as still as glass (Rev 4:6). Four Ezekiel-like living creatures,

representing all creation (see Ezek 1:4-24; cf. Is 6:1-7), cry out from their preeminent position "in the middle, encircling the throne" (Rev 4:6), "Holy, holy, holy is the Lord God, the Almighty one, the one who was and is and is to come" (Rev 4:8).

Day and night, without ceasing (Rev 4:8), the four living creatures provide unparalleled perspective. Covered with eyes "in front and in back" (Rev 4:6) and "all around and inside" (Rev 4:8), the four living creatures offer unique wisdom from the inner circle of God's throne room.[2] As such, their perpetual canticle shouldn't be glossed over, for it centers heaven's worship on one key theme: the identity of God.

The tripartite "Holy" bellows like the beat of a drum rhythmically reciting the same message: "There is no one like our God." He is singularly unique. Set apart. Beyond replication. Beyond fabrication. Beyond expression or comprehension, for words cannot contain him even as temples cannot house him.

Which is why Exodus 3:14 is so startling. Scandalous, even.

As Moses stumbled upon holy ground in the barren desert, he accosted God with a question as simple as it is absurd: What is your name? (Ex 3:13). The problem is that *words limit*. And names intentionally delimit. Demarcate and fix boundaries so that *this* one can be distinguished from *that* one (Gen 2:19-20). But, by definition, God is limitless. Boundary-less. "Alpha and Omega" (Rev 1:8), beginning and end, the one "who was and is and is to come" (Rev 4:8).[3] Thus, to give Moses an answer, to limit himself in a name, denies a central element of his identity: the one who cannot be contained in a name. For words cannot contain the infinite one, the one who is "Holy, holy, holy."

Even still, God answers. He responds to Moses with a name: "I am who I am" (Ex 3:14). He replies with a movement of grace: "You tell them: I AM has sent me to you" (Ex 3:14). In a name, God moves toward us. For us. Limiting himself so the limited can know him, even if only in part.

That's what he did (action), because that's who he is (identity).

---

[2] Pseudo-Dionysius identifies the inner circle of celestial beings (especially cherubim and seraphim) as those with the highest levels of divine knowledge due to their proximity to the throne (*The Celestial Hierarchy* 6.1–7.4).

[3] The threefold "who was and is and is to come" appears throughout a variety of scenes in Revelation, emphasizing the eternality of God. It is used for God the Father multiple times (Rev 1:4, 8; 4:8), twice omitting "is to come" to emphasize present judgment (Rev 11:17; 16:5). Four times in Rev 17:8 [2×], 10-11, evil parodies the trifold formula, highlighting its divine significance. Other phrases such as "beginning and end" and "first and last" also emphasize God's eternality (Rev 1:8, 17; 2:8; 21:6; 22:13).

PERCEIVING TRUE POWER

The four living creatures continue their celestial psalm by qualifying God's uniqueness still further. He is holy because *his power pervades all.* He is the "Almighty one," the *pantocrator,* which literally means "the one who commands all things and all people."[4]

Our definitions of power, though, war with our understanding of God's identity. Typically we define power with gradients of might, not acts of service; with swords of sovereignty, not self-sacrifice—especially not for our enemies. But the power of the Almighty God in Revelation 4 is defined through the imagery of Christ in Revelation 5: Jesus sovereignly enthroned as a slain Lamb.

Such a move is not just narratival or exegetical but theological and essential. Creation craves God and is restless until it finds its rest in him.[5] The New Testament is quite clear: to know Jesus is to know God. To study Jesus is to study God. For Jesus doesn't just imitate the Father; he *exegetes* the Father (Jn 1:18).[6] He explicates the Holy One. Jesus enfleshes what heretofore was invisible (Col 1:15), what was viewed yet through a muddy mirror (1 Cor 13:12), beheld but only through a veil (2 Cor 3:12-18).

Yes, God went through great lengths to reveal himself before the fall and thereafter, from prophets to theophanies to limiting himself in a name, but his own still did not know him. We still could not see him. And so, with one voice, all of creation cries out, "Lord, show us the Father, and that will be enough" (Jn 14:8). In response, Christ clarifies our exegetical lens: "Whoever has seen [the Son] has seen the Father" (Jn 14:9).

As in Exodus 3, God limited himself to a time and at a place in the womb of Mary, in the flesh of Jesus Christ (Jn 1:1, 14). In Jesus, the physical and the nonphysical become one; in him is union of "uncreated and created, impassible and passible," seen and unseen.[7] Thus, the Revelation of Jesus Christ thins the veil between heaven and earth, for Jesus incarnates "the radiance

---

[4]Johannes P. Louw and Eugene A. Nida, "παντοκράτωρ, ορος," in *Greek-English Lexicon of the New Testament: Based on Semantic Domains,* 2nd ed. (New York: United Bible Societies, 1996), 12.7.

[5]Augustine, *Confessions* 1.1.1. See also Pseudo-Dionysius, *Divine Names* 4.4-7, 10-13.

[6]In biblical interpretation, "interpreting a text" is referred to as *exegesis,* which comes from the Greek word ἐξηγέομαι, used in Jn 1:18. It means to explain or to make fully known or to draw the meaning out of.

[7]Maximus the Confessor, *Ambigua ad Thomam* 2.2.

of God's glory and the exact representation of his being" (Heb 1:3 NIV) so that, in a movement of grace, "God's glory [is unveiled] in the face of Christ" (2 Cor 4:6).

As such, our definitions of the Holy God, the Almighty Father, must be discipled by the Revelation of Jesus Christ. And nothing is off-limits or out of reach. Definitions of glory (Mk 10:35-45), definitions of victory (Rev 12:11), definitions of justice (Mt 5:38-48), definitions of monotheism (1 Cor 8:6), and yes, even definitions of power.

In Revelation 5, John is overcome and overwhelmed at the sight of a scroll resting in the Father's hand, a revelation from God sealed with seven seals (Rev 5:1). Yet no one is found worthy to open the scroll (Rev 5:2-3). No one mighty enough to wrest it from the clutches of the king.

So John weeps (Rev 5:4). Bitterly. Desperate for a message from the Lord to satisfy the loneliness and the confusion of life on Patmos and life under the Roman Empire. John sobs, helpless and hopeless.

Then, like a good shepherd, one of the twenty-four elders from Revelation 4 comforts John with a redefinition of power: "Don't cry. Look! The Lion of the tribe of Judah. The root of David. He has conquered [νικάω], and he is able to open the scroll and its seven seals" (Rev 5:5). With blurry eyes, John looks, in search of power, seeking, like most, the strength of a Lion. But all he finds is a Lamb, "appearing as if it had been slaughtered." Slain yet standing sovereign "in the middle of the throne" (Rev 5:6).

This juxtaposition of a Lion and a Lamb is not incidental. It defines, or redefines, the *pantocrator* of Revelation 4, the "Almighty" that sets apart the eternal God as holy. The power and worth of Rome was secured through the annihilation and at times crucifixion of enemies. But the power and worth of Christ was acquired through the affliction and mutilation as a victim of crucifixion himself (Rev 5:9). In Revelation 5, it's *because* Jesus is the one "who was slaughtered" (Rev 5:12) that all of heaven worships him and finds him worthy "to receive power and wealth and wisdom and strength and honor and glory and praise" (Rev 5:12). Humanity's definition of power, then, is mocked with the heavenly revelation of victory through Christ's cross. This insight excites all of creation: "I heard every creature in heaven and on earth and underneath the earth and on the sea, and all that is in them, saying: 'To the one sitting on the throne and to the Lamb be praise and honor and glory

and power, for ever and ever!'" (Rev 5:13). The slain Lamb exegetes the Almighty Father, bringing both clarity and concern to a people caught in the shadow of the empire.

THE BRIDGE TO THE DIVINE

Revelation 4–5 unveils *who* God is and celebrates *what* God has done. For action flows from identity. And as Christians, our identity is rooted in Christ. Created by Christ. Transformed by the slain Lamb.

In Revelation 5:8-10, the voices of the four living creatures and twenty-four elders unite to sing a "new song." A song celebrating Christ's sacrifice as not just a promise for heaven one day but a new creation on earth today:

> With your blood you redeemed for God
> persons from every tribe and tongue and people and nation.
> And you formed them into a kingdom and priests to our God,
> and they will be kings on the earth. (Rev 5:9-10)

The cross of Christ, an act of the Almighty God, liberates us and transforms us into a "kingdom and priests." But make no mistake, like Paul's "body of Christ" (1 Cor 12:27), the title "kingdom and priests" is more than just a label or a name tag to be worn. It's an identity. And every identity comes with a mission.

This isn't the first time Revelation invokes Christ's sacrifice as a catalyst for transformation, and even in similar language. In the opening verses, John sings, "To the one who loves us and has freed us from our sins by his blood, and has formed us into a kingdom and priests to his God and Father—to him be glory and power for ever and ever. Amen" (Rev 1:5-6).[8] The opening words of the Revelation of Jesus Christ celebrate our liberation and our transformation through the blood of the slain Lamb. The slain Lamb who is the king of a kingdom fashioned by the ministry of priests.

---

[8]The reference to "freed us from our sins by his blood" alludes to the liberation of Israel in the final exodus event, when the blood of the lamb was spread on the doorposts (Ex 11:1–12:42). Similarly, "kingdom and priests" alludes to Ex 19:3-6, when God told Moses to instruct Israel, "And now, if you obey my voice fully and keep my covenant . . . you shall be for me a kingdom of priests and a holy nation" (Ex 19:5-6). Unfortunately, the rest of the Old Testament documents how Israel did not in fact obey God or keep the covenant, resulting in Israel's exile (i.e., the exodus in reverse). Yet Christ's faithfulness satisfies the conditional "if you obey my voice fully," resulting in the fulfillment of the promise in those who follow him, i.e., the "kingdom and priests" (Rev 1:6).

In the Old Testament, priests were the bridge between heaven and earth, between humanity and God. Through sacrifices, offerings, and blessings, the priests mediated God's holy covenant to earth's festering wounds (Lev 16:1-34). Similarly, Christ is our "great high priest" (Heb 4:14) who offers an eternal sacrifice as the slain Lamb (Heb 10:12-14), allowing us to "approach the throne of grace with boldness" (Heb 4:16). Thus, in both instances, priests pierce the veil, bridging what we can see with what we cannot. Our ministry, as the body of Christ, is no different. But only if we understand power as defined by the identity and actions of the slain Lamb.

Revelation 1:9 characterizes our priestly kingdom as one of "suffering" and "patient endurance in Jesus." A kingdom that conquers the dragon, "that ancient serpent called the devil and Satan" (Rev 12:9), not with swords or weapons of mass destruction. For our battle is "not against flesh and blood" (Eph 6:12) but against an enemy that lurks in the shadows just beyond the veil. An enemy conquered "by the blood of the Lamb" (Rev 12:11) *and* by the willingness of each saint to take up their cross and die as Christ did (Rev 12:11). In Jesus, we are a kingdom of priests whose mission for the Almighty God is to be a bridge beyond the veil, even for those who oppose us. Even if it means we suffer as Christ suffered.

Jesus' identity and ministry craft who we are and dictate what we do. The slain Lamb, therefore, is more than mere imagery or symbol without substance. It's a revelation. A bridge that spans heaven and earth, God and humanity, the beyond and what's right before us. It's a mission to be embodied. It's a clarion call from God to his own to *remember who you are*.

BEYOND THE VEIL

Sometimes I wonder if the American church suffers from a severe case of amnesia. If we've forgotten who we are. If we've lost sight of our King crowned in glory with thorns that pierce his brow. If we've exchanged the power of the slain Lamb for Supreme Court justices, a majority in the House and the Senate, and our political party's president sitting in the Oval Office. Especially during election season, Christians seem to carry a cross to find their next victim instead of being the sacrifice themselves. Fear governs our actions as vitriol dictates our speech. We lambast any who disagree with our party line

and incessantly repeat the slogans of our favorite political pundits, forgetting the chants of "Holy, holy, holy" that rest just beyond the veil.

The day after President Barack Obama was elected to his second term, I did something stupid. I got on social media. The anger, outrage, and at times blatant racism that filled my feed was overwhelming. Especially coming from the very same people who taught me Jesus in Sunday school as a kiddo. The more I scrolled, the more I became confused.

One post in particular caught my attention. The woman curtly wrote, "When I heard the results last night, I wept because I was so angry and scared. In fact, I cried myself to sleep last night."

Out loud, mouth open, eyes fixed to my screen, I yelled, "What?!?!"

I shook my head, trying to piece together what I was taught about Jesus and what I was witnessing from Christians. I knew responding online would do nothing, but my mind was racing with questions: "You cried yourself to sleep last night? Over an election? When was the last time you cried yourself to sleep over a child caught in sex trafficking? When was the last time you cried yourself to sleep over orphans and widows caught in the crossfire of a war they didn't start and never wanted? When was the last time you cried yourself to sleep over lost souls who die every day without Jesus?"

Social media rewards folly over wisdom. Many posts should never be written. Much of what crosses our minds doesn't deserve to be spoken or recorded for any to see or hear. Yet Jesus was right to draw our attention to the thread connecting our heart to what we say: "The things proceeding out of a mouth come from the heart, and that makes the person profane" (Mt 15:18). Our words unveil our allegiance, where we put our trust, where our faith truly resides. In Rome. Or in God's throne. But we cannot pretend to adequately serve two masters. "Either you will hate the one and love the other, or be devoted to the one and scorn the other" (Mt 6:24). And Revelation leaves little room for negotiation.

As Christians, we need to remember that regardless of who wins an election, the four living creatures are still singing, the twenty-four elders are still bowing, and God is still sitting sovereign on his heavenly throne. We need to remember that regardless of the political issue, we were never called to follow a donkey or an elephant. We were called to follow the slain Lamb.

As Christians, we need to remember *who we are* in light of *who he is*. We are the kingdom of the crucified King. The priests of the risen Lord. The bridges between humanity and divinity that pierce the veil between heaven and earth, offering healing and hope to all. Enemies included.

GOING DEEPER

THE TOOL: Historical background. Revelation was written to real people at a real time going through real issues. Historical background invites the reader to see the world through the eyes of first-century Christians. Watch this video (www.ivpress.com/wood-3a) and wrestle with the following:

1. Empathy is defined as "seeing the world through another person's eyes—their experiences, their emotions, their context."

   ➤ How does practicing empathy help with historical background?

   ➤ What insights can empathy offer into the biblical text?

   ➤ What insights can empathy offer into today's world?

2. What other ways do you find historical background useful?

3. If you were a Christian in the first century, what do you think your biggest struggle would be? Your biggest fear? Your greatest joy?

THE TEXT: The power of Christ (Rev 4:1–5:14). The Revelation of Jesus Christ redefines words such as *victory, suffering, power,* and *monotheism.* Christ's identity removes the veil from our eyes, allowing us to see as God sees. Watch this video (www.ivpress.com/wood-3b) and answer the following:

1. In Revelation 4:11, the twenty-four elders worship God because he created all things and sustains their being.

   ➤ Reflect on the creation account in Genesis 1. What type of God is revealed? What characteristics of God come to the forefront? Is he threatening? Gentle? Rude? Considerate?

   ➤ How does a good theology of creation draw us closer to Jesus?

2. Revelation 5:5-6 offers a majestic picture of Jesus as a slain Lamb. Put yourself in the time of the disciples, view the Roman world through their eyes, and listen to Jesus' words on power through their ears.

> What do you see? Would you have argued with Jesus like Peter? Would you have jostled for "the greatest in the kingdom" like James and John?

> How would you respond?

THE TAKEAWAY: Creating a new creation. We don't learn by merely reading or listening. We also learn by creating, fashioning something as an interpretation of what we've encountered in God's Word. What follows is a practice of sanctified imagination, where you create something from the imagery of Revelation 4:1–5:14. Here's how it works:

---

1. Re-read Revelation 4:1–5:14. Allow the images to prayerfully stimulate your imagination.

2. Partner with the Spirit to create something new: a poem, a song, a painting, a set of prayers, a liturgical service, or something else entirely. For inspiration, see

> Albrecht Dürer's wood carving titled "The Four Horsemen" (ca. 1497–1498): www.ivpress.com/wood-3c.

> Jennie Lee Riddle's "Revelation Song," based on Revelation 4 (performed by Kari Jobe): www.ivpress.com/wood-3d.

3. Share your creation with someone you love and trust.

4

WORSHIP IS WAR
(Revelation 6:1–8:5)

Politics, Propaganda, and the Power of Story

———

*Sovereign Lord, the holy and true one, how long until you
judge the earth dwellers and avenge our blood?*

REVELATION 6:10

THE LOBBY WAS TENSE. Two daughters, one spouse, and no agreement
on how to remember their mom. I sat with windows to my back; they surrounded the coffee table, filled with unkept magazines; and stories filled the
space between. Stories of pain, frustration, joy, laughter, oddities, quirks, and
isolation. Stories about their mom.

Two weeks earlier, I sat beside her in the hospital. Machines whizzing and
whirling, providing oxygen and end-of-life care. Her family sat at the foot of
her bed, witnessing each labored breath.

She had called the meeting. Asked for my presence. Invited me into this
sacred space.

The family didn't know what she had planned. They even seemed a bit ap-
prehensive. Unsure of what she might say or whether she'd say anything at all.
Or at least anything coherent.

Her illness had come on quite rapidly. At least from the children's perspective. She was a private woman, keeping even her diagnosis to herself for
the last six months. Now, with only days left, all was laid bare.

She held my hand and whispered, "I wish I could've done more." Her eyes glistened and her voice trailed off as she repeated, "I just wish I could've done more."

Too often in moments like these, the living feel the need to fill the space with words. The dying, however, understand no words will suffice. Silence is best embraced, not merely endured.

She turned her head, closing her eyes, as her breath rattled a deep mystery. Each breath vying to be her last. For fifteen minutes or so, we all sat silent. Watching. Waiting. Praying.

She startled awake, almost as if she'd been pulled back from beyond the veil. She blinked her way over to me, both seeing and appearing to see past me.

"I'm scared," she whispered.

"Of what?" I asked.

Her lip quivered. Her pupils enlarged and then contracted. She stared into silence.

"Of dying?" I whispered.

"That . . . that . . . and," she stammered, "that I haven't done enough."

"My dear friend," I leaned in, "he's so proud of you. He's so excited to hold you. He loves you so much."

Her gaze held me in the silence for several minutes. Finally, I asked, "What would you like me to pray?"

She slowly turned her head toward her children, closed her eyes, and let out a long sigh. "Pray," she rasped, "pray that when I close my eyes, I see Jesus with his eyebrows raised and not lowered."

Now, in the lobby, after her death, her children shared stories. For hours, they sorted through each memory like unopened boxes littering the family attic, exchanging anecdotes about their mom like gifts wrapped with words such as *fierce*, *private*, *loyal*, and *chili dogs*. Stories about parties she would plan for dinner guests she never invited. Stories about rules never spoken but always obeyed, like to never write in pen or to avoid direct eye contact even with your loved ones. Stories about elaborate Thanksgiving feasts with mounds of food piled on folding tables that actually tipped over multiple times. In that sacred space, with each sacred story, the daughters wrestled with questions of the past, a void in the present, all unsure how to take the next step into the future. Into a world without their mother.

The stories were the balm and the burn, the cure and the source of the pain itself. At times one of them would say, "Gosh, we're messed up." Silence would fill the space. Only to be interrupted with another story that would elicit a nod of the head or rippling laughter or just more tears.

THE POWER OF STORIES

Stories are powerful. They heal. They wound. They convict. They create. Communities preserve them. Families relive them. Nations wield them, for good and ill. Stories move us, transform us, guide us, and give us meaning, purpose, and an understanding of *who we are*. Stories create worlds.

Identities, both individual and communal, are birthed by stories. Tethered to and anchored by stories. Stories of wounds done to us or by us craft our personalities, our triggers, and our defenses. Stories of heroes known to us or created by us inspire our actions, our dreams, and even our grammar. Oftentimes, stories are summarized by slogans (*E pluribus unum*), sometimes smothered with shame ("I always mess everything up"), and sometimes saturated in grace ("Christ makes me new"). Sometimes a song or a phrase triggers characters, plots, and all the emotions that come with a shared story.

Stories shape us, compel us, intrigue us. Stories blur the lines of who we are and who we want to be. This is why trillions of dollars are spent on blockbuster movies each year. This is why millions of people willingly swab and mail their DNA to catch a glimpse of ancestral trees. This is why preachers are taught that if you're losing your audience, just tell a story. The congregation will always respond with rapt attention.

Why? Because we are storied beings. Each person, each family, each community a tapestry of interweaving stories.

It comes as no surprise, then, when the New Testament begins with five books of stories. Stories that recount our beginnings, our foremothers and forefathers. Stories of a new covenant sealed in blood and promising an abundant life. Stories that flow from a story still prior: the Old Testament.

The Old Testament endlessly employs the power of story to craft God's people. To fashion their ethics, to dictate their allegiance, to define who they are and where they belong. These stories are told and retold time and again, harnessing repetition to form the identity of a nation.

Take, for example, the exodus. After nine devastating plagues, Pharaoh refused to loosen the bonds of slavery, hardening his heart to Moses' persistent plea, "Let my people go" (Ex 5:1; 7:16; 8:1, 20; 9:1, 13; 10:3). Before the final plague unleashed (Ex 12:29-30), God instructed Moses and Aaron to orient Israel's calendar around a meal: the Passover (Ex 12:1). A feast embedding the exodus story in each emblem.

To this day, the Passover meal consists of bitter herbs and bread without yeast (Ex 12:8) to remind Israel of the bitterness of Egyptian slavery and the purification of sin from their midst. The feast centers on hope found in consuming the slain Lamb whose blood, in the exodus, painted the doorframe (Ex 12:22) as a plea and a pledge for mercy and grace in the face of death. Consuming the meal, then, is a means of ingesting the story, becoming the story, actively participating in God's narrative.

And not only one time but annually. At the dawn of each new year. Orienting all time and space around the exodus story. As the calendar cycles anew, the feast prompts the question, "What is the meaning of this ceremony?" In response, God commands Israel to retell the story (Ex 12:26-27). The story of God's faithfulness, the story of God's redemption. The story of when God brought his people out of Egypt, through the Red Sea, into the wilderness, and to the base of Mount Sinai, where his law delivered his will through his story: "I am the LORD your God, who brought you from the land of Egypt, from the house of slavery. You shall have no other gods before me" (Ex 20:2-3).

The story of the exodus reveals God to his people and, by extension, reveals God's people to themselves. The story shapes them, guides them, anchors them in identity and action. This is why even the great Shema (Deut 6:4-5; cf. Mt 22:34-40), which both commands allegiance and celebrates God's identity, invokes the exodus story with a cautionary imperative: "Guard yourself so that you do not forget the LORD, who brought you out from the land of Egypt, from the house of slavery" (Deut 6:12). The community and posterity are to be covered in the commands rooted in the story: "Recite them to your children. Talk about them sitting at your home and walking along the road and at your lying down and at your rising. Bind them as a symbol on your hand and as an emblem on your forehead. And write them on the doorframe of your house and on your gates" (Deut 6:7-8). The

exodus story saturates the mundane and the generations to come, for identities are created by repeating the story.

Without surprise, then, the exodus story significantly shapes the story of the New Testament. The exodus provides the grammar, contours, and imagery in the Gospels, Paul, and the later letters. Christ's ministry breaks the bonds of sin's slavery, liberates the lost and the oppressed at the cross, and offers a new law written on the hearts of his disciples.

In Revelation, the exodus influences much. The exodus crafts Revelation's worship, redefining power and praise through the Passover's slain Lamb (Rev 5:6-14). The exodus molds all three sets of seven, especially the plagues of the trumpets (Rev 8:1–9:21) and the bowls (Rev 16:1-21).[1] The exodus shapes the identity of God's people as a "kingdom and priests" (Rev 1:6; 5:10), a promise offered to Israel at the base of Mount Sinai by God himself (Ex 19:3-6). Each allusion to the exodus reminds the reader of God's faithfulness in the past in the face of oppressive evil and his longing for all to repent (Rev 9:20-21).

In Revelation, then, allusions to Exodus and, indeed, the whole Old Testament, are more than mere parallels. They are an interweaving of stories. An unfolding of God's narrative. An articulation of the Revelation of Jesus Christ from "in the beginning" up to the present day. Thus the Revelation of Jesus Christ is not a new story but the continuation of an age-old one. The fulfillment of a narrative left unresolved by rebellion and sin. The climax of a tale that begins before time and echoes with increasing intensity as each chapter of the canon unfolds.

WHEN STORIES COLLIDE

Stories have power. Stories birth identities, create cultures, structure space and time, and define allegiances. Stories are where nations are born and kingdoms collide.

The seven seals of Revelation 6 recount a story of conflict. Each scene unfolds fresh confrontation. Clashes in the cosmos between the heavens and

---

[1]*Trumpets:* first trumpet (Rev 8:7) = hail plague (Ex 9:13-35); second trumpet (Rev 8:8-9) = blood plague (Ex 7:14-24); fourth trumpet (Rev 8:12) = darkness plague (Ex 10:21-29); fifth trumpet (Rev 9:1-12) = locust plague (Ex 10:1-20); sixth trumpet (Rev 9:13-19) = death plague (Ex 11:1–12:30). *Bowls:* first bowl (Rev 16:2) = boil plague (Ex 9:8-12); second and third bowls (Rev 16:3-7) = blood plague (Ex 7:14-24); fifth bowl (Rev 16:10-11) = plague of darkness (Ex 10:21-29); sixth bowl (Rev 16:12-14) = frog plague (Ex 8:1-15); seventh bowl (Rev 16:17-21) = hail plague (Ex 9:13-35).

the earth, collisions between the kingdom of Christ and the empire of Rome, discord between God and his own.

In the fifth seal (Rev 6:9-11), God is confronted by martyrs crying out from under the altar in heaven, "Sovereign Lord, the holy and true one, how long until you judge the earth dwellers and avenge our blood?" (Rev 6:10). Blood that stained the ground like that of Abel (Gen 4:10) and testified to the injustice of their death at the hands of evil. For, like Christ, they were living sacrifices (Rom 12:1), slain because of their witness to the Word of God and their faithfulness to Christ's call. Yet now they contest, "When will you make this right? When will you correct the wrongs of earth? When will you wield your sovereignty in a new exodus?"

Ironically, this demand for justice is spoken in the presence of the slain Lamb, executed on a Roman cross after a verdict of innocence (Mt 27:24-26). It's God's response, however, that clarifies the purpose and the message of the seven seals even as it confuses and frustrates those longing for vengeance: "And each of [the martyrs] was given a white robe, and they were told to rest a little longer until the complete number of their fellow servants, their brothers and sisters, were killed just as they themselves had been" (Rev 6:11).

From humanity's perspective, and especially that of the Roman Empire, this response is laughable if not nonsensical. First, the martyrs' demand is met with a request for more patience ("rest a little longer") and a revelation that more of them must die. Even more confounding, they're given a "white robe," a symbol of victory, the uniform worn by citizens of Rome at a triumphal procession celebrating a great military conquest.[2] But the martyrs, as evidenced by their death, are not victors but failures, casualties of a story and an empire that far surpasses the sovereignty of their crucified king, who couldn't keep them alive. Or so the story goes.

In the seven seals, the kingdom of God and the empire of Rome collide. Neither empire governed by the same story. Neither kingdom sharing the same perspective or the same definitions of words such as *victory* or *sovereignty*, *peace* or *death*. The Roman Empire exalted generals and sought sovereignty through fear and the sword; Christ's kingdom worships a slain Lamb and reigns supreme through sacrifice and self-denial. The question of the

---

[2]Plutarch, *Aem.* 32.2; Juvenal, *Satirae* 10.45; cf. Ovid, *Tristia* 5.5.

martyrs, then, is governed more by the metric of Rome than the perspective of heaven. Something the seals intend to correct by exposing the folly of Rome's sovereign narrative.[3]

THE CONTEXT OF CONQUEST

In Revelation 6:1, heaven is captivated, the slain Lamb holding the scroll secured with seven seals (Rev 5:1-2, 8). The Lamb opens the first seal, prompting heaven to speak ("Come!") and earth to encounter the effect.[4] The first of four horsemen appears on a white horse.[5] The rider is equipped for war and crowned with sovereignty (Rev 6:2). "He rode out," the text highlights, "as a conqueror bent on conquest" (NIV).

Conquest colors the canvas of Rome's story. The origin of Rome is beleaguered with the fratricide of Remus at the hands of Romulus, both the twin sons of Mars, the god of war. Conquest governed Roman transfers of power. When Octavian (later named Augustus) conquered Marc Antony at the Battle of Actium (31 BCE), the rise of the principate was the demise of the republic. Conquest dictated Roman imagery in the agora, symbolism in poetry, and even relationships with celestial deities secured by Roman rituals, religion, and worship.

The Roman story of conquest saturated the empire. With icons and slogans, static and enacted propaganda, Rome declared to the literate and the unlettered a narrative summarized by three key messages: (1) Rome was the ruler of the kings of the earth, (2) Rome was favored by the gods, and (3) Rome was the bearer of *pax*. Three mutually supportive messages, heralding a tale for all to embrace and support. Or face the consequences of conquest.[6]

In Virgil's epic poem, the *Aeneid*—a masterpiece commissioned by Augustus, written circa 30–19 BCE—the goddess Venus grieves over the

---

[3]Shane J. Wood, *The Alter-Imperial Paradigm: Empire Studies and the Book of Revelation* (Leiden: Brill, 2016), 71: "The sovereign narrative is the ideology of 'how the world should be' from the dominant perspective, which is implemented in the public transcript through imperial propaganda (static and enacted) and the threat of violence."

[4]Each of the first six seals has vocalization of some sort: heavenly voices cry out, "Come!" in the first four seals (Rev 6:1, 3, 5-6, 7), martyrs in heaven cry out for vengeance in the fifth seal (Rev 6:10), and the evil of earth cry out in fear in the sixth seal (Rev 6:16-17). The seventh seal, however, disrupts the pattern with silence in heaven (Rev 8:1), creating intrigue and suspense in the narrative arc.

[5]See Suetonius, *Dom.* 2.6.

[6]Wood, *Alter-Imperial Paradigm*, 77-109.

apparent plight of the Trojan people (1.227-253) and her son Aeneas (1.259). In response, Jupiter, "the Father of men and gods" (1.254-255), unveils the legacy of Aeneas, the descendants of the Homeric hero, climaxing with Augustus and the Roman people: "For these I set no bounds in space or time; but have given empire without end . . . [to] the Romans, lords of the world, and the nation of the toga. Thus is it decreed. . . . From this noble line shall be born the Trojan Caesar, who shall extend his empire to the ocean, his glory to the stars, a Julius [Augustus], name descended from great Iulus!"[7] What the gods ordained, Augustus secured and celebrates in the opening lines of his *Res gestae divi Augusti*: "The Accomplishments of the divine Augustus, by which he subjected the whole world to the rule of the Roman people."[8]

To perpetuate the story of worldwide dominance, Rome harnessed every opportunity to inscribe its sovereignty into the collective memory of the plebs, from architecture to parades to inscriptions and even currency. Coins, in fact, were a unique emissary for the Roman sovereign narrative.[9] The coin's limited space required potent imagery to creatively communicate the story; the empire-wide necessity for money ensured its broad distribution.

Consider, for instance, the use of the globe in various coins from various emperors to communicate the same message: Rome is the ruler of the kings of the earth.

In all three coins, the obverse is filled with the conventional profile of the emperor crowned with a laurel wreath (symbolizing victory) and abbreviations adorning the circumference with honorific titles. On the reverse of Galba's coin (fig. 4.1), the caption heralds the "victory of Rome," while imagery defines the scope: the goddess Roma stands in full military garb with her right foot planted on the globe, indicating world domination. Similarly, Vitellius depicts Victory with a flowing train, holding a laurel wreath and once again standing on a small orb, signifying global sovereignty (fig. 4.2).

---

[7] Virgil, *Aeneid* 1.267-296, in *Ecologues, Georgics, Aeneid*, trans. H. R. Fairclough, 2 vols., LCL (Cambridge, MA: Harvard University Press, 1916).

[8] The *Res gestae divi Augusti* was written by Augustus himself, entrusted to the Vestal Virgins, inscribed on bronze tablets, and, after his death, displayed at the entrance of his mausoleum in the Campus Martius in Rome.

[9] Under Augustus, the production of imperial coinage was brought under the direct control of the emperor, apart from the Senate. Such a shift was due to the significance of imperial coinage for the distribution of emperor-specific propaganda. For more discussion, see Wood, *Alter-Imperial Paradigm*, 65-66, 72, 81.

Figure 4.1.
Galba: *RIC* 1.60 (68 CE).
Roma stands on a globe
in victory

Figure 4.2.
Vitellius: *RIC* 1.16 (69 CE).
Winged Victory stands
on globe triumphantly

Figure 4.3.
Titus: *RIC* 2.162 (79-81 CE).
Vespasian hands Titus
a globe

Not to be outdone, on the Flavian coin, minted in 79–81 CE, two figures are etched on the reverse, each facing the other, with an orb in between (fig. 4.3). The figure on the left is the emperor Vespasian, the right his son Titus; the orb is the world.

The globe, in all three coins, announces the victory and dominance of an empire bent on conquest. Each tells its version of the same story heralding the same message: the Roman Empire is the ruler of the kings of the earth.

WORSHIP IS WAR

In the Roman narrative, though, global domination wasn't just a result of military prowess. Imperial conquest was the result of divine favor. A consequence of Roman worship. As Dionysius of Halicarnassus (60–7 BCE)

explains, "To understand the success of the Romans, you must understand their piety."[10] In other words, the Roman Empire was the ruler of the kings of the earth *because* Rome was favored by the gods. Conquest, then, was a result of worship, because in Rome, as in Revelation, *worship is war.*

Indeed, the four horsemen in the first four seals of Revelation 6 are surrounded by worship. Before the first horseman, in Revelation 4–5, John's isolation on Patmos is translated into a celestial key, where worship "day and night without ceasing" (Rev 4:8) fills the heavenly halls with hymns "to the one sitting on the throne and to the Lamb" (Rev 5:13). After the fourth horseman, the fifth seal's heavenly altar (Rev 6:9) begets a context of temple worship through sacrifice. In the sixth seal, evil earth dwellers pray to their idols, "Hide us from the face of the one sitting on the throne and from the wrath of the Lamb" (Rev 6:16).[11] In Revelation 7, more hymns of praise are offered to "the one sitting on the throne and to the Lamb" (Rev 7:10, 12, 15-17). Worship even anchors the imagery in the seventh and final seal (Rev 8:1-5), when all of heaven stops silent (Rev 8:1) to receive "the prayers of all the holy ones" as an incense offering "on the golden altar before the throne" (Rev 8:3). Worship, then, is the context of the four horsemen, even the one bent on conquest. For in Revelation, as in Rome, *worship is war.*

At the outset of Augustus's reign in 31 BCE, Rome was in desperate need of repair. A civil war, in which Romans spilled the blood of Romans, had damaged not just city structures but their relationship with the gods themselves. "Your fathers' guilt," Horace cautions Augustus, "you still must pay, Roman, until you have rebuilt the temples and restored all the ruined sanctuaries with the dark images of the gods stained with smoke."[12] Sparing no expense, Augustus renovated every damaged temple, "omitting none which at that time stood in need of repair."[13] Not satisfied with mere restoration,

---

[10]Quoted in R. M. Ogilvie, *The Romans and Their Gods in the Age of Augustus* (London: W. W. Norton, 1969), 8.

[11]Evil humanity's call for the "mountains and rocks" to "fall on us" alludes to Hos 10:8, where "idolatry" saturates the context (Hos 10:1-7; 11:1-2; cf. Apocalypse of Elijah 2:29-34). Mountains, even in Jewish literature (e.g., Ex 19–20), were considered sacred intersections with the gods. Similarly, "rocks" (or "stones") were veiled references to idols crafted from earth's resources (cf. Ex 20:3; Ps 115:4-8; Is 2:19-21; 44:6-20; Hab 2:18-19). The image in Rev 6:16, then, is evil humanity calling on their deities to protect them from the great day of God's wrath.

[12]Horace, *Carmen saeculare* 3.6.

[13]Augustus, *Res gest.* 20, in *Velleius Paterculus and Res Gestae Divi Augusti*, trans. Frederick W. Shipley, LCL (Cambridge, MA: Harvard University Press, 1924).

Augustus constructed new temples to various deities, transforming the cityscape of Rome with his piety.[14]

Pious devotion, so the story goes, secures the favor of the gods.[15] Thus, to challenge, undermine, or reject Roman worship was a national security issue. For if Roman conquest was secured through the favor of the gods, then religious devotion was essential throughout the entire empire. By everyone. No exceptions. Christians included. To neglect the worship of the gods threatened Rome's ability to access the heavenly storehouses filled with divine treasure. Chief among them: *pax* ("peace").

THE SPOILS OF WAR

In Revelation 6:3-4, a second horse appears, this time a "fiery red one." The second seal and the two thereafter follow the same pattern as the first: (1) the seal is opened by the Lamb; (2) a living creature cries, "Come!"; (3) a horse gallops onto the scene affixed with a rider; and (4) a description explains what this horseman contributes to the others. While the first horseman is "a conqueror bent on conquest" (Rev 6:2), the second horseman is "given power to take peace from the earth and to make people slaughter each other" (Rev 6:4). Riding together, the two horsemen wage war that doesn't proffer *pax* but removes it. Regardless of the imperial propaganda.

The Pax Romana ("Peace of Rome") was both a promise and a threat; it was a treasure and a terror of the Mediterranean—for *pax* was secured through subjugation and the sword (cf. Rev 6:4). Augustus illustrates: "I extended the boundaries of all the provinces which were bordered by races not yet subject to our empire. The provinces of the Gauls, the Spains, and Germany. . . . *I reduced to a state of peace.*" Conquest was the conduit through which a region was offered *pax*, oftentimes, as Augustus later explains, through unparalleled brutality: "Very large forces of the enemy . . . were cut

---

[14]Jupiter Tonans: Dio Cassius, *Hist. Rom.* 54.4.2. Mars Ultor: Dio Cassius, *Hist. Rom.* 54.8.3. Apollo: Dio Cassius, *Hist. Rom.* 53.1.3. William Charles Korfmacher, "Vergil, Spokesman for the Augustan Reforms," *Classical Journal* 51, no. 7 (1956): 330-31.

[15]So pervasive was the message that Roman piety resulted in Roman conquest that Tertullian (160–240 CE), a church father, wrote, "However, having been led thus naturally to speak of the Romans, I shall not avoid the controversy which is invited by the groundless assertion of those who maintain that, as a reward of their singular homage to religion, the Romans have been raised to such heights of power as to have become masters of the world [*ut orbem occuparint*]. . . . This, forsooth, is the wages the gods have paid the Romans for their devotion" (*Apology* 25 [*ANF* 3:39]).

to pieces in battle and many towns were captured."[16] Violence was the Roman path to peace, annihilation and oppression the twin agents of *pax*.

Roman peace, then, was quite often discerned only through the eye of the beholder. Calgacus (ca. 83/84 CE), a British chieftain, called the Romans "robbers of the world" after his defeat. "If the enemy be rich," he decries, "they are rapacious; if he be poor, they lust for dominion; neither the east nor the west has been able to satisfy them." The Roman lust for conquest is cavernous and the Roman *pax* a farce. "To robbery, slaughter, plunder," he continues, "they give the lying name of empire; they make a wasteland and call it peace."[17] *Pax*, while a divine gift, was wielded by the Roman Empire as a weapon with endless appetite for all.

Revelation 6 confronts the Roman story by unveiling the Roman deception. Bent on conquest (the first horseman), Rome doesn't bring *pax* but removes "peace from the earth" (the second horseman), resulting in economic devastation and widespread death wherever they trod—both reflected in the final two horsemen. The third horseman, riding a black horse, holds "a balance scale in his hand" (Rev 6:5), with the heavenly declaration, "A quart of wheat for a day's wages, and three quarts of barley for a day's wages. But do not damage the oil and the wine" (Rev 6:6). Exorbitant inflation with prices threatening the ability to provide daily bread and the basic necessities of life, yet the luxuries of oil and wine unmolested. Roman conquest prospers the privileged even as it devastates the poor.

Yet the propaganda of *pax* painted quite a different picture, rendering the pillage and the plunder as the pathway to abundance for all. Consider the lower register of the Ara Pacis Augustae altar ("the altar of Augustan peace").

The altar was dedicated in 9 BCE in the Campus Martius, and its upper register is adorned with legendary figures who populate the Roman sovereign narrative: Remus and Romulus—the twin sons of Mars and founders of the sovereign city; Aeneas—the Trojan ancestor of the Roman populace; Roma— the patron goddess seated on foreign weaponry collected as spoils of war; and Pax—the goddess enthroned on the earth with luxury overflowing.[18]

---

[16]Augustus, *Res gest.* 26 (trans. Shipley). See also Tacitus, *Agricola* 20.1; *Ann.* 12.33.

[17]Tacitus, *Agricola* 30, in Alfred John Church and William Jackson Brodribb, trans., *The Agricola and Germania of Tacitus* (London: Macmillan, 1877).

[18]Augustus, *Res gest.* 12.

Figure 4.4.
The Ara Pacis
Augustae altar (front)

Figure 4.5.
The Ara Pacis Augustae
altar (upper register:
front left). Remus
and Romulus

Figure 4.6.
The Ara Pacis Augustae altar
(upper register:
front right). Aeneas

Figure 4.7.
The Ara Pacis Augustae altar
(upper register: back right).
Roma seated on pile
of weapons

Figure 4.8.
The Ara Pacis Augustae altar
(upper register: back left).
The goddess Pax enthroned

The lower register, however, portrays creation's response to Roman peace. The circuitous vine contains flowers and fruits, plants present in all seasons, and both wild and cultivated vegetation flowing through the floral scroll. The bounteous *pax* bestows so much blessing that the vegetation violates the laws of nature in celebration.

Figure 4.9.
The Ara Pacis Augustae altar
(lower register). Floral scroll

What the altar depicts, Tibullus (55–19 BCE) narrates:

Meanwhile let Peace tend our fields. Bright Peace first led under the curved yoke the cows about to plow the fields; Peace nourished the vine plants and stored the grape juice so that pure wine might flow for the son from the father's jar. In Peace shine the hoe and plowshare, but decay masters the sad arms of the harsh soldier in the darkness. . . . Then come to us, nourishing Peace, and hold the wheat stalk in your hand, and let fruits pour out in front of your shining breast.[19]

---

[19]Tibullus, *Elegies* 1.10.45-50, 67-68, quoted in Barbette Stanley Spaeth, "The Goddess Ceres in the Ara Pacis Augustae and the Carthage Relief," *American Journal of Archaeology* 98, no. 1 (January 1994): 91.

The Pax Romana is sovereignty secured and perpetuated through plundering and war recast as the font of abundant blessing and peace itself. Coins proclaimed it, altars portrayed it, poets romanticized it, and emperors administered it in practice and propaganda.[20] Yet the fourth horseman unveils the true spoils of Roman peace: "And I looked, and behold, a pale horse. The name of the one sitting upon it was Death, and Hades was following behind him" (Rev 6:8).

WEAPONIZING WORSHIP

In times of suffering, it's easy to view worship or prayer as passive or irresponsible responses to real problems. Vengeance whispers promises it can't deliver; resentment seeds anger into our imagination, envisioning the blood of our enemies satiating our pain. Yet the worship of Revelation 4–5 calls Christians to a different vision, an alternative story where the slain Lamb secures sovereignty through sacrifice. Where God's martyrs receive white robes in celebration of a victory unseen by the stories of empire. In Revelation, worship brings confrontation and comfort, clarity and a call. In Revelation, worship is war.

In Revelation 6, the seven seals confront the story of Rome. Challenge the claims of empire. Collide with the definitions and narratives of the imperial elite. Unveil the Roman message for what it is: a satanic deception. The seven seals tell a different story from what's sold in the Roman sovereign narrative. Roman conquest (Rev 6:1-2) doesn't provide *pax* and prosperity for all (Rev 6:3-4); it produces predictable patterns that privilege the rich and devastate the least of these (Rev 6:5-6), parading death through the streets, with Hades following close behind (Rev 6:7-8). And Christians are not exempt from this timeless tale. As the fifth seal and the cross of Christ proclaim, the sandals of the sovereigns are stained with the blood of the saints, who cry out in a loud voice, "Sovereign Lord . . . how long until you avenge our blood?" (Rev 6:10).

Yet, where eyes of earth see victory, heaven spots defeat; where eyes of earth pander for justice, heaven proclaims a victory already secured (Rev 6:11). What's needed is worship to thin the veil, to dissolve the illusion of Rome's story. So heaven ignites with praise (Rev 7:9-17), yet grows silent for half an hour (Rev 8:1) to allow the prayers of the saints on earth to be heard in the halls of heaven (Rev 8:3-4). It's worship that unveils this heavenly insight

---

[20]Claudius: *RIC* 1.21; Galba: *RIC* 1.279, 323; Otho: *RIC* 1.3, 4; Domitian: *RIC* 2.364.

woven through the revelation of Jesus Christ: what happens on earth affects heaven, and what happens in heaven affects earth.

Worship, then, is more than just singing or talking to God. Worship is the entry point to our story. Worship is the means through which God crafts our identity. Worship is the means by which all other stories are confronted and curated, repelled and revealed, reminding us amid the toil and the turmoil that Jesus Christ is "the ruler of the kings of the earth" (Rev 1:5). Regardless of what Rome claims.

In life and at death's end, we stand secure in Christ's story when we believe that worship is war. The battleground of cosmic and regional forces. The weapon we wield even in the presence of our enemies. Or so the story goes.

GOING DEEPER

> **THE TOOL:** Genre. If you ask the wrong questions, you'll still find an answer. But in Bible study, the goal is to learn *how* to ask the questions the text intends to answer. Watch this video (www.ivpress.com/wood -4a) and wrestle with the following:

1. Name your favorite genre of music.
   - List the components you expect to find in a song from this genre.
   - List the things you don't expect to find in a song from this genre.
   - How does this observation of musical genre affect your understanding of biblical genres?

2. Name five stores you've visited in the past week.
   - Do different stores follow different genres?
   - Are there certain items you know you can find in one store that you're confident won't be available in another? Why?

3. How does the discussion of genre affect your interpretation of other biblical books?
   - What insights does the epistolary genre have on the book of Romans?
   - What insights does the prophetic genre have on chapters such as Matthew 24?

> **THE TEXT:** When Christ pierces the veil (Rev 6:1–8:5). Time and again, the book of Revelation demonstrates that the veil between heaven and earth is not as thick as we assume. What happens on earth affects heaven, and what happens in heaven affects earth. Watch this video (www.ivpress.com/wood-4b) and answer the following:

1. In the chaos of the four horsemen (Rev 6:1-8) or even the dissolution of the world (Rev 6:12-17), it's easy to forget that God is in control, standing sovereign over each seal.

   › How does the presence of the Lamb in the seven seals affect how you see struggles in your own life?

   › Do we long for vengeance on our enemies like the martyrs in the fifth seal (Rev 6:9-11), or do we respond to our enemies as Christ did, with forgiveness?

   › What's at stake if we choose to forgive instead of avenge?

2. Revelation 8:1-3 suggests that when we pray, God listens. To every word. To every tear shed in that sacred space.

   › If you truly believed this, how would it change your perspective on prayer?

   › How would it affect the blessings and curses you speak throughout each day?

> **THE TAKEAWAY:** Partnering with silence in prayer. In Revelation 8:1-5, heaven partners with silence to receive the prayers of the saints. Following their example, this ancient Christian prayer practice partners with silence on earth to receive words from heaven. Here's how it works:

1. *Invitation*

   › Begin your prayer time by inviting the Holy Spirit into your space.

2. *Scripture and silence*

   › Recite aloud Psalm 46:10, "Be still and know that I am God."

> After you say the last word, give three to five minutes of silence to receive whatever the Lord wants to say.

> Note: It's normal to struggle with mental distractions preventing you from focusing on the Lord. Whenever that happens, gently guide your thoughts back to God without criticism or judgment.

3. *Drawing closer to silence*

> Recite aloud Psalm 46:10, leaving off the last word, "Be still and know that I am."

> After you say this abbreviated version, give three to five minutes of silence to receive whatever the Lord wants to say.

4. *Deepening our presence with God*

> Recite aloud an even smaller portion of Psalm 46:10, "Be still and know."

> After you say this abbreviated version, give three to five minutes of silence to receive whatever the Lord wants to say.

5. *Obeying God's command for silence*

> Recite aloud an even smaller portion of Psalm 46:10, "Be still."

> After you say this abbreviated version, give three to five minutes of silence to receive whatever the Lord wants to say.

6. *Partnering with silence in prayer*

> Recite aloud an even smaller portion of Psalm 46:10, "Be."

> After you say this abbreviated version, give three to five minutes of silence to receive whatever the Lord wants to say.

7. *Gratitude to God*

> Spend a couple of minutes thanking God for meeting you in this time of Scripture and silence.

> Write down anything the Spirit revealed to you.

> End your prayer time by reciting Psalm 46:10 in its full form, "Be still and know that I am God."

5

THE TENDERNESS OF GOD
(Revelation 8:6–11:19)

Unveiling Evil and the God of Pursuit

When Christ calls a man, He bids him come and die.

DIETRICH BONHOEFFER,
THE COST OF DISCIPLESHIP

GOD HAS ALWAYS BEEN TENDER WITH ME. More so than I've been with myself.

I've always struggled with grace. Not for others, so much. But as a recovering legalist, I'm always on trial in my own head, and the verdict's always guilty.

Grace feels like an intrusion, a disruption to my pattern of self-hatred and self-lashing. But that's because it is. Grace *is* a divine intrusion. A tender interruption. A movement toward me even as I move against and away from myself.

In some sense, even though I've grown up in the church, I feel like I'm being introduced to God all over again. Step by step. Story by story. Truth by truth. The basics of the faith are startling me anew with their depth, with what they're asking of me, revealing to me, tenderly calling me to.

Every month or so, I meet with my spiritual director, a wise, tender, holy eighty-year-old man. He's slow to speak, allowing me to ramble without end. He laughs often, not at me but in response to a conversation with the Lord I can't always hear. He's tender with me, prayerfully listening as I grope in the

darkness for something I desperately want that he knows simply won't satisfy. He shows me God by showing me endless grace.

Several weeks ago, I was in a particularly dark place, and he was patiently allowing me to fully express my frustration. After I exhausted all words, he paused. Sat silent. Honestly, for a bit too long for my taste. And then he asked this tender question, "Shane, what do you want from God?"

Without hesitation, I fired back, "Two things: One, I don't want to get hit. I want to do enough so that he doesn't have a reason to backhand me. Two, I want to know he's proud of me."

He nodded his head. Gently smiled. And after quiet consideration he asked a second question: "Okay, but what do either of those have to do with being God's beloved?"

I slightly tilted my head, a combination of "I don't understand" and "I don't approve of the question."

"Well," he continued, "I only ask because our children do things, at times, we're proud of, and at other times, things we aren't proud of. But does that change how much we love them?"

I was stunned. Unable to respond. For the realization was setting in, that after all these years of following God, teaching God, pursuing God, I still resisted his tenderness, still overlooked his love, still didn't understand the purpose and place of grace.

LOVE-LACED LOOPHOLES

Grace stands at the center of the Revelation of Jesus Christ. At the center of the throne, hand in hand with the slain Lamb. Grace pervades the Scripture, old and new. Refusing to allow one jot or tittle to appear without being laced with love. Grace is the binding of the Bible, the pages that tenderly hold both red and black ink. Grace pervades even as we resist. Grace beholds even as we cower, hiding our faces from the one who sits on the throne and the Lamb.

But grace will not be ignored. Will not be dismissed by accusations of death or set aside by deceptions of sin. I struggle, as do many others, to believe I'm worthy of grace. To believe I'm not irreparable. To believe that beauty is found even in my flaws. To believe that when I face death, hell will not be following close behind, awaiting a long embrace.

Not long ago, after teaching in a church service, a young woman approached, deeply troubled by the story that began the previous chapter. She began mid-thought, "But how do you know?"

A bit confused, I replied, "I'm sorry?"

"You told the woman on her deathbed, he's proud of her," she nervously smiled. "But how do you know? How do you know she won't close her eyes and open them to an angry Jesus? I mean, how do you *know*?"

She became frantic, quickening her pace and intensity, "I mean, maybe she's just *right* on the line, just *right* on the line of getting into heaven, I mean, what if she thought she was in, but she actually *just* missed it, I mean, *just* missed it, I mean, *how do you know*?"

She blinked herself out of the small rant, apparently forgetting where she was and who she was actually worried about.

I paused. Nodded. Gently replied, "Well, I *don't* know. But I do know *him*. I do know who *he* is. I do know that all over Scripture God reveals himself to be a God not looking for loopholes to kick us into hell but just the opposite. He's a God of grace."

Even in the beginning, grace abounds. To protect Adam and Eve, God taught his newborn image bearers how to properly navigate the bounty and barriers of Eden: "You may eat freely from any tree in the garden, but from the tree of the knowledge of good and evil you must not eat, because on the day you eat from it you will certainly die" (Gen 2:16-17). Yet when both male and female consumed the forbidden fruit, they didn't immediately die. Yes, death entered the scene, altering their fate, grammar, and patterns of thinking. But ingesting the fruit didn't end the story. It extended the epic tale of God's grace, his continued pursuit of his beloved creation.

God provided a ram to take humanity's place on the altar (Gen 22:1-19). He offered mercy for fifty, forty, twenty, or even ten righteous ones in rebellious cities (Gen 18:16-33). He allowed not one but ten opportunities for Pharaoh to repent (Ex 7:14–12:30). In the desert, he sent bread and meat from heaven to feed and nourish his own (Ex 16:4-15). Their grumbling didn't turn him away; their accusations didn't deter his grace from meeting Israel at the base of Mount Sinai in the form of his holy law (Ex 19:1–20:21). Grace pervades each text; loopholes of love abound in the Law and the Prophets.

Even before the exile, Israel saw visions of grace, faith blooming as God's holy law was implanted "in their minds" and written "on their hearts" (Jer 31:33). Even during the exile, Israel received visions of mercy, hope flourishing as their "heart of stone" was replaced with "a new heart" (Ezek 36:26), intimacy unfolding with images of "one like a son of man, coming with the clouds of heaven" to replace their exile with a kingdom that knows no end (Dan 7:13-14). Time and again, rebellion is persistently confronted with grace, separation relentlessly bridged by mercy. For the Old Testament stubbornly pursues loopholes of love to pave the way for Christmas.

Grace seems to know no limits, perceives no boundaries, refuses to recoil at any obstacle. Grace persists. Seeks to make all things new. Reaches across chasms, "not wanting anyone to perish but everyone to give way to repentance" (2 Pet 3:9). You. Me. Even the greatest enemies in our story.

ANNIHILATING YOUR ENEMIES

There are two ways to annihilate your enemy: kill them or convert them into a friend. The first is death's default, death's immediate reaction to opposition, whether by word or deed. The second takes longer and costs more, and to many is just plain foolish. At least to those who are perishing (1 Cor 1:18). Either way, though, your enemy is annihilated. Ceases to exist. No longer lingers.

John Perkins, the civil rights luminary, stood on the stage, calling us in attendance to obliterate our enemies.[1] Just advocating for the second option. The costly one.

Peering into the crowd, he recounted each swing of the police baton his body absorbed in a jail cell behind closed doors. No witnesses to the bludgeoning but him and them.

"As they were raining blows down on my body," he recalled, "I looked up and saw the faces of demons. White demons."

His voice shook. The audience held a collective breath. His frail frame held a holy pride. Not one that leads to a fall but a pride that bears witness to a power birthed by grace few have felt and even fewer have lived to retell. His eyes glazed over, blurring the present auditorium with the jail cell of times gone by.

---

[1]Speech given at College Heights Christian Church, Joplin, MO on May 4, 2014.

"I remember thinking," he confessed, "if I had a bomb, I'd push the button and kill us all."

The honesty in this statement seemed to pierce space and time, lingered longer in my mind than the recording revealed: "I'd push the button."

Pain is powerful, tempting even giants of the faith to fall. Pain at the hands of another offers fantasies of a different sort. The vengeful heart won't be satisfied until its enemy gets ten times worse. Even then, the pain asks for more. Demands more. Longs for more than mere retribution, but complete annihilation: "How long until you avenge our blood?" (Rev 6:10).

But as Perkins continued, I realized we were in the presence of a saint of a different sort. Something more akin to a slain Lamb or a crucified King.

"But then I remember thinking," he paused, "'if I pushed the button, well, then I'd be just like them. Filled with hate.'"

He paused again, allowing the incense of his words to rise to heaven.

"So, I decided right then," his cadence and volume increasing, "I committed to God right then, that I would be an agent of love. *God's* agent of love. I'd respond to their blows with love."

It's impossible to understand grace, to truly comprehend its scandalous nature and deafening call, until you hear it ask you to forgive the greatest enemy in your story. Until you hear grace demand you do the same as your crucified King: forgive the greatest enemy in your story (Lk 23:34). The babysitter who molested you, the father who left you, the mother who neglected you, the sister or brother who sold you, the friend who betrayed you, the community who forgot you, the boss who defamed you, the church who belittled you. Forgive the greatest enemy in your story.

Now, to be clear, a call to forgiveness isn't a call to persist in dangerous or harmful relationships of any sort. If you're in an abusive situation, the first step of grace isn't forgiveness but to remove yourself from the danger entirely. And no, reconciliation and forgiveness are not the same. Reconciliation necessitates the presence of all parties involved, whereas forgiveness doesn't even require the offending party. When the victimizer persists in unsafe and/or harmful behavior, they prevent reconciliation from being a safe option to pursue. But for the victim, forgiveness is still possible. Necessary. Essential for true liberation and healing.[2]

---

[2]For my own story of healing from sexual abuse, see Shane J. Wood, *Between Two Trees: Our Transformation from Death to Life* (Abilene, TX: Leafwood, 2019), 97-126.

Indeed, grace isn't grace at all until it confronts your greatest wound. Until it asks you to forgive your greatest enemy. If, as Christians, we do the bidding of grace, we will eternally obey the command, "Love your enemies, and pray for those persecuting you" (Mt 5:44), because our enemies will be our neighbors and friends in the heavenly community paved with gold and grace.

Scandalous? Yes. Grace? Without question.

Worship is war, but as Christians, we wield the weapon of grace. With our neighbors. With ourselves. With our enemies. For between kill or convert, Christ calls us to the latter. That's who he is: grace. And, in Revelation, who you worship, you become.

GOD'S STRATEGY OF GRACE

On the surface, the seven trumpets of Revelation 8:6–11:19 appear to be a divine denial of everything written above. A betrayal of Matthew 5:44. A renunciation of grace. The trumpets seem to depict a vengeful God viciously torturing his enemies in a Dante-inspired murderous affair. Yet as the text unfolds, the imagery unveils a different revelation altogether: God's willingness to break any barrier to reach his enemies with grace.

The first six trumpets appear anything but gracious. The first four trumpets, like the first four seals, target the earth. The first trumpet unleashes a hailstorm (Rev 8:7) before a third of the sea turns into blood in the second trumpet (Rev 8:8). Not to be outdone, in the third trumpet, a star named Wormwood poisons a third of the waters (Rev 8:10-11) as the fourth trumpet assaults the sun, darkening the day and night by, once again, one-third (Rev 8:12).

The fifth and sixth trumpets alter the target ever so slightly, from the earth to the earth dwellers, from creation to evil humanity, a shift signaled by an eagle crying out a trinity of "woes" (Rev 8:13). In the fifth trumpet, hell is unlocked, and a fiendish army pours forth with "the angel of the abyss," aptly named "Destroyer" at the helm (Rev 9:11). Unlike the four horsemen, this infernal legion doesn't assail the earth or God's people (Rev 9:4); they relentlessly torture their own (Rev 9:5). Evil mercilessly tormenting evil. The sixth trumpet intensifies the attack as sulfurous cavalry (Rev 9:17) annihilate a third of the earth dwellers with murderous rage. Hell obliterating the vile. Their own.

Yet none of this is done outside God's sovereign hand. A thread of divine authority is woven throughout the tapestry of merciless evil. The trumpets are each sounded by heavenly angels (Rev 8:2); the limits of evil are governed by heavenly permission (Rev 9:4-5, 13-14); and even the abyss is unlocked (Rev 9:1) by a key secured by Christ at his death and resurrection (Rev 1:18). It's not a jailbreak but a divine plan guided by God's sovereign will.

God's goal, though, is far from sinister; it's a movement of grace. Not pernicious but merciful. A divine strategy to obliterate the enemy by converting them into a friend. After the sixth trumpet, Revelation 9:20-21 laments: "And the rest of humankind who were not killed in these plagues *still did not repent* of the deeds of their hands *nor stop* worshiping demons and idols of gold and silver and bronze and stone and wood that are not able to see or to hear or to walk around. *Nor did they repent* of their murders or their sorcery or their sexual immorality or their thefts." The target was never torture but repentance; the goal was never punishment but conversion. Into a friend. Into one of God's own children. Not through coercion but through revelation. An unveiling. Of evil. Of their master. Of the consequences for entrusting yourself to the arms of death.

EVIL'S UNVEILING

Violence is evil's native tongue, the grammar of death. Not love. Not faithfulness. But unrestrained violence. Not just against opposition, mind you, but against all. Even their own. Violence, according to evil, solves all issues and satisfies all desires; it provides peace and security, victory and prosperity, love and well-behaved children. Violence crafts the "pattern of this world" (Rom 12:2 NIV) and dictates all interactions, whether with an enemy or one's own. The trumpets put this strategy of evil on full display.[3]

The fifth trumpet, for example, unlocks the abyss. Allows the will of hell to invade the earth. Without delay, earth is undone, returned to a state of "formless and void" (Gen 1:2) as darkness covers creation, the smoke of the abyss undoing the light of the sun in a simulation of *un*creation (Rev 9:2). Torture ensues, not of those that belong to God but of earth dwellers. Of devoted followers of the evil one (Rev 9:4-5), unveiling the abyss as a barrier

---

[3]For discussion on humanity's "union with death" and "death as our native tongue," see Wood, *Between Two Trees*, 53-65.

of grace protecting the earth from evil—those devoted to God and not. Here the barrier is unsealed, and evil unleashes its fury on its own.

As shocking as forgiving one's enemy may be, to destroy your own, those loyal to you and your cause, is far more unsettling. Something far beyond the word *sinister*. Grace is, without question, scandalous, but an evil elated by the agony of evil has no parallel. Yet, it's unsurprising. Violence knows not loyalty; it is not disciplined in fidelity. Violence done by someone doesn't prevent violence done to them. In fact, it almost assures a violent return, physically, psychologically, or otherwise.

Sympathy does little to alter the course of evil. Pain of the other, even to the point of death, is indeed the goal. Not mercy. Not comfort. Not even presence. So, in Revelation 9:6, as the agony of the earth dwellers matures into despair, they seek the embrace of their master, the arms of death. But all they receive is abandonment: "And in those days people will earnestly seek Death but absolutely will not find it; they will desire to die, but Death will flee from them."

Conversely, grace is moved by sympathy, obliterates isolation, heals the harmed, and pursues all that is lost. So, in Revelation 1:9-16, God collapses cosmology to meet John on Patmos, annihilating his loneliness with a tender touch and a gentle appeal: "Do not fear" (Rev 1:17). Grace converts John's weakness into strength through the presence of Life (2 Cor 12:1-10).

Grace creates, resurrects, and makes all things new. Grace gives light, life, and hope to the forgotten and the forlorn. Grace woos everyone, small and great, slave and free, enemy and friend, to moments of transformation.

The goal of the trumpets is to unveil evil, to expose evil by offering an opportunity for its will to be done on earth as it is in the abyss. Unfettered, evil attends to its own with violence, only to abandon its own in their time of need. Even still, the earth dwellers do not repent, refuse to abandon hope in the hell that has abandoned them. Which, to some extent, unveils the character of the earth dwellers as well.

Even before the lock to the abyss was unfastened, earth dwellers demonstrated an aversion to healing, an allergy to grace. At the sound of the third trumpet, "a great star" (Rev 8:10) named Wormwood (ἄψινθος) falls from the sky, igniting an insightful wordplay. Wormwood (which means "bitter") turns a third of the waters "bitter" (ἄψινθος), which causes a great number of

people to die "from the waters that were made bitter [ἄψινθος]" (Rev 8:11). Oddly enough, wormwood is not a poison but a medicine: "a bitter-tasting herb used as *a cure* for intestinal worms."[4] Yet, discipled by death, the earth dwellers receive the medicinal herb as a poisonous pollutant, transforming what should bring life into a plague of destruction.

But this is nothing new. The same inversion is seen all throughout Scripture. Movements of God in the heavens and on the earth are consistently received by sinful humanity as a threat or a reason to abandon God altogether. After Adam and Eve ingested the fruit of death, God's approach prompted the image bearers to flee in fear (Gen 3:10), mutating the author of life into a toxic threat to hide from and even accuse of treachery (Gen 3:12). Love's approach is like poison for those infused with death, those blinded by evil. Those who look into the sky and refuse to see the stars as "the works of [God's] fingers" (Ps 8:3) or the product of the "breath of his mouth" (Ps 33:6), the same breath that infused humanity with life (Gen 2:7). Instead, through the eyes of death, stars are transformed into idols, deities that demand child sacrifice and violence to their own (2 Kings 17:16-17; 21:5-6; see also 2 Chron 33:2-6; cf. Deut 4:19; 17:2-3). Even when the star of heaven announced the birth of love incarnate (Mt 2:1-10), Herod was moved not to jubilation but to a murderous rage (Mt 2:16-18). Time and again, as grace draws near, humanity's cry of "Hosanna in the highest" (Mt 21:9) is replaced with chants of "Crucify him!" (Mt 27:22-23). For death distorts, not clarifies; perverts, not purifies.

Consistently and without fail, God approaches fallen humanity with arms of grace, and humanity responds with violence done to themselves, to others, and to God himself. Thus, how evil receives God's pursuit is just as important, if not more so, than whether God pursues at all. For if medicine falls from heaven, if grace draws near, but humanity cannot perceive him, doesn't have the capacity to receive him, then the Lord of life will always be received as poison.

THE GRACE OF GOD'S WITNESS

Yet God does draw near. Persistently. That's who he is. That's who he calls us to be. For in Revelation, who you worship, you become.

---

[4]Johannes P. Louw and Eugene A. Nida, eds., *Greek-English Lexicon of the New Testament: Based on Semantic Domains*, 2nd ed. (New York: American Bible Society, 1996), 79.43, emphasis added.

Following God's lament in Revelation 9:20-21, God's pursuit begins anew in Revelation 10. A mighty angel descends from heaven clothed with glory (Rev 10:1) and "holding in his hand a little scroll" (Rev 10:2). Like prophets of old (Ezek 3:1-3), John is told to eat the scroll, merging the message with the messenger (Rev 10:8-10). Without delay, John is instructed, "You must prophesy again about many peoples and nations and tongues and kings" (Rev 10:11). You must go speak to them again, preach to them again, communicate a message of hope and grace to the unrepentant again.

God's grace is relentless, undeterred by humanity's rebellion. His love transforms rejection and lamentation into witness and pursuit. The tragedy of Eden was met with the call of Abram, whose descendants would be "as numerous as the stars in heaven" (Gen 22:17; cf. Gen 15:5). The mourning of Israel was met with the call of Moses, who led God's people on dry ground across the Red Sea (Ex 14:21-22). The calamity of the exile was met with the call of countless prophets, whose voices sing in concert the story of the coming King appointed by God as a "light for the nations so that my salvation can extend to the ends of the earth" (Is 49:6). And now, at the end of Revelation 10, the hellacious torment of the trumpets is confronted with the call of John to once again witness to the tireless grace of the crucified King.

Revelation 11 centers on two figures, summarized with one word, *witness* (μάρτυς). This word is used three times in Revelation before chapter 11: twice for Jesus (Rev 1:5; 3:14) and once for one of his followers (Rev 2:13). And a common theme links each usage: victory through suffering.

In Revelation 1:5, the story of Jesus is retold in a trinity of titles: "the faithful witness [ὁ μάρτυς, ὁ πιστός] [cross], the firstborn from the dead [resurrection], and the ruler of the kings of the earth [ascension]." The *suffering* of the cross proffers *sovereignty* through the victory secured in the empty tomb, a message told in short to the church of Laodicea, "These are the words of the Amen, the faithful [πιστὸς] and true witness [μάρτυς] [suffering], the origin of God's creation [sovereignty]" (Rev 3:14).[5] A message of suffering and sovereignty merges with the messenger in Revelation 2:13: "I know where you live [church of Pergamum], the place of Satan's throne. And

---

[5] The word *Amen* (Ἀμήν) is used seven times in Revelation (Rev 1:6, 7; 3:14; 5:14; 7:12; 19:4; 22:20), each time in the context of sovereignty secured through suffering.

yet you hold fast to my name. You did not deny your faith in me even in the days of Antipas, my faithful witness [ὁ μάρτυς μου ὁ πιστός], who was killed among you where Satan resides."

Antipas doesn't just cling to the cross; he carries it. He embraces suffering as the path to victory. And his example is not exceptional but the call and command for all Christians: "Fear nothing of what you are about to suffer," Jesus says to the church of Smyrna. "Look, the devil is about to cast some of you into prison to tempt you. You will suffer affliction for ten days. Be faithful [πιστὸς], even to the point of death [suffering], and I will give to you the crown of life [sovereignty]" (Rev 2:10). The story of Christ's victory over the grave shapes our identity and curates our call, transforms our actions and guides our worship, challenges Christians, both past and present, to not just recite the story but to embody the story itself.

WHO YOU WORSHIP, YOU BECOME

Worship isn't just something we do; it's something done to us. Something that transforms us. In worship, we experience revelation and reorientation, unveiling God to us and us to us. We collide with God, come face to face with the crucified King gazing at our grasps for power. In worship, we are undone even as we are re-created into the image of the slain Lamb. We encounter the one crucified "in the beginning" (Rev 13:8), who now becomes our end. His identity and actions become our own.

In Revelation, who you worship, you become, and Christians worship Jesus, the faithful witness, who bids us come and die (Mt 16:24). Whose blood was shed for us even when "we were enemies of God" (Rom 5:9-10). So, as astonishing as it may be (Rev 17:7), it's unsurprising that the final occurrence of *witness* (μάρτυς) appears in Revelation 17:6, where the great prostitute is "drunk on the blood of the holy ones, the blood of the witnesses [μαρτύρων] to Jesus."[6] As witnesses to Christ, we testify as Christ did. With our lives. For Jesus isn't just "the beginning and the end" (Rev 22:13); he is *our* beginning and *our* end.

---

[6]Throughout Revelation, God's people are most commonly called "holy ones" (ἁγίων), typically translated "saints" or "God's people" (Rev 5:8; 8:3-4; 11:18; 13:7, 10; 14:12; 16:6; 17:6; 18:20, 24; 19:8), which derives from God's designation in Rev 4:8 as "Holy, holy, holy" (ἅγιος, ἅγιος, ἅγιος). Conversely, evil humanity is most commonly called "earth dwellers" (κατοικούντων ἐπὶ τῆς γῆς), betraying where their true allegiance lies (Rev 3:10; 6:10; 8:13; 11:10; 13:8, 14 [2×]; 14:6; 17:8).

Thus, the fate of the prophetic pair in Revelation 11 is known by the mere mention of the word *witness* (Rev 11:3). Like Christ, the two testify (Rev 11:3-6), are killed in Jerusalem (Rev 11:7-8), resurrect on the third day (Rev 11:11), and ascend to heaven (Rev 11:12). The two witnesses image the body of Christ, double entendre intended. The two witnesses both retell Jesus' story and depict the church's ministry as the hands and feet of Christ.

Who you worship, you become.

In response to our cries for vengeance (Rev 6:9-11), God calls us to "prophesy again" (Rev 10:11), to bear witness to the crucified King again, to pronounce once again God's pursuit of rebellious humanity through the story of Jesus now lived in and through the body of Christ. We are called to witness, even if it means we experience the same fate as Christ.

In the Revelation of Jesus Christ, the cross isn't merely a beacon of salvation; it's a call to do what Jesus did. To take up our cross and forgive the greatest enemy in our story, come what may. A call to witness even in the face of suffering.

Suffering, though, isn't God's goal or desire but a divine strategy to undo the tragedy of Eden. A divine strategy to disrobe the character of evil, to reach God's enemy discipled by death, to provide a path to repentance and grace through sacrifice and suffering. A divine strategy employed on the cross of Calvary and enfleshed by the two witnesses in Revelation 11.

And the strategy works.

After the death and resurrection of the two witnesses (Rev 11:7-11), they ascend to heaven as "their enemies watched" (Rev 11:12). Creation quakes (Rev 11:13), as at the cross (Mt 27:51), to bear witness to God's grace, to God's pursuit of his enemy through his body. As astonishing as it may be, repentance graces the scene: "[the evil ones] were terrified, and they gave glory to the God of heaven" (Rev 11:13).

What the torture of the abyss couldn't accomplish, the testimony of the two witnesses did: annihilation of God's enemy. Not by killing them but by converting them into friends.

THE MESSAGE OF THE TRUMPETS

The Revelation of Jesus Christ is a story of pursuit. God became flesh to find us in our wandering. God lay in the clutches of death to seek those

languishing in the valley of its shadow. God ruptured the tomb to rescue us from the long loneliness that threatened to consume creation. Revelation reveals a God of pursuit and an enemy of abandonment.

The trumpets, in the end, are about unveiling the character of the characters in the Revelation of Jesus Christ, the good and the evil. The pursuit of hell tortures its own, while the pursuit of God targets even his enemies with grace. Yet the earth dwellers, discipled by the deceit of death, can't distinguish medicine from poison, heaven's gaze from divine wrath. Thus, thinning the veil is a comfort to some but a threat to many. The response is governed by who you worship.

But even when enemies of God refuse to repent, he doesn't relent. He calls his own to prophesy anew, to participate in Christ's story. To embrace the cross as not just what gets you out of hell but the shape through which God's relentless grace pierces a grace-less world.

As the body of Christ, who at the Lord's Supper ingests Jesus' flesh and blood, we become what we eat. The message merges with the messenger. The message compels us to witness, come what may, bringing clarity to not only *how* to fight the war but *who* the war is actually against. The *true* enemy unveiled in Eden yet disguised by empire and the greatest enemies in our story: Satan.

GOING DEEPER

THE TOOL: Symbols. Symbols have power. They move masses and unite nations. Symbols pierce the veil to apprehend what words can't seem to reach. Watch this video (www.ivpress.com/wood-5a) and wrestle with the following:

1. Find a symbol online or driving down the street (could be from a brand, a sign, etc.).
   - What features stick out to you (be as specific as you can)?
   - What emotions ignite as you reflect on the symbol?
   - Does the symbol come with a call to action?
2. List as many symbols from the Bible as you can.
   - Why does God communicate in symbols?

> ➤ Do symbols target our heart, our head, our hands, or some combination of all three?

3. If symbols have power:

> ➤ What dangers do they possess?

> ➤ What positive attributes do they contain?

> ➤ How can a church or community harness this power?

THE TEXT: The call of Christ (Rev 8:6–11:19). The New Testament refers to the church with the symbol "body of Christ." The New Testament offers the symbol as more than just a label, but as an identity that comes with a mission. Watch this video (www.ivpress.com/wood-5b) and answer the following:

---

1. Many assume our witness comes with words of confrontation, protests, or public displays of faith.

> ➤ What ways can we witness without using words?

> ➤ How do our lives testify to the goodness of a God who loves his enemies?

2. Revelation 11:13 describes the only time in the book where evil repents and worships God.

> ➤ What does this say about the connection between our worship (i.e., union with God) and our witness (e.g., evangelizing the world)?

> ➤ When do churches have the most impact for a lost world?

THE TAKEAWAY: Interpreting Scripture with Scripture. The Bible is in conversation with itself from Genesis 1 to Revelation 22. When texts are difficult to understand, an important principle of interpretation is to allow Scripture to interpret Scripture. Here's how it works:

---

1. Download this document (www.ivpress.com/wood-5c), which lists Old Testament allusions in every verse of Revelation.

2. Find the section that lists Revelation 11:3-6.

3. Read Revelation 11:3-6 in your Bible, and then read each Old Testament allusion for this text.

4. For each allusion, ask these questions:

› What is the parallel in this Old Testament text and Revelation 11:3-6?

› What are the implications for the imagery in Revelation 11:3-6?

› Are certain symbols defined in the Old Testament that are now employed in Revelation 11:3-6?

› What is the overall importance of this Old Testament parallel for Revelation 11:3-6?

NOTE: Not all parallels will be easy to understand, but wrestling with the parallel will provide deeper insight into the conversation between the two texts.

6

THIS IS YOUR ENEMY
(Revelation 12–14)

Disrobing a Deceptive Target

And they conquered [the dragon] by the blood of the Lamb
and by the word of their testimony, for they didn't
covet their lives in the face of death.

REVELATION 12:11

IT WAS LATE AT NIGHT the day before I turned twenty-nine. A birthday filled with the unexpected.

I was on a plane from Colorado to Missouri. Almost home after a long weekend at a church teaching and preaching on Revelation. I was exhausted.

Deboarding the plane was normal. We taxied to the jet bridge; the "fasten seatbelt" light went off; a small burst of noise rippled through the plane, a mixture of clanking buckles and the clanging of overhead bins. I stood up. Not to deboard. But to stretch my legs and watch from the back row as each row gathered their belongings and stepped out into the aisle.

Walking up the jet bridge, I remembered, "Oh, yeah . . . tomorrow's my birthday." I smiled. Slightly shrugged. The day had been so long that I felt disconnected from everything.

Stepping out into the airport, I was reminded how late it actually was— most lights were out, dimming the entire terminal, and each store and

restaurant sealed with a pull-down, see-through gate. I let out a tired but grateful sigh. And then I noticed commotion just ahead.

A large group of people gathered under a television. A strange sight in an airport after hours. As I approached, I sensed their excitement, picked up on their chatter, watched their heads turn side to side with expressions of both shock and possibly celebration. A gentleman on the edge threw up his hands and yelled, "Hell yeah!"

Confused, my gaze shifted from the crowd to the screen, "Breaking News: Osama bin Laden Killed."

My first thought was, "We got the sucker." But my second thought stretched well into my birthday and beyond: "But he didn't know Jesus . . ."

I was confused. Conflicted. Deeply unsettled and agitated.

I was well aware of the evil he orchestrated. I remember where I was when I saw the second plane crash into the south tower on 9/11. I remember where I was when I decided to go to the Middle East the summer after 9/11 to minister to Muslims. I remember the wars that dominated the decade leading up to my twenty-ninth birthday, each of the four horsemen galloping in events ignited by this man.

Yet I was struggling. Uncertain how to feel or think or move amid the jubilation around me. I'd preached that morning a message of grace, challenging the congregation to forgive as Christ forgave. That semester I'd been teaching the book of Acts, and I marveled at the transformation of Saul of Tarsus into Paul the apostle: a radical militant who terrorized the early church, overseeing and spearheading violence on God's own (Acts 7:57-8:3; 9:1-2), yet an enemy who was converted into a friend, who preached and expanded Christ's love to the ends of the earth (Acts 9:3-31; 12:25–14:28).

Standing in the airport, I froze. I lowered my head as tears swelled. I didn't know what to do, what to think, how to respond. I just stood still. Trying to process the celebration of a lost soul (Rev 11:9-10). Straining to understand which kingdom was celebrating, which kingdom had advanced, which kingdom had won, which kingdom's agenda had been furthered by this man's death.

Standing in a darkened terminal, surrounded by high fives and "Hell yeahs," I struggled with this haunting question: As a Christian, what does victory over the enemy look like?

A DRAGON IN BETHLEHEM

Figure 6.1.
Family photo of Shane J.
Wood's family nativity
scene with a red dragon

My family nativity scene includes a dragon. Which I know is weird, even if biblical.

For over twenty years, I've placed the manger with Joseph peering down at his blossoming family, staff in hand; with wise men bowing down, gifts in hand; with Mother Mary reaching out both hands to cradle the Creator of the universe crafted in her womb. And also a red dragon, lurking in the background.

It's a fixture in our family, an understood expectation, like the star atop the tree or stockings over the mantle. So much so that my son Zion came home from kindergarten one day a bit exasperated.

"Dad?"

"Yeah, buddy."

"Is there a dragon in the Christmas story?"

"Yeah. . . . Why?"

"Well, that's what I was telling my friends at recess, but nobody believed me!"

I couldn't hold back the belly laugh. Picturing this theological argument at the monkey bars overlooking the seesaw and slide was just too much.

"Well," I collected myself with giggles still teeming, "just know you are more theologically accurate than they are."

But, to be fair, a dragon in a nativity scene does merit explanation. For kindergartners or otherwise.

In Revelation 12, the narrative arc of the Revelation of Jesus Christ seems to reset. The seals are already broken, and the sound of the trumpets no longer echoes. Yet Revelation 12 doesn't begin another set of seven. Instead of the

seven bowls of Revelation 15–16, Revelation 12 begins with an enigmatic woman "clothed with the sun," standing on the moon (Rev 12:1; cf. Rev 1:16).

This narratival disruption, though, is no mistake or later interpolation. It's a literary strategy. A dramatic device to regather the reader's attention, to reorient the story's melody, to illuminate a topic and a message essential for what's to come and what has been.

The stage darkens. The spotlight shines. The cosmic woman crowned with "twelve stars on her head" (Rev 12:1) stands center stage. The reader's attention is transfixed. Frozen by her grandeur. Even though her identity is still veiled.

In Revelation 12:2, the woman's intrigue is enhanced with unexpected tension: "She was pregnant, and she shrieked from the birth pains and agony of giving birth." Heavy breathing, unbridled pain, harrowing contractions, impossible pushing against the curse of Eve. The trimesters have passed, and the cosmic woman is about to give birth.

And we don't even know her name.

Yet in Revelation 12:5, we get a clue: "And she gave birth to a male child who is to 'rule all the nations with an iron scepter.'"

That's Psalm 2:9 (LXX). A messianic psalm. A song that begins with tension: nations conspire, kings of the earth rage "against the Lord and against his anointed one," with battle cries shrieking, "Let us break their bonds and let us cast off their shackles" (Ps 2:1-3). God chuckles at the arrogance of his enemy, rebukes them out of hand, and installs his "king on Zion" (Ps 2:4-6). A king unlike any before or after. A king who holds more than a title but a relationship with God unique in history and posterity: "You are my son; today I have begotten you. Ask me, and I will give to you the nations as your inheritance and the ends of the earth as your possession. You will rule them with an iron scepter" (Ps 2:7-9 LXX). The child of Revelation 12, then, is God's anointed son from Psalm 2. The Jewish Messiah. The Christian Jesus.

Thus, on some level, the woman is Mary.[1] And, however cosmic the scene may seem, on some level we're in Bethlehem. At Christmas. Peering anew at the nativity.

---

[1]Symbols by nature are multifaceted. Indeed, there's an appropriate range of meaning governed by a text's context (i.e., a symbol can't mean anything we decide), but a symbol can have multiple referents simultaneously. Thus, Mary as the woman in Rev 12 isn't the *only* possible interpretation of the symbol.

Yet this is anything but a silent night, even if it is a holy one. In Revelation 12:3, a new character emerges not found in the birth narratives of Matthew or Luke or in the Christmas pageants at your home congregation. Yet a character essential to acknowledge and unveil: "Behold, a great red dragon with seven heads and ten horns and seven crowns on its heads" (Rev 12:3).

In Revelation, there's always more beyond the veil, just beyond what the eye can see. In times of tribulation, the Apocalypse unveils a God who is near, moving toward us with a tender touch and a calming command, "Do not fear" (Rev 1:17). In times of tranquility, the Apocalypse reveals an enemy who is imminent, lurking in the shadows with sinister schemes and violent intent. For even in Bethlehem not all was calm, for "the dragon stood before the woman who was about to give birth, so that when she gave birth it might devour her child" (Rev 12:4).

This passage, though, changes more than just our nativity scenes. It changes our understanding of what rests beyond the veil. It changes our perception of a silent night and scenes of seeming tranquility. It changes our perception of the story altogether, translating local pain into a cosmic key, struggles with Rome into conflict with the great red dragon. Revelation 12's interruption, then, strategically reveals the identity of the *true* enemy lurking just beyond the veil: "that ancient serpent called the devil and Satan, the one deceiving the whole world" (Rev 12:9).

UNCOVERING OUR ENEMY

It's easy to forget who the true enemy is, both in our story and in the stories that craft us. Past wounds prioritize the people who've hurt us most—an abusive parent, an adulterous spouse, a traitorous friend, a tyrannical boss. Present pain seeks meaning or at least someone to blame, believing that vengeance or "accountability" will satiate the bloodlust of our trauma. But pain left untransformed is simply transferred from one person to another.

Our agony deceives us into wasting kingdom energy, arguing with anyone online or everyone nearby, believing that if we are right and they are wrong, then by some twisted economy we are made whole or at least justified in our self-pity and anger at others. Some self-medicate by creating conflict with neighbors or refusing to forgive an estranged child or working to divide a church over preferences clothed in scriptural prooftexts, forgetting that even

Satan can quote the Bible to prove a point. Still others exhaust their witness in the political sphere, attacking the Roman eagle or the Republican elephant or the Democratic donkey, truly believing they're attacking the most significant enemy in God's story. Revelation 12, however, confronts this satanic deception by deemphasizing the regional in view of the cosmic, by decentralizing Rome with the red dragon gracing center stage.

Revelation 12 deliberately disturbs Revelation's cycles of sevens. A strategic disruption of Christmas to reveal what deception conceals. To seize the reader's attention, to disciple the Christian's perception, to usher into the foreground what so far has been obscured in the background: the true enemy. The red dragon.

In Revelation 1–11, Satan is present, just out of focus. Only mentioned in passing in the letters of Revelation 2–3 (Rev 2:9-10, 13, 24; 3:9), the dragon doesn't appear alongside the four horsemen in Revelation 6 or amid the smoke rising from the abyss in Revelation 9, and not even among the earth dwellers celebrating the death of the two witnesses in Revelation 11. The diabolical presence may be assumed, but the foreground of the first eleven chapters is populated by characters and circumstances that obscure our view of the true enemy resting just beyond the veil. The loneliness of Patmos (Rev 1) shrouds Satan's schemes. The enemies of the church (Rev 2–3) distort the dragon's presence. Roman conquest that devours peace, economies, and the lives of many (Rev 6) veils the devil as the true enemy.

That is, until Revelation 12.

Now the background becomes the foreground. The veil thinned to reveal beyond doubt the true enemy of this ancient story. In the final eleven chapters, the dragon moves center stage. No longer lurking or prowling but on full display, harvested out of the shadows to expose the ancient serpent in all his villainy.

In Revelation 12, violence and failure compose the chords of the first several verses of Satan's spectacle. His attempt to devour the Christ child (Rev 12:4) is thwarted by a heavenly ascension (Rev 12:5). Without delay, "the dragon and his angels" take arms against heaven itself (Rev 12:7), but "Michael and his angels" (Rev 12:7) overpower the satanic soldiery, hurling them down to the earth (Rev 12:8-9). "Filled with fury" (Rev 12:12), the dragon pursues the mother of the Christ child (Rev 12:13-15), but creation swallows

the satanic assault, leaving the woman unscathed (Rev 12:16). Time and again, failure spews forth as the appetite for violence proves impossible to satisfy. Satan spirals into blind rage ever further, now turning his vitriol "against the rest of her offspring, the ones keeping God's commands and holding fast to the testimony [μαρτυρίαν] of Jesus" (Rev 12:17).

Revelation 12 leaves little doubt: the *true* enemy of the church of Jesus Christ is Satan. Not Rome. Not bin Laden. But the dragon, "that ancient serpent called the devil and Satan, the one deceiving the whole world" (Rev 12:9), now filled with fury and murderously pursuing the faithful witnesses of Jesus Christ. A story that continues even into the present.

THE ONSLAUGHT OF EVIL: THE BEAST FROM THE SEA

History and the world today bear witness to this important truth: evil isn't creative. Then again, it doesn't have to be. Each generation falls for the same temptations time without end. Lust claimed the heart of David even as it parades the city streets of today. Violence plagued the mind of Saul just as it seduces governments of today. Selfishness stained the actions of Achan just as it slithers down the aisle of every church service critiqued by another worshiper today. The same stories saturated with the same sins separated by thousands of years.

Evil isn't creative, but it doesn't need to be to lead the world astray (Rev 12:9). The world is discipled and disciplined in the grammar of death, fluent in the serpent's native tongue of lies and deception. So, as the dragon stands "on the shore of the sea" (Rev 13:1), humanity awaits not with bated breath, not uncertain of what's about to unfold, for the onslaught of evil proceeds with predictable patterns uncovered in Genesis 3 and repeated in every epoch thereafter: distortion, deception, and displays of worship, all laced with threats and acts of violence.

At the beginning of Revelation 13, the dragon hovers by the waters of the sea, conjuring chaos from chaos. As in Daniel 7, a beast emerges from the sea. Unlike Daniel 7, it's only one beast, not four. "And I saw a beast coming up from the sea, having ten horns and seven heads, and on his horns ten crowns and on his heads blasphemous names. And the beast I saw was like a leopard and his feet like a bear and his mouth like the mouth of a lion" (Rev 13:1-2; cf. Rev 12:3). A single beast, yet a *distortion* of God's creation. The beast isn't identified with a single animal but an amalgamation: a leopard, a

bear, a lion (Rev 13:2). A melding of three that, not incidentally, mirrors the first three beasts in Daniel's vision:

beast 1: "The first was like a lion." (Dan 7:4)

beast 2: "And there was another beast, a second one, looking like a bear." (Dan 7:5)

beast 3: "After this, I was watching, and there was another one like a leopard." (Dan 7:6)[2]

As discussed in chapter one, Revelation is in dialogue with the story of the Old Testament. Not ignoring it or attempting to replace it but rereading the sacred text through the lens of the Revelation of Jesus Christ. Parallels persist, then, even if they're reshaped in the image of Jesus.

Thus the parallel to the beasts of Daniel 7 reminds us that the story of Revelation isn't new. The red dragon has been lurking since the days of Eden, yet now disrobed through Christ Jesus, exposing the patterns of evil enlisted to enslave humanity for millennia. The distortion of creation in Revelation 13, then, is as predictable as the *deception* that follows.

In Revelation 13:3, the beast appears to receive "a fatal wound," a type of deathblow. The fatal wound, however, is healed, a type of resurrection. The charade elicits the intended response: "And the whole earth marveled and followed the beast." As the pattern predicts, the *deception* unfolds into *displays of worship*: "And people worshiped the dragon because he gave authority to the beast, and they worshiped the beast saying, 'Who is like the beast? And who is able to war against it?'" (Rev 13:4).

Evil is a destroyer, not a creator. In fact, evil can't create at all; it can only distort what God wooed into existence and called good. But, time and again, male and female submit to the patterns of evil anew, believing this time the distortion will deliver them from pain, the deception will protect them from suffering, the idols will provide the life they've always wanted. Oddly enough, when evil produces what it can *only* offer—more pain, more suffering, more isolation, more loneliness—we turn to God and arrogantly shake our fists,

---

[2]Further parallels include that the beasts originate from the sea (Rev 13:1; Dan 7:3); Revelation's beast has the same total number of heads as the four beasts in Dan 7 and the same number of horns (Rev 13:1; Dan 7:7); that they're given authority to rule (Rev 13:2, 4-5; Dan 7:6); that they're connected to arrogant utterances (Rev 13:5-6; Dan 7:8, 11); and that they war against God's people (Rev 13:7; Dan 7:19, 21).

decrying injustice and spewing the same blasphemy as the beast (Rev 13:5-6). Indeed, who you worship, you become. For better or worse.

Unfortunately, the veil between heaven and earth is not as thick as we would hope. Removed from heaven (Rev 12:8-10, 12), the dragon and his followers can't translate their defamation into a celestial assault, unable to storm the steps of heaven's hill. So, their violence shifts its gaze from the holiness of heaven to the holy ones on earth: "[The beast] was given power to make war against the holy ones and to conquer them" (Rev 13:7). Distortion breeds deception and matures into displays of worship that ultimately war against God and "the ones keeping God's commands" (Rev 12:17). An onslaught of evil as predictable as humanity's perpetual fall.

EVIL'S ENCORE: THE BEAST FROM THE EARTH

Revelation 13, though, hasn't exhausted evil's unveiling quite yet. Revelation 13:11 highlights a peculiar development: the dragon and the beast from the sea are joined by "another beast, coming up from the earth." It's true, Daniel 7 has more than one beast, but none of them come out of the earth. Each beast—lion, bear, leopard, and the other—all come from the sea (Dan 7:2-3). Such a shift isn't incidental but an intentional development unveiled by the Revelation of Jesus Christ. Something pushing the interpreter beyond the veil.

In Daniel 7, each beast represents a different kingdom, a different iteration of empire pretending to be God as they assail God's people (Dan 7:15-17, 23-26). As tempting as it is to follow suit, to reduce Revelation's "sea beast" to the Roman Empire, the addition of the second beast "from the earth" modulates the image into a Christocentric key, signaling to the reader that a stilted one-to-one parallel to the Old Testament will not satisfy the imagery or the intent.[3] Revelation is unveiling something more, thinning the veil to uncover an enemy far superior to any single kingdom, something impossible to summarize with any particular empire.

---

[3]For the beast from the sea as Rome, see Wilhelm Bousset, *Die Offenbarung Johannis*, 5th ed. (Göttingen: Vandenhoeck & Ruprecht, 1906), 358-74, 418-26; R. H. Charles, *A Critical and Exegetical Commentary on the Revelation of St. John*, Vol. 1, International Critical Commentary (Edinburgh: T&T Clark, 1920), 1:345-67; G. B. Caird, *The Revelation of Saint John*, Black's New Testament Commentaries 19 (repr., Peabody, MA: Hendrickson, 1999), 170-73; Adela Yarbro Collins, *Crisis and Catharsis: The Power of the Apocalypse* (Philadelphia: Westminster, 1984), 148; Elisabeth Schüssler Fiorenza, *Revelation: Vision of a Just World* (Minneapolis: Fortress, 1991), 84-87; and others.

The second beast follows the satanic pattern of the first: distortion, deception, displays of worship (all laced with violence). The earth beast appears with "two horns like a lamb," yet with a peculiar *distortion*: "It was speaking like a dragon" (Rev 13:11). The beast performs "great signs," reminiscent of the two witnesses in Revelation 11:5, "even causing fire to come down from heaven to the earth in full view of the people" (Rev 13:13 NIV). Those "great signs," however, don't seek to reveal but to conceal: "Through the signs, it deceived the earth dwellers" (Rev 13:14). *Deception* designed to captivate onlookers and usher them into *displays of worship*: "[The beast from the earth] instructed the earth dwellers to make an image [εἰκόνι] in honor of the beast who was wounded by the sword and yet lived" (Rev 13:14). Thus, the deception of the first beast—the pseudo-resurrection—intermingles with the great signs of the second beast to entrance the onlookers and to entice them to pledge allegiance to the satanic kingdom saturated in violence: "And [the beast from the earth] was given power to give breath [πνεῦμα] to the image [εἰκόνι] of the beast from the sea, so that the image [εἰκὼν] could speak and force all who might refuse to worship the image of the beast [εἰκόνι] *to be killed*" (Rev 13:15). The second beast rehearses evil's predictable pattern, but not without revelatory power. The beast from the earth enacts a parody of Genesis 1—God's creation "in the beginning" (Gen 1:1; cf. Rev 4:11)—and unveils the complete picture of the *true* enemy. Let me explain.

In the beginning, God created the cosmos by bringing order from chaos, by whispering the words "Let there be light" into the darkness "over the surface of the deep" (Gen 1:1-3). In Revelation 13, the dragon conjures the two beasts from chaos to plunge creation back into the darkness of the void. In Genesis 1, as each day passes, God offers command after command to usher life into its place. In Revelation 13, as each beast appears, the dragon offers deception after distortion to usher life into a hellish abyss. God's creative act is parodied by evil's attempt at *un*creation. And the second beast offers the climactic parallel.

In Genesis 1, the sixth day disrupts the imperative pattern of the first five days ("Let there be . . .") with a subjunctive, with a divine consultation: "Let us make humankind according to our image [εἰκόνα] and according to our likeness" (Gen 1:26 LXX).[4] A holy idea that matures into a movement of

___

[4]John Behr, *John the Theologian and His Paschal Gospel: A Prologue to Theology* (Oxford: Oxford University Press, 2019), 211-12.

grace. God plunges his hands into the earth to create man from the dust of the ground just before an impossible image of intimacy: God animates humanity by breathing "the breath of life" into his nostrils (Gen 2:7 LXX). A merging of God and his creation, a vivification in the same vein as Jesus breathing on his disciples so they may "receive the Holy Spirit [πνεῦμα ἅγιον]" (Jn 20:22).

In Revelation 13:14-15, the second beast also crafts an εἰκών, this time an image of an *un*holy us. An idol celebrating the deception of the first beast, "who was wounded by the sword and yet lived" (Rev 13:14; cf. Rev 13:3, 12). The beast from the earth distorts God's act of intimacy by giving "breath" (πνεῦμα) to the image, giving life to the εἰκών in order to bring death to "all who might refuse to worship the image" (Rev 13:15).

Revelation 12–13, therefore, is a parody of Genesis 1, an act of *un*creation intent on plunging God's good work into chaos and darkness. Yet, it does more than just parallel; it clarifies. Unveils. It reveals the dragon, the beast from the sea, and the beast from the earth as an *un*holy trinity. A cosmic enemy far beyond the boundaries of any earthly empire. A parody of God the Father, God the Son, and God the Holy Spirit.

A TALE OF TWO TRINITIES

When God "became flesh and dwelled among us" (Jn 1:14), insight overwhelmed our senses. The Revelation of Jesus Christ altered categories, revised definitions, exegeted the Father on our behalf (Jn 1:18). God pervades the Old Testament, yet always encountered through a veil. Ever present yet never fully seen. Always guiding, wooing, and challenging, but never on full display. Shrouded in the background, content with others on center stage. In Jesus Christ, though, the background became the foreground, the veil removed by the "image [εἰκὼν] of the invisible God" (Col 1:15). The God of the forms burst into the cave to dispel all shadow with his glorious light.

The economy of God unveiled through the actions of Christ, particularly on the cross, brought clarity even if received as confusion. Through the incarnation, those with eyes to see could hear God speak as three persons, even though one being. The Trinity, then, wasn't born in Christ but unveiled, bringing to the foreground what was always present in the blurred

background: "Let *us* make humankind according to *our* image and ac cording to *our* likeness" (Gen 1:26).[5]

Still further, revealing the Holy Trinity also unveils the enemy. Clarity of one is enhanced by the contrast of the other. In Revelation 13, parody progresses from acts of creation and *un*creation to contrasts of the Holy Trinity with the *un*holy trinity.

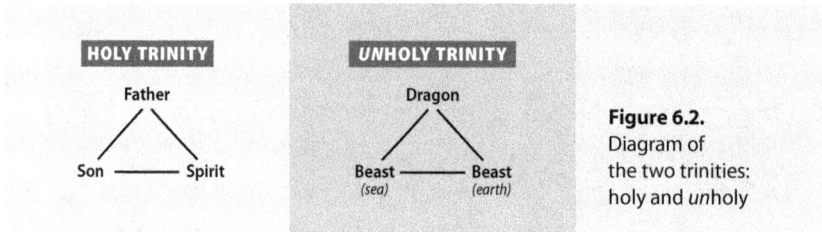

HOLY TRINITY

Father

Son ——— Spirit

UNHOLY TRINITY

Dragon

Beast ——— Beast
(sea)   (earth)

Figure 6.2.
Diagram of
the two trinities:
holy and *unholy*

For instance, each person of the Holy Trinity is mocked by persons of the *un*holy trinity. The slain Lamb (Jesus) is paired with the beast from the sea: the presence of horns (Rev 13:1; cf. Rev 5:6), the possession of diadems (Rev 13:1; cf. Rev 19:12), the inscription of a name (Rev 13:1; cf. Rev 19:12), the reception of authority (Rev 13:2; cf. Rev 5:7), the recipient of worship (Rev 13:4, 8; cf. Rev 5:8-10, 12-13), the leader in war (Rev 13:7; 19:19; cf. Rev 19:11, 15), and the (apparent) death and resurrection of each (Rev 13:3; cf. Rev 1:5, 18; 5:6; 13:8).

Similarly, the Spirit of God in Revelation parallels the beast from the earth: the second beast is intimately connected to the first beast (Rev 13:12, 15), as the Spirit is intimately connected to the Son (Rev 5:6; 19:10; 22:6); the second beast performs a ministry of proclamation (Rev 13:13-14; 16:13; 19:20; 20:10), and the Spirit proclaims as well (Rev 2:7, 11, 17, 29; 3:1, 6, 13, 22; 22:17); the earth beast coerces humankind to worship evil (Rev 13:12, 14-15), as the Spirit guides humanity to worship God alone (Rev 1:10; 4:2, 5; 21:10). In Revelation, the Spirit of God and the beast from the earth are bridges between humanity and divinity—neither receiving worship directly but both channeling humankind to contexts of worship.

---

[5]For a hermeneutic of Old Testament texts as trinitarian conversations overheard by the prophets (i.e., prosopological exegesis), see Matthew W. Bates, *The Birth of the Trinity: Jesus, God, and Spirit in New Testament and Early Christian Interpretation of the Old Testament* (Oxford: Oxford University Press, 2015).

The actions of these first two pairs (Jesus/sea beast, Spirit/earth beast) are directly connected to the authority and aims of the third pairing: the one on the throne (God the Father) and the red dragon (Satan). Satan bestows his authority on the beast from the sea (Rev 13:2) and even allows the beast to be worshiped by humanity alongside the dragon (Rev 13:4). The dragon's authority is used by the sea beast to war against God and his followers (Rev 13:7; cf. Rev 12:7, 17) through slander (Rev 13:6; cf. Rev 12:8-10, 12) and physical dominance (Rev 13:7, 10; cf. Rev 12:4, 7-8, 17). The beast from the earth—who has the voice of a dragon (Rev 13:11)—completes the *un*holy trinity by advancing the dragon's agenda (Rev 13:15-17) through the dragon's sovereignty (Rev 13:12).

Similarly, the authority and aims of God the Father are shared and enacted by the Son and the Spirit. In Revelation, the Father's authority extends to the Son (Rev 2:26-27), as evidenced by parallel titles, shared worship, and both reigning from the throne of heaven.[6] The Son uses this authority to bring resolution to the rebellious (Rev 2:4-5, 14-16, 20-23; 3:1-3, 15-20; 6:12-17; 19:11-21) and transformation to the faithful (Rev 1:5-6; 2:10, 17, 26-27; 3:12, 21; 5:9-10; 7:14-15; 20:4-6), both of which directly assault the aims of evil. Like the beast from the earth, the ministry of the Spirit completes the Holy Trinity, advancing the aims and authority of God by guiding humanity to worship the Son and the Father—for in Revelation, worship is war (Rev 8:1-5; 13:4, 8, 12, 15; 14:7, 9, 11; 15:4; 16:2; 19:20; 20:4).[7]

Humanity, then, is confronted with a tale of two trinities. Two trinities targeting uncompromised worship, two trinities demanding unrivaled fidelity. Both trinities gathering followers to do their will on earth as it is beyond the veil—the *un*holy trinity through deception (Rev 12:9; 13:14; 16:13; 19:20; 20:8, 10; cf. Rev 2:20) and the Holy Trinity through sacrifice (Rev 1:4-6; 5:9-10; 7:14-15).

Thus Revelation's tale of two trinities requires a response from the reader. A decision. A pledge of allegiance to the Holy Trinity or to the other. A

---

[6]Parallel titles: "Alpha and Omega"—Rev 1:8; 21:6 (the Father) and Rev 22:13 (the Son); "Beginning and End"—Rev 21:6 (the Father) and Rev 22:13 (the Son). The parallel title "the First and the Last" is also used of the Son in Rev 1:17; 22:13. Shared worship: The same "four living creatures" and "twenty-four elders" who worship God the Father (Rev 4:6-8, 10-11) also worship the Son, both alone (Rev 5:8-10) and along with the Father (Rev 5:13-14). See also Rev 5:11-12; 7:9-10. Both reigning on the throne in heaven: Revelation 4:2-6 (the Father) and Rev 5:6 (the Son). See also Rev 3:21; 7:9-10, 17; 22:3.

[7]See also Steven J. Friesen, *Imperial Cults and the Apocalypse of John: Reading Revelation in the Ruins* (Oxford: Oxford University Press, 2001), 176, 209; Leonard Thompson, *The Book of Revelation: Apocalypse and Empire* (Oxford: Oxford University Press, 1990), 53-73.

commitment that transforms you into their image on earth. Their will on earth. Their presence on earth. For in Revelation, who you worship, you become. You enact. You manifest—their appearance, their actions, and even their seal of allegiance.[8]

As such, the tale of two trinities is also a tale of two groups: the holy ones and the earth dwellers, the bride of Christ and the great prostitute, the new Jerusalem and Babylon, the church and the Roman Empire. Two groups who speak a different grammar, wield a different sword, and celebrate different definitions of war and conquest.

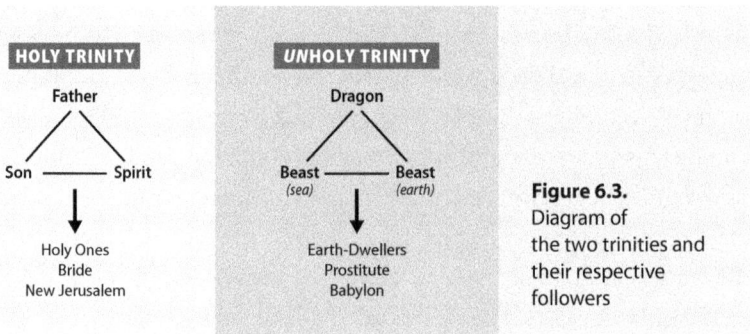

Figure 6.3. Diagram of the two trinities and their respective followers

HOW TO KILL A DRAGON

Revelation resounds with a message missed by many commentators and Christians today: Rome isn't the true enemy; Satan is. The *un*holy trinity is. Humanity's regional conflict and compromise is only part of a much larger cosmic battle between the two trinities. To misunderstand this essential principle threatens more than just misreading a text but Christ's kingdom as a whole. How to fight, who to fight, and what victory even means are dictated by who is the *true* enemy. If Rome: violent revolution; if Satan: cruciform sacrifice even for our adversaries.

---

[8]Appearance: The prostitute in Rev 17:4 and Babylon in Rev 18:16 are dressed in the color κόκκινος, which is the color of the beast in Rev 17:3 (cf. Rev 18:12). Similarly, the bride of the Lamb (Rev 21:9) brilliantly shines like jasper (Rev 21:11), as did the one on the throne (Rev 4:3). Actions: The followers of the *un*holy trinity blaspheme (Rev 16:9, 11, 21; 17:3; cf. Rev 2:9; 13:1, 5-6) and deceive (Rev 2:20; 18:23; cf. Rev 12:9; 13:14; 19:20; 20:8, 10). The followers of the Holy Trinity sacrifice (Rev 2:13; 13:10; 17:16; cf. Rev 1:5, 18; 5:9) and witness (Rev 2:13; 17:6; cf. Rev 1:5; 3:14). Seal of allegiance: The followers of the *un*holy trinity receive the χάραγμα of the beast on their foreheads (Rev 13:16-17; 14:9, 11; 16:2; 19:20; cf. Rev 20:4); the followers of the Holy Trinity receive the σφραγίς of God on their foreheads (Rev 7:2; 9:4; 14:1).

To understand Satan's trinity as the *true* enemy, however, doesn't trivialize or demean the evils of first-century Rome or the sins of twentieth-century racism. Indeed, there are times to speak against oppressive systems, confront tyrannical leaders, and overthrow racist rulers. But the voice of John Perkins and John of Patmos clarify the goal, sharpen the tactics, and reveal the uncomfortable truth that even if Osama bin Laden is killed, Satan's kingdom marches on unscathed. The head of the snake untouched. But if our enemy is converted into our friend, Satan's kingdom struggles to find its footing.

The revelation of the *un*holy trinity, then, doesn't overlook the evils done to us or by us but situates every evil in the context of the cosmic battle, clarifying both who the *true* enemy is and *how* to win the war. Destroying Rome does little to upend the dragon's agenda, for another Babylon is always waiting in the wings. Indeed, history discloses what Revelation 12–13 unveils: every empire falls and is followed by another and another on end. If Rome falls, like Egypt and others before, another empire will emerge, crafted in the image of the dragon and the two beasts. To target only the regional, therefore, misses the mark, settles for something far less than what God intends.

Consider Christ's arrest, recorded in all four Gospels (Mt 26:47-56; Mk 14:43-50; Lk 22:47-53; Jn 18:1-14). Jesus' kingdom is confronted by a contingent of troops and a wayward disciple. What ensues in Gethsemane clarifies. To the surprise of all, Jesus rejects Peter's sword (Jn 18:10-11) and refuses to unleash twelve legions of angels to annihilate the soldiery (Mt 26:53). Why? Rome is too small. Too little of a target. Too small a victory. Too insignificant to be considered God's true enemy.

God's battle is cosmic, not regional; against the bondage of sin and death, not Pilate and the empire. Jesus is not, then, indifferent to the trials and inquiries that follow, just focused on a greater target. One more grand than any single empire, past or present. A target birthed in Eden, not by the principate. A target beyond the reach of swords and slings and arrows, even as it slithers in the shadows of each empire. Jesus embraces the cross not pragmatically ("Rome is too big to fight!") but purposefully, deliberately, consciously—for an enemy beyond the veil necessitates a weapon fit to pierce the veil. So Christ employs self-sacrifice and the forgiveness of enemies to assault the true target: the *un*holy trinity.

And Revelation calls Christians to do the same.

In Revelation 12:10-12, after the dragon's heavenly defeat at the hands of Michael, a celestial choir sings a song of "salvation" that celebrates "the kingdom of our God, and the authority of his Christ" (Rev 12:10). Like all hymns in the Apocalypse, the psalm is an interpretative key, a melodic translation of the story. In the center of the hymn, the reader is taught how to kill the cosmic tyrant: "And they conquered [the dragon] by the blood of the Lamb and by the word of their testimony [μαρτυρίας], for they did not covet their lives in the face of death" (Rev 12:11). In the economy of Christ, slaying dragons occurs through the cross of Calvary *and* through the willingness of Christians to witness in the same way. To sacrifice in the same way. To suffer as Christ suffered.

In the economy of any empire, this is foolish. Asinine. A sadistic fantasy that denies reality and deserves to be mocked. Yet Revelation is unrelenting. The text refuses the overture of the enemy, singing the same message time and again through hymns and proverbial calls to action:

If anyone has an ear, let him hear:

> If anyone is to be taken as a prisoner of war, as a prisoner of war he
>   goes off.
> If anyone is to be killed by the sword, by the sword he is to be killed.

This requires patient endurance and faithfulness [πίστις] from the holy ones. (Rev 13:9-10)

To slay the dragon, Christians can't use the weapons of the empire; they must use a cruciform metric of victory. One that doesn't equate death with defeat, as employed by the onlookers at the foot of the cross (Mt 27:39-44), but instead trusts that triumph over the true enemy is paved by the blood of the slain Lamb. The Revelation of Jesus Christ, then, doesn't just reveal *who* the true enemy is but also *how* to kill this enemy: through the cross and cruciform living.

This same message sung in Revelation 12:11 and proclaimed in Revelation 13:10 is depicted with startling imagery in Revelation 14:1-20. The Lamb stands triumphantly on Mount Zion (Rev 14:1) with his followers close by. Followers branded with the name of God (Rev 14:1) and committed to "following the Lamb wherever he might go" (Rev 14:4), even to a cross. Like Christ, their lives are a living sacrifice, "firstfruits offered to God and to the Lamb" (Rev 14:4).[9] In

---

[9]See Ignatius, *To the Ephesians* 1.1. For Christ as firstfruits, see 1 Cor 15:20, 23; cf. 1 Clement 24:1.

Revelation 14:13, a voice from heaven compels Revelation's reader to see death from a different vantage: "Blessed are the dead, the ones dying in the Lord from now on."[10] Jesus' resurrection transformed the cross's tragedy into a triumph, inverting our expectations and unveiling death "in the Lord" as the path to blessing. To victory. To conquest over the dragon.

The imagery, however, intensifies by transforming an Old Testament image into a startling depiction of grace. In Isaiah 63, a cryptic figure appears robed with splendor (Is 63:1) yet with garments stained crimson, "like one who treads in the winepress" (Is 63:2). When asked, "Why are your garments red?" (Is 63:2), the hero announces: "I have trodden the winepress alone, and there was not a man from the nations with me. I trod them in my anger and trampled them in my wrath. Their blood spattered on my garments, and I have stained all my clothing. . . . I trampled the nations in my anger. And I made them drunk in my wrath, and I poured their blood on the earth" (Is 63:3, 6). The grisly scene envisions blood splattering as the enemy is trampled underfoot like grapes crushed in a winepress. An image striking in its ferocity and gruesome in its display.

Revelation 14:14-20 invokes this "winepress of God's wrath" (Rev 14:19) but inverts it from an image of unbridled anger into an image of endless grace. Into an image of Christians living in the shape of the cross. Into an image of destruction of the true enemy through the sacrifice of Christ and those following him.

In Revelation 14:14-18, angelic figures emerge from the temple in heaven ready for harvest. A heavenly voice commands an angel to reap the earth, for "its grapes are ripe" (Rev 14:18). The angel obeys, gathering the grapes and throwing them "into the great winepress of God's wrath" (Rev 14:19). The imagery climaxes in Revelation 14:20: "And [the grapes] were trampled [ἐπατήθη] in the winepress outside the city, and blood [αἷμα] flowed from the winepress as high as the horses' bridles for 1,600 stadia."

Revelation 14:20 contains three key elements that transform the winepress in Isaiah 63 through the Revelation of Jesus Christ. First, in Revelation, the word *blood* (αἷμα), when referring to a human, is used only in reference to Jesus (Rev 1:5; 5:9; 7:14; 12:11; 19:13) or one of his followers (Rev 6:10; 16:6 [2×]; 17:6;

---

[10]Revelation 14:13 is the second out of seven beatitudes in the book of Revelation (Rev 1:3; 14:13; 16:15; 19:9; 20:6; 22:7, 14).

18:24; 19:2).[11] Second, the only prior use of the word *trampled* (ἐπατήθη) in Revelation is in Revelation 11:2, where the "holy city" (i.e., the church on earth) is trampled by "the Gentiles," a depiction of persecution enacted in the death of the two witnesses (Rev 11:3-10) and envisioned in the hymn of Revelation 12:11 (cf. Rev 19:15).[12] Third, the connection between blood and wine in Revelation 14:20 also occurs in Revelation 17:1-6, where the great prostitute is intoxicated on "the wine of her sexual immorality" (Rev 17:2), later defined as "the blood of holy ones, the blood of the witnesses [μαρτύρων] of Jesus" (Rev 17:6; see also Rev 18:24). Taken together, these three elements unveil an insight comparable to the hymn of Revelation 12:11 and the call of Revelation 13:10, an insight dependent on the blessing of Revelation 14:13 and the example of the saints "following the Lamb wherever he might go" (Rev 14:4): the evil nations aren't the grapes of wrath, for Christians took their place, just as Christ took ours.

Unlike in Isaiah 63, the winepress in Revelation 14 isn't an image of vengeance on the enemies of God crushed underfoot like grapes but an image of Christians sacrificed like Christ for those led astray by the *un*holy trinity. The river of blood is a river of grace, high and deep, that, like Wormwood, provides healing for those willing to step into the winepress, yet poison for those who refuse to repent.[13] Without question, this calls for "patient endurance and faithfulness from the holy ones" (Rev 13:10; cf. Rev 1:9). Yet the cosmic secret of how to destroy the enemy of Eden has now been disclosed: to kill a dragon, you need much more than anger and a sword; you need a cross and cruciform living.

REMEMBER WHO THE ENEMY IS

I remember it was cold outside. Rain lightly tickled the windowpane of the library in Prague, Czech Republic. Inside, a short silence filled the room as

---

[11]Blood (αἷμα) is also used of creation (Rev 6:12; 8:7-8; 16:3-4), but never in reference to the earth dwellers.

[12]In Revelation, "the holy city" (τὴν πόλιν τὴν ἁγίαν) is always in reference to God's people (Rev 11:2; 21:2, 10; 22:19), in contradistinction to "the great city" (τῆς πόλεως τῆς μεγάλης), which is always in reference to rebellious humanity (Rev 11:8; 16:19; 17:18; 18:10, 16, 18-19). For more on Rev 11:1-2, see Shane J. Wood, *The Alter-Imperial Paradigm: Empire Studies and the Book of Revelation* (Leiden: Brill, 2016), 116-20.

[13]Also, Rev 14:20 references 1,600 stadia (4 × 4 × 10 × 10). In Revelation, four is a number of completion attached to the earth (e.g., Rev 5:9; 7:1; etc.). Ten is a number of completion attached to a time period of suffering or persecution through which God proves to be faithful (so Dan 1:6-20; Rev 2:10; etc.). Taken together, the 1,600 stadia emphasize suffering and persecution on earth through which God proves to be faithful—just like the cross of Christ.

the interpreter finished the last line of my lecture, titled "Suffering and Victory in the Book of Revelation." The audience was filled with both young and old, Christians and the curious.

I caught eyes with the interpreter, who broke the silence and announced the question-and-answer time would now commence. The first several questions were quite typical: the mark of the beast, the rapture, the 144,000, and so on. Nothing out of the ordinary for a lecture on Revelation. That is, until an older gentleman spoke up.

His voice was raspy, his face weathered by life and strain. In a soft voice, he spoke, causing all of us to lean in just a little to discern what he was saying. I leaned toward the interpreter who matched the man's volume, quietly relaying each word.

"He says, 'I've grown up in Prague my entire life *as a Christian*. I remember the revolution. I remember when the communists were driven away. I remember the celebration in the streets. I also remember life *before* all this. I remember the suffering my family went through at the hands of a godless government. The fear Christians lived in each day.'"

The interpreter paused as the man's emotion glistened in his eyes. His lip quivered with intensity. No one dared move. All could sense the holy moment unfolding.

"I remember," he continued, "my father disappearing for days at a time for questioning. My mom would fight worry with cleaning and quoting Scripture. It was truly a frightening time."

Once again, he paused. Silence stilled the room. Then he looked up, locked eyes with mine, and taught us all a lesson far more insightful than anything in the lecture.

"Even still, I find being a Christian today far more difficult than living under the communists."

Without thinking, I blurted out, "What? Why?!?!"

"Well," he said, furrowing his brow, "back then, I knew who the enemy was. They wore uniforms. Now," he looked around the room, "I don't know who the enemy is. The enemy could be anyone. Now the enemy blends in."

I was dumbstruck. Humbled by this insight only evident to those discipled by suffering, familiar with an enemy devoted to deception and destroying the good. Sure, anti-God governments terrorize with distortion, deception, and

displays of twisted worship, laced with layers of violence. But the satanic trinity loves the background, longs to lurk undetected, sowing tares among the wheat, tempting all to believe that all we see is all there is.

Evil distorts. Parades good in the streets, twisting theology and God's graciousness into a crown of deception that pierces each brow with false images of the divine one.

Evil deceives. Shifts with each shadow, distorting the light and casting confusion where truth longs to reign.

Evil demands worship. Seeks to dismember each limb of the body of Christ, or at the very least convince Christians to fight the wrong enemy.

"If only," evil quips, "I can get them to fight for themselves."

"If only," evil muses, "I can get them to silence the prophets and promote the merchants in their fold."

"If only," evil cries, "I can get them to stare into the face of Christ and see a menacing figure intent on imprisoning them instead of liberating them in an exodus."

It's easy to forget who the enemy is. It's easy to live life without ever acknowledging the dragon, especially if we are insulated in luxury or emboldened by anger. Carefully curated lives thicken the veil, pretending there is no enemy. There is no accuser. There is no dragon lurking in the shadows of our schedules or behind the mangers of our heart. Pretending there's no enemy brings a strange solace, even if it leaves us vulnerable to attack.

But Revelation 12–14 confronts this naiveté, thins the veil between the visible and the not, revealing that even in the most tranquil of moments, even on the most silent of nights, there's more to the story. More to be seen. More to unveil. Dragons are prowling, beasts are emerging, and kingdoms are masquerading as masters of the universe they didn't create and can't control.

Revelation 12–14 clarifies the enemy. Unveils the *un*holy trinity. Unearths the accuser from the shadowy background and brings the ancient serpent center stage, disrobing Satan, the master of deception, and his beasts of chaos.

Unveiling the enemy changes more than just our nativity scenes and the questions we ask in darkened terminals. It changes what we celebrate, how we define victory, whom we target as the enemy, and even how we engage the fight as a whole. To see the enemy clearly demystifies the target and simplifies our response. Shifts our gaze from the sword to self-sacrifice, from grasps of

power to acts of service, from political allegiances to unrivaled devotion to the slain Lamb.

No, this isn't merely a call to an ethic, or a political or apolitical position. It's a call to transformation. It's a call to "follow the Lamb wherever he might go" (Rev 14:4), even if he goes to a cross. It's a call to confront the *un*holy trinity with "the blood of the Lamb" (Rev 12:11) and with the willingness of Christians to witness as Christ witnessed, to die as Christ died, to live as the body of Christ.

GOING DEEPER

> **THE TOOL:** Structure. Revelation has an unfamiliar organization of thoughts. At times the reader must strain to see any logic in the narrative's structure. Watch this video (www.ivpress.com/wood-6a) and wrestle with the following:

1. Read Matthew 4:1-11 and Luke 4:1-13. The temptation of Jesus is told by two authors from two different perspectives.

   ‣ What differences do you notice?

   ‣ What similarities?

   ‣ If Matthew's Gospel emphasizes kingdom and Luke's Gospel emphasizes broken humanity, how does each author accentuate his point here?

2. Watch your local news tonight and pay attention to the structure.

   ‣ What do you notice? Do they retell events?

   ‣ If so, how does each time differ?

   ‣ What is the benefit of structuring the news like this?

   ‣ How could you infuse this type of structure in other areas of your life?

> **THE TEXT:** The enemy of Christ (Rev 12:1–14:20). It's hard to win the battle if you don't know who the enemy is. The targets may be mistaken, the weapons do more harm than damage, and chaos ensues. Watch this video (www.ivpress.com/wood-6b) and answer the following:

1. If Satan is the true enemy, how do we win the battle?

   ‣ What tactics work against this enemy?

   ‣ What actions seem good but actually advance the enemy's agenda?

   ‣ How does this insight change how you treat the church? Politics? Your family?

2. In Revelation 13, deception is a key strategy of the *un*holy trinity. Reflect on a time when you were deceived by someone or something.

   ‣ What made the message so believable?

   ‣ What was the turning point that unmasked the deception?

   ‣ Has there been a time when you used deception?

   ‣ What was the key for making the deception believable?

> **THE TAKEAWAY**: Looking for Revelation in the everyday. Each Christmas I add a dragon to my nativity scene as a reminder that we are in a battle. What follows is a challenge to do something similar. Here's how it works:

1. Look through the book of Revelation for an image to incorporate into your everyday life.

   ‣ The image should be a reminder that the veil between heaven and earth is not as thick as we assume.

   ‣ It could be something you create or something you buy.

2. Incorporate the image into your everyday life.

   ‣ Affix the image in a key location that you interact with on a consistent basis as a persistent reminder that we are in a war and God is closer than we presume.

   ‣ Why? Because we aren't just studying the Word of God. We're committing to allow it to permeate every area of our lives.

7

THE MESSAGE IN THE MEANTIME
(Revelation 15–16)

Christ, Our Deeds, and the Death of Death

Behold! I come like a thief. Blessed is the one keeping watch and
remaining clothed, so as not to go around naked and shamefully exposed.

REVELATION 16:15

LIFE IS FILLED WITH LIMINALITY. Transitions from one stage to the next, one phase to another, one season to whatever comes thereafter. As we wean, we learn to walk, or at least stumble in a quasi-coordinated fashion. Gibberish gives way to grammar as diapers graduate to pull-ups and potty-training. Preteens limp through puberty, navigating different degrees of freedom and constraint, rebellion and restriction, all the way up to and through their diploma, which announces the next phase of life: adulthood.

As young adults, we leave the nest in flight with promises and possibilities as expansive as the horizon. Ideals unfold into habits, for better or worse, and life lumbers toward more milestones of transition: marriage for some, children for others, midlife crises for all, and retirement as a goal for many, though few are prepared to apprehend it. The end of work commonly accompanies a loss of identity, a muddling of meaning and purpose and questions of mortality. Each transition, each liminal birth and rebirth, however small or grand, reminds us and prepares us for the *final* transition. Moving from the lushness of life to the liminality of the grave. Life's final rite of passage: death.

I'm writing this chapter in Houston, Texas, sitting in a small enclave in the Lanier Theological Library. I'm surrounded by death. Each enclave hosts a table and chairs surrounded by countless books with a plaque overhead naming the deceased donor whose collection now populates this space: "Trude Dothan," "Alan Segal," "Larry Hurtado," and other luminaries now living beyond the veil. To my left is a jar encased in glass, ancient pottery that housed a portion of the Dead Sea Scrolls for almost two millennia. The ornate ceiling is covered in beautiful artistry, each panel framed by crosses uniquely crafted to invite reflection on the mystery of Christ's sacrifice. The space is alive, even if it's saturated in death.

Settling in to write, I caught eyes with a senior scholar, a man who graciously greeted me with a warm handshake and undeserved hospitality. For several minutes, he patiently explained the layout of the library, drawing my attention to the artifacts of C. S. Lewis and various resources I might need for this book. Then, without warning, the death surrounding us merged with our conversation.

He mentioned the name of a collection, the name of a scholar I'd met while working on my dissertation. A scholar, he disclosed, who had been one of his close friends for more than thirty years. A scholar who had died in the not-too-distant past.

"Well," he recalled, "several years ago, my child passed away from cancer."

The comment shifted the moment. His gaze became distant and softened, almost as if the memory had pierced the veil of the present.

"And, well," his voice deadened, "I just . . . I just couldn't face the death of my good friend as well."

He stammered a bit as his eyes fixated on something before us but beyond us.

"I did, though, get to see him several weeks after my son's death. It was wonderful. His blood levels were great. He was feeling fine. We went to shops, walked around, played the guitar in his living room. He even danced with his wife."

I knew now that the veil between the present and the past was quite thin. Almost as if he could see the lovely couple swaying back and forth—eyes locked, arms embraced, smiles wide, lost in a lifelong love now entering liminal space. The unknown passage of death.

"I left for home," he continued, "and I thought, 'He's not sick. He can't be dying.' But just six weeks later: he was gone."

DEATH THE TEACHER

I have a lot to learn from death. Despite its tyrannical grip on the living, it has a lot to teach us about life. How to live. What truly is sacred.

Each day's stress would loosen its grip if we were discipled by death. Death unveils how often we make what is small so big, majoring in the minors of life. Noises that once overstimulated us are no longer unwelcome. Titles that once defined us no longer hold value. In the presence of death, all seems to become clear. Lucid. Obvious and without obscurity.

The desert fathers and saints of old speak of death as a companion or guide.[1] Saint Francis even had the audacity to bestow death with the familial status "sister."[2] Indeed, by humanity's invitation (Gen 3), death *is* omnipresent, infused into each person and pattern of the wind, offering its instruction at all times and in all locations. Yet we ignore it, avoid it, refuse to reflect on it, attempting to pretend it doesn't exist at all. Yes, death is the "last enemy to be destroyed" (1 Cor 15:26), but that can happen by converting death into a friend. Or even family. In Christ alone, *sister* death becomes a guide, a friend, a teacher filled with wisdom and insight, instructing its students how to live. *Truly* live.

This might be why the Western world is drowning in depression and anxiety. We've insulated ourselves from death and as a result have forgotten how to live. The old and dying are pushed out of our homes (and theirs) into retirement villages or hospice wings of hospitals, so we don't have to look at them if we don't choose. We use dyes to purge the gray in our hair, cosmetic procedures to erase the wrinkles in our faces, and in every image on the streets and on our screens, youth is equated with beauty, because the younger you are, the more distant you are from death. In our quest to kill this great enemy, we've lost our ability to live. To live well. To live as Christ did.

---

[1]Origen, *Commentary on John* 6.36; Evagrius of Pontus, *Foundations* 9; *To Eulogius* 18.19; 19.20; 21.23; *Vices* 6; Maximus the Confessor, "On The Lord's Prayer," in *The Philokalia: The Complete Text Compiled by St Nikodimos of the Holy Mountain and St Makarios of Corinth*, compiled by St. Nikodimos of the Holy Mountain and St. Makarios of Corinth, trans. G. E. H. Palmer, Philip Sherrard, and Kallistos Ware (London: Faber and Faber, 1981), 2:300. Cf. Ignatius, *To the Ephesians* 7.2, *To the Magnesians* 5.1-2, *To the Smyrnaeans* 4.2; Athanasius, *On the Incarnation* 27.1-4.
[2]Francis of Assisi, "The Canticle of the Creatures," 12.

Death never meant to be a great teacher; its goal was more sinister. Something more akin to a warden or a slave owner. Death didn't intend to be a conduit for life; it still tries to resist its calling. Instead of wisdom, death chooses to distribute fear. Fear of the unknown, fear of the grave, fear of what rests beyond the veil.

The mystery of Christ crucified, though, reveals a God who unveils death as a guide for how to live. That is, if we choose to face it. Embrace it. Convert it into a friend.

Jesus didn't bypass death, avoid death, or even cling to equality with God as a loophole out of death. He exposed death for what it is: a distortion of transformation. A corruption of the beauty only found in times of transition. Seasons of liminality. Avenues of becoming *new* because you've been *reborn*. This is why Jesus demands, "If anyone wants to follow me, let them deny themselves and take up their cross daily" (Lk 9:23). This is why Paul celebrates that we're "always carrying around Jesus' death in our body, so that the life of Jesus might be manifested in our body" (2 Cor 4:10). This is why Revelation 14:13 unveils, "Blessed are the dead, the ones dying in the Lord from now on." Because embracing death instead of avoiding death allows us to live. *Truly* live.

LIFE IN THE LIMINAL SPACE

I know some may insist that thus far this chapter is an exercise in morbidity or mere philosophical musings divorced from Revelation or even the gospel as a whole. But meditating on death isn't morose when done in Christ. It's an invitation. A summons to contemplate the meantime. The space in between. The truth only visible in the liminal, however small or grand. However terrifying or mundane.

At the end of the first century, Christians in Asia Minor were *in* liminal space and *entering* liminal space. The church was birthed into a time of transition: after Christ's first coming yet before his second. But as each moment unfolded ever further away from the foot of the cross, anxiety heightened and memories faded. For now, John, the last living apostle, was exiled on the island of Patmos, and there was little hope for his return, especially at such an advanced age.[3] Imperial tension was escalating, and questions were

---

[3] The traditional date of John's exile is during Domitian's reign (81–96 CE), roughly fifty years after the life of Jesus (Irenaeus, *Against Heresies* 5.30.3). According to tradition, John returned from exile to

increasing: Where is God? Is this winning? Is this the kingdom Christ envisioned? What will become of the church after John's death? Has Rome won? Is there any hope?

Christians were caught between conflict and conviction, tension and turmoil, eternity and time. Time polluted by perceptions of power—how it's acquired and how it should be used. Time confused by commentaries on victory—how it's attained and how it should be measured. Time arrested by the clash of two cities (Babylon and new Jerusalem), the procession of two women (the great prostitute and the bride of Christ), and the marching of two armies (the earth dwellers and the holy ones) belonging to their respective trinities (*un*holy and holy). Time consumed by the strain and the struggle of the meantime.

In times of transition, we labor to find our bearings. We flounder to find our footing. We lash out at those we love even as we lament our aggression. We build walls with abrasive tones and sour looks, hoping the angst will protect us from the pain and the onslaught we can't see or outflank. In times of transition, we flail. Emotionally. Spiritually. Relationally.

Liminality challenges the well-worn saint and the middle school teen all the same. Unsure of where to go or what to do or how to survive, we forget who we are, where our hope resides, and how to take even the smallest steps without stumbling or falling altogether. Thus, during the meantime, the basics are essential. Pausing, creating space, intentionally reminding ourselves of what's true: God is love, he knows not how to abandon, and come what may, his faithfulness will overcome.

THE MESSAGE IN THE MEANTIME

The Revelation of Jesus Christ unveils its message through interludes. Interruptions in the narrative. All three sets of seven—seals, trumpets, and bowls—contain an interlude between the sixth and the seventh. The sixth seal is broken in Revelation 6:12-17, the seventh in Revelation 8:1-5, with an interlude in between (Rev 7:1-17). The sixth trumpet sounds in Revelation 9:13-21, the seventh not until Revelation 11:15-19, with an interlude in between

---

live in Ephesus (Clement of Alexandria, *Quis dives salvetur* 42; Eusebius, *Ecclesiastical History* 3.20) until his death in the reign of Trajan (98–117 CE) at an advanced age (Irenaeus, *Against Heresies* 2.22.5; 3.3.4; Jerome, *De viris illustribus* 9).

(Rev 10:1–11:14). The sixth bowl is poured out in Revelation 16:12-14, yet before the seventh in Revelation 16:17, red letters interrupt the black ink with another, albeit much smaller, interlude: "Behold! I come like a thief. Blessed is the one keeping watch and remaining clothed, so as not to go around naked and shamefully exposed" (Rev 16:15). The interlude pattern isn't incidental or mere rhetorical flare. It's calculated. A coordination of the message and the meantime, since life is lived there anyway.

Like the three messages of the Roman sovereign narrative, each message from each interlude is a tributary of the same river.[4] Three threads of the same braid. As each set of seven approaches its iteration of the end of the world, the message in the meantime summits with a call to Christians, first century or otherwise.[5]

The ascent begins with the seals and a question.

After the appearance of the four horsemen (Rev 6:1-8) and the martyrs under the altar in heaven (Rev 6:9-11), the sixth seal begins with an earthquake, a crimson moon, and a blackened sun (Rev 6:12). The celestial apogee turns tragic as the stars fall to the earth (Rev 6:13) and the heavens recede "like a scroll being rolled up" (Rev 6:14). Mountains move, islands upheave (Rev 6:14), and fallen humanity hides in caves, crying out to the rocks, "Fall on us and hide us from the face of the one sitting on the throne and from the wrath of the Lamb!" (Rev 6:15-16). The end is nigh; hope scatters. A desperate query is voiced: "For the great day of their wrath has come, and who can stand?" (Rev 6:17).

Death's frightful mien pales in comparison to the possibility of judgment. Which is why many find greater solace in *nothing* after we die than even a modicum of accountability postmortem. The vulnerability of a judgment day is simply unbearable. Even for most Christians.

Years ago, my oldest son, Zion, was in the passenger seat recounting conversations from Wednesday night church. When he's excited, his pace quickens as his six-foot-three frame becomes more involved, animating each person's comment and response.

"And so, you know, I told him, 'Well, when I get to heaven—I mean, *if* I get to heaven . . .'"

---

[4] (1) The Roman Empire is the ruler of the kings of the earth, (2) Rome is favored by the gods, and (3) Rome is the bearer of *pax*.

[5] Seals = Rev 6:12-17; trumpets = Rev 11:15-19; bowls = Rev 16:17-21.

"Whoa," I interrupted midsentence, "What do you mean *if*?"

"I mean, you know," he hesitated, "I think I'll get in."

I parked the van and looked him straight in the eyes, "What makes you think on judgment day you'd have anything to worry about?"

"I don't know," he shrugged, a bit surprised. "I just didn't want to be arrogant about it or anything."

"Hey," I said apologetically. "I'm sorry I responded like that. It's just, you're covered with the blood of Jesus, and as long as you walk with him, you don't need to worry about *if*. Now, it's just *when*."

He smiled. We hugged. And we both went inside a bit lighter.

But his hesitation reminded me of the question at the end of the sixth seal: "The great day of God's wrath has come, and who can stand?" It's essential that Christians are able to answer this question. Confidently so. Our mission depends on it. Our witness moved by it. Our ability to endure the meantime directly affected by it. Which is why Revelation 7, the interlude between the sixth and seventh seals, emphatically offers an answer.

THE MESSAGE IN THE MEANTIME, NO. 1:
THE INTERLUDE OF THE SEALS

Revelation 7:1-8 is located on earth and centered on the number four, a number of completion usually attached to the earth. Four angels stand guard "at the four corners of the earth," preventing the "four winds of the earth" from spreading across "the earth or on the sea or on any tree" (Rev 7:1), that is, until a seal is affixed to "the foreheads of the servants of God" (Rev 7:3). A seal of protection, of ownership, of grace. In Revelation 7:4-8, "the number of the ones having been sealed" is announced as "144,000 from every tribe of the sons of Israel" (Rev 7:4), followed by a list of twelve tribes, with the number 12,000 affixed to each, beginning with the tribe of Judah.[6]

The list, though, contains an anomaly: Dan and Ephraim are removed and replaced with Joseph and Levi. Jewish literature prior to Revelation already signaled the removal of Dan and Ephraim for acts of rebellion, but the addition of Joseph (Egyptian royalty) and Levi (God's priests) identifies this group on

---

[6]Typically, the Roman Empire was populated with roughly 20 to 26 legions, each with approximately 4,000-6,000 soldiers. Thus, the 144,000 on earth could be seen as not just 12 sets of 12,000 but 24 sets of 6,000, or 24 legions of the Holy Trinity on earth.

earth as "a kingdom and priests" (Rev 1:6; 5:10) led by the Lion of the tribe of Judah (Rev 5:5).[7] In Revelation 14:1-5, this same 144,000 is similarly depicted, sealed with God's name "on their foreheads" and "*standing* on Mount Zion" (Rev 14:1). Their commitment to Christ is highlighted by saying, "They are the ones following the Lamb wherever he might go" (Rev 14:4). Even to the cross.

The number 144,000 reiterates this same portrayal. In Revelation, as in all apocalyptic literature, numbers should be weighed, not measured. The text isn't counting individuals on earth from 1 to just past the number 143,999 and stopping just before 144,001. The number holds a symbolic weight compiled by its constituent parts: $12 \times 12 \times 10 \times 10 \times 10$.

The number twelve is a number of completion usually attached to God's people. Yes, the twelve tribes of Israel, but also the twelve disciples, both of which the churches of Asia Minor and Christians today can trace their spiritual lineage from. The twenty-four elders first seen in Revelation 4, then, hold significant symbolic weight: 12 + 12. The complete number of God's people + the complete number of God's people.

If the number twelve punctuates the identity of the 144,000, the number ten stresses their context: conflict. Ten is a number of completion usually attached to a time period of suffering or persecution through which God proves to be faithful. A definition derived, as before, from the Old Testament.

Consider Daniel 1:1-20. The Babylonian Empire destroyed the city of Jerusalem and its holy temple, carrying cultic items and Yahweh's people into exile. Into liminal space (Dan 1:1-2). Among them was Daniel, the apocalyptic prophet, and some of his companions, Shadrach, Meshach, and Abednego (Dan 1:6-7). Unable to obey all of God's commands, especially without the temple, Daniel and his countrymen resolved to keep the dietary laws, refusing the royal food and wine (Dan 1:8). The Babylonian official, however, pressed Daniel to be reasonable. The king of Babylon had "assigned your food and drink" and would hold the official responsible if they were not well fed (Dan 1:9-10). In response, Daniel made a request: "'Please test your servants for *ten* days, and let them give us vegetables to eat and water to drink.

---

[7]For Dan, see Testament of Dan 5:4-8; cf. Jer 8:16-17. For Ephraim, see Ps 78:9-11; Is 9:8-12; Hos 5:1-15; cf. Josh 16:1-17:17; Judg 1:28-29. For postbiblical rabbinic literature especially critical of Dan, see Hermann Strack and Paul Billerbeck, *Commentary on the New Testament from the Talmud and Midrash*, ed. Jacob N. Cerone, trans. Joseph Longarino, Vol. 3 (Bellingham, WA: Lexham, 2021), 3:941-42.

And let them compare our appearance and the appearance of the young men eating the fine food of the king, and deal with your servants according to what you see.' And [the official] agreed to their proposal, and he tested them for *ten* days" (Dan 1:12-14). The result revealed God's faithfulness even amid the suffering of the exile. After "ten days," Daniel and his companions "appeared healthier and better nourished than all of the young men eating the fine food of the king" (Dan 1:15). In fact, after questioning them, the king "found them *ten* times better than all the soothsayer-priests and enchanters in his whole kingdom" (Dan 1:20).

The number ten carries symbolic weight that confronts conflict and suffering with God's faithfulness. This is why, in Revelation, the church of Smyrna, a congregation caught in the throes of conflict (Rev 2:9), is told, "Fear nothing of what you are about to suffer. Behold, the devil is about to cast some of you into prison that you might be tempted, and you will have affliction for *ten* days" (Rev 2:10). Translation: you will go through a time period of suffering and persecution through which God will prove to be faithful. The same is true with the 144,000, although it contains a trinity of tens.

Taken together, the 144,000 are the complete number of God's people caught in conflict and suffering on earth, but as in days of old, God will prove his faithfulness. He will overcome. And on the great day of God's wrath, Christians on earth will be able to *stand*.

But this doesn't exhaust the answer to the question, "Who can stand?" Two more groups emerge in Revelation 7:9-11. This time in heaven.

In Revelation 7:9, John sees "a great multitude that no one was able to count." No numbers or tribal names affixed to this celestial crowd. Yes, this multitude is *from* the earth, as indicated by the fourfold "every nation, tribe, people, and tongue" (Rev 7:9), but now, they're *in* heaven "wearing white robes" (Rev 7:9), clothed in victory. Like the 144,000, they endured suffering on earth (Rev 7:14), but they overcame the onslaught, cleansing their robes "in the blood of the Lamb" (Rev 7:14). Now they're "*standing* before the throne and before the Lamb" (Rev 7:9). Thus, this great multitude mirrors the 144,000 but is not the same group. The great multitude is Christians, but they've died, are in heaven, and are able to stand.

The final answer to "Who can stand?" is found in Revelation 7:11, "All the angels were *standing* around the throne and the elders and the four living

creatures." The angels were standing, that is, until "they fell before the throne on their faces" (Rev 7:11), worshiping God with a song containing a sevenfold celebration: "Amen! Praise and glory and wisdom and thanks and honor and power and strength to our God for ever and ever. Amen!" (Rev 7:12).[8] The worship scene is central for those "who can stand." Christians on earth can stand because they fall before God in worship; Christians in heaven can stand because they fall before God in worship; all angels in heaven can stand because they fall before God in worship.

Just like John in Revelation 1:17, the posture positions God's servants to see him clearly. To pierce the veil. To look beyond the liminal space, the transitions littering life, and even beyond death itself to this liberating truth: "On the great day of God's wrath, servants of God can stand." A message that's as humbling as it is emboldening.

THE MESSAGE IN THE MEANTIME, NO. 2: THE INTERLUDE OF THE TRUMPETS

The upheaval in the space in between, both small and great, clouds our vision and shrouds our souls with insecurity. Especially in times of suffering. Particularly in the presence of death. As tensions teem and empires collide, the cosmic battle between two trinities can be confusing. So the message in the meantime simplifies what appears so bewildering: in Christ, you can stand. You are spiritually secure (the seals).

But this isn't mere escapism, a message that simply says, "When you die, you go to heaven." Indeed, for those in Christ, that's true. But the message of heaven extends to action on earth. In fact, in the New Testament, whenever the end times are invoked, it's always in the context of how to live like Christ *in the present.*

Consider 2 Peter 3:1-11. The letter is written to churches struggling with false teachers who are mocking Christians about the delay in Christ's second coming (2 Pet 2:1–3:4). After offering assurances and explanations (2 Pet 3:5-9), the letter depicts the unpredictable "day of the Lord" as "a thief" equipped with consuming fire to purify the heavens and the earth (2 Pet 3:10).

---

[8]Seven in Jewish literature is a number of completion usually attached to creation or the creative act (see Gen 1). For more numbers in the book of Revelation, see "Appendix: Interpreting Numbers in Revelation."

This *end*, though, brings clarity to the present. To the earth, right now. "Since all these things are thus to be destroyed, what sort of people ought you to be?" (2 Pet 3:11).

In Revelation, the message in the meantime follows the same design. The interlude of the seals begins with the question, "In the end, who can stand?" and concludes with the answer, "You can, Christian! Whether alive on earth or alive in heaven, as God's servant, in the end, you can stand." The interlude of the trumpets builds on this message with a call for the present: "So, get out there and witness, Christian! Even if it costs you your life."

As discussed in chapter five, the two witnesses of Revelation 11 mirror the life of Christ. Their "testimony" (μαρτυρίαν) concludes with their murder in Jerusalem, the city "where also their Lord was crucified" (Rev 11:7-8). The earth dwellers celebrate their deaths by "sending gifts to one another" (Rev 11:10). But three and a half days later, "the breath [πνεῦμα] of life from God went into them, and they stood on their feet" (Rev 11:11), resurrected like Christ. Terror gripped the onlookers as a voice from heaven ushered the two witnesses "up into heaven in a cloud" (Rev 11:12), ascending to the abode of God like Christ.

The parallels to Jesus in this trumpet interlude extend beyond the plot, including the descriptions of the two witnesses as well. The two witnesses are "the two olive trees and the two lampstands" that "stand before the Lord of the earth" (Rev 11:4), an allusion to the prophetic vision in Zechariah 4:1-14. There, Zechariah asks the angel attendant, "What are these two olive trees on the right of the lampstand and on its left?" (Zech 4:11). After a short exchange, the angel replies, "These are the two anointed sons who *stand* near the Lord of all the earth" (Zech 4:14 LXX): the king and the high priest.[9] Two offices fulfilled by Christ and entrusted to his church as "a kingdom and priests" on earth (Rev 1:6; 5:10).[10]

---

[9]G. K. Beale, *The Book of Revelation*, NIGTC (Grand Rapids, MI: Eerdmans, 1999), 576-79. In Zechariah, the anointed ones refer to Zerubbabel and Joshua.

[10]The ministry of the two witnesses echoes two luminaries from the Old Testament: Elijah and Moses. Like Elijah, the two witnesses "have power to shut up the heavens so that it will not rain" (Rev 11:6; cf. 1 Kings 17:1), and, also like Elijah, miraculous fire delivers the two witnesses from their enemies (Rev 11:5; cf. 1 Kings 18:16-40). Like Moses, the two witnesses "have power to turn the waters into blood" (Rev 11:6; Ex 7:14-24), and, also like Moses, various plagues were at their disposal to further their message (Rev 11:6; cf. Ex 8:1–12:30). Moses and Elijah are quintessential figures commonly associated with the Law (Moses) and the Prophets (Elijah), a shorthand way of referring to the entire

The two witnesses, therefore, don't merely retell Christ's story. They embody the truth of 1 John 2:6, "Whoever says, 'I abide in Jesus' must live as Jesus lived"; they image the adage, "Who you worship, you become"; they celebrate the cruciform mystery, "And they conquered [the dragon] by the blood of the Lamb and by the word of their testimony [μαρτυρίας]" (Rev 12:11).

The interlude of the trumpets builds on the message between the sixth and seventh seals. Essentially so. "Since you can stand, Christian, since you are spiritually secure, church, get out there and witness, come what may." For in Christ, death is no longer a barrier to be feared but a passing through the veil, an ascension in the clouds, a transition from the 144,000 to the great multitude.

THE MESSAGE IN THE MEANTIME, NO. 3: THE INTERLUDE OF THE BOWLS

Compared to the seals and the trumpets, the interlude of the bowls is quite small, although not less significant or profound. In Revelation 16:15, between the sixth and seventh bowls, Jesus interjects with the emphatic, "Behold ['Ιδού]!" The same exclamation used by the comforting elder in Revelation 5:5 to soothe John's sobs with "the Lion of the tribe of Judah," the same word used by the one on the throne in Revelation 21:3 to quiet suffering's lies with divine presence: "The dwelling place of God is now with humanity, and he will dwell with them." Yet here, Jesus employs "Behold ['Ιδού]!" to highlight his coming ("I come like a thief") and the blessing that bestows a calling: "Blessed is the one keeping watch and remaining clothed, so as not to go around naked and shamefully exposed."

There's a theology of nudity in Revelation, and by extension a theology of clothing. The arrogance of the Laodicean church, for example, blinds them to their spiritual poverty. They brazenly announce, "I am rich, and I have accumulated wealth, and I need nothing" (Rev 3:17). But Jesus confronts their pride with a theology of nudity/clothing: "But you do not understand that, actually, you are miserable and pitiful and poor and blind and naked [γυμνός]. I advise you to buy . . . white clothes [ἱμάτια] to wear, so that your shameful

---

Old Testament. Not coincidentally, Moses and Elijah appeared at Jesus' transfiguration (Mt 17:1-13), where a voice from heaven commands, "Listen to [Jesus]!" (Mt 17:5), echoing Mt 5:17, where Jesus clarifies, "Do not think that I have come to abolish the Law or the Prophets; I have not come to abolish them but to fulfill them."

nakedness [γυμνότητός] won't be exposed" (Rev 3:17-18). The only other reference to naked/nakedness in Revelation is the fate of the great prostitute destroyed by the *un*holy trinity: "They will make her desolate and naked [γυμνὴν]" (Rev 17:16). In contrast, the twenty-four elders around the throne are "dressed in white" (Rev 4:4), similar to the great multitude in heaven (Rev 7:9, 13) and the angels entrusted with the seven bowl plagues (Rev 15:6; cf. Rev 10:1; 11:3; 12:1). Thus, as in the Garden of Eden (Gen 3:7), clothing or lack thereof discloses allegiance. Which trinity the agent(s) worships. Unlike Eden, though, in Revelation, nakedness denotes devotion to evil, while devotion to Christ results in being clothed.

Still further, to be "dressed in *white*" indicates not only devotion to Jesus but *victory* in Christ. To the church of Sardis, Jesus confronts their façade of spiritual vitality (Rev 3:1-3) by reminding them that he will "come like a thief," that they "will not know" the time of his arrival (Rev 3:3). Nevertheless, Jesus identifies "a few people in Sardis who have not soiled their clothes [ἱμάτια]" (Rev 3:4). To these faithful few, Christ promises, "The one who conquers [νικῶν] will be clothed in white garments [ἱματίοις]" (Rev 3:5). Such a vision is realized in Revelation 19:14, when Jesus, "dressed in clothes [ἱμάτιον] dipped in blood" (Rev 19:13), rides triumphant on a white horse with "the armies of heaven" galloping close behind "clothed in fine linen, white and clean" (Rev 19:14). Allegiance to Christ clothes Christians in garments of conquest, heralding victory in the face of suffering.

One additional passage links the bowl interlude with the previous interludes in the seals and the trumpets. In Revelation 19:6-8, "a great multitude" in heaven erupts in praise (Rev 19:6). The occasion for their jubilation is nuptial: "The wedding of the Lamb has come," they cry out, "and his bride has prepared herself" (Rev 19:7). The radiant woman stands in stark contrast to the great prostitute. Her matrimony connotes fidelity, while prostitution assumes the opposite; marriage thrives on self-sacrifice, while harlotry propagates selfishness. The great prostitute ends naked (Rev 17:16); the radiant bride wears "fine linen, bright and clean" (Rev 19:8). Yet it's the parenthetical at the end of Revelation 19:8 that offers further insight for Revelation 16:15, "(For the fine linen stands for the *righteous acts* of the holy ones)." Clothing is connected to ethics. To what you do. The deeds that display your devotion.

Deeds play a significant role throughout the entirety of Revelation. To five out of the seven churches in Revelation 2–3, Jesus says, "I know your deeds [ἔργα]."[11] For the faithful, there's nothing more comforting to find in red letters. But for the rebellious, nothing could be more terrifying. *Deeds* matter. Significantly so. To the church of Sardis, Jesus writes, "I know your deeds [ἔργα], that you have a reputation of being alive, but you are dead. Wake up and strengthen what remains that is about to die, for I have not found your deeds [ἔργα] complete before my God" (Rev 3:1-2). All throughout the Apocalypse, what you do and what you don't do matter.

In Revelation 14:13, a voice from heaven pronounces, "Blessed are the dead, the ones dying in the Lord from now on." The Spirit responds with the affirmative "Yes!" and a clarifying caveat: "They will rest from their labors, for their *deeds* [ἔργα] will follow them." Similarly, in the judgment scene before the "great white throne" (Rev 20:11), the dead appear before books laid open (Rev 20:12). With ledgers in hand, "The dead were judged according to their *deeds* [ἔργα]" (Rev 20:12). Even in Christ's final discourse, an announcement signaled by the same "Behold! [Ἰδού]" from Revelation 16:15, Jesus focuses on our deeds: "Behold! I am coming soon. My reward is with me, to repay to each person according to their work [ἔργον]" (Rev 22:12).

At this point, the righteous among us rise up, fearing "works-righteousness," summoning Paul to the stand to wield the salvific summation dispensed to the church of Ephesus: "For by grace you are being saved, through faith . . . *not by deeds* [ἔργων] so that no one may boast" (Eph 2:8-9). Without question, there's but one deed that saves us, and that's the work of Jesus Christ on the cross of Calvary. The salvific act of the slain Lamb. Yet, even in Ephesians 2 our deeds *matter*. "For we are God's workmanship," Paul continues, "having been created in Christ Jesus *to do good works* [ἔργοις]" (Eph 2:10). Indeed, we are not saved *by* our works, but we are saved *for the purpose* of doing good works. And with Paul, Revelation agrees.

The message in the meantime, the three threads of Revelation's three sets of seven, challenges Christians bewildered by conflict to remember the basics of our faith. First, in Christ, you are spiritually secure (the seals). Because of

---

[11]Ephesus: Rev 2:2; Thyatira: Rev 2:19; Sardis: Rev 3:1; Philadelphia: Rev 3:8; Laodicea: Rev 3:15.

his great deed on the cross, on the great day of God's wrath, you can stand. Whether alive on earth or alive in heaven, as God's servant, you can stand secure in his grace. So, get out there and witness, even to the point of death (the trumpets). As the kingdom and priests, the royal bridges between humanity and divinity, our lives must conform into the shape of Christ's cross. A cruciform witness that assails the *un*holy trinity with a testimony of grace communicated not just with words but with our lives. For the content of our witness is populated by our deeds (the bowls).

As followers of the slain Lamb, we clothe ourselves with Christ, walking as he walked, living as he lived, even in the valley of the shadow of death, where there's much evil to fear. But the interludes illuminate the dark path in the liminal space, providing clarity and the way forward. That is, for those with ears to hear what the Spirit is saying to the churches.

CONFRONTING THE SEA

Revelation 15 startles at its opening. Not with the seven angels who carry the final plagues or with the song of Moses (Ex 15) translated into a Christocentric key (Rev 15:3-4). But with the choir who sings this song. The choir victorious over the *un*holy trinity. The choir of faithful followers "*standing* [ἑστῶτας] beside the sea" (Rev 15:2). The same sea where evil and chaos emerged in the dragon's act of *un*creation (Rev 13:1). The same sea from which the beast, the parody of the Son, surfaced to unleash torment and deception on the earth dwellers (Rev 13:2-10). The same sea that, in Revelation 4, stood still before the throne, "as a sea of glass, like crystal" (Rev 4:6), afraid or unable to move in the presence of the sovereign one seated on the throne.

The sea, in Revelation and throughout Jewish literature, is a stock symbol for evil and chaos. The four beasts in Daniel 7 all emerge from the sea, because that's where evil and chaos reside. In the cavernous abyss just below the bow of the ship that had swallowed many, drawing them down to the dark depths beyond the reach of any onlooker. Not surprisingly, then, in Revelation 21, the new heavens and the new earth emerge with an important caveat: "And the sea was no more" (Rev 21:1). Evil is eradicated in the new Eden, chaos purged by the love of God and the sacrifice of his Son.

Here in Revelation 15, Christians *stand* by the sea. Boldly. Without fear. Victorious. For the blood of the Lamb and their cruciform lives alter their relationship with evil. Shift their understanding of "sister" death.

In Christ, the veil between heaven and earth is pierced by death. Traversed by death. In Christ, our mortality is no longer paved by shame or mourning but is the avenue for union with God. Intimacy with God. The very presence of God. Not because he needed death to draw near but because we chose death in the beginning. Searching for his bride, God finds us cowering from death in its shadow; so he shines his light of love to illuminate our escape.

In the liminal space, in Christ alone, death becomes our teacher. A path of clarity. An invitation to transformation. An avenue of intimacy. Death reminds us of who we are and who God is. Death clarifies what matters and compels us to make amends, understanding that the burdens of this life—the secrets, shame, lies, and grudges—don't belong beyond the veil. Death invites us to see what is and not what will be. For as death approaches, what *will be* disintegrates, leaving us often with the wish that we'd done more.

Yet, as the end draws near, a new clarity emerges. Death isn't what it always appeared to be. Death masqueraded as an ending, a barrier to joy, peace, and productivity. But as it approaches, death is unveiled as a door to heaven. Not one reserved for the prophet of Patmos alone (Rev 4:1) but one offered to all. Open to all. One that sings a song so ancient and yet so familiar, so cold and yet so inviting, so foreign and yet so intimately interwoven into the fabric of our souls that we can't help but hum the tune we didn't know we knew.

In Christ, death's smell morphs from a stench into incense, an offering of praise, a feast filled with faces of times gone by, some you know quite well and others who need an introduction. A banquet where Christ comes dressed in white, with the hem of his robe stained in crimson, inviting all to come near, encouraging all to feast. A meal in honor of your safe passage, in celebration of your victory. In Christ. Through Christ. Because of Christ.

And as his eyes catch yours, a smile spreads across your face as you see the radiance of God's glory with his eyebrows raised. Not lowered.

He whispers, "You are secure, dear one. Go be my witness, come what may. For the sea can no longer harm you. Stand firm, my child, for in the face of death, your deeds will rise."

GOING DEEPER

> **THE TOOL:** Application. The purpose of Revelation isn't to predict. Revelation's target is you. The transformation of the reader into the image of the crucified Christ. Watch this video (www.ivpress.com /wood-7a) and wrestle with the following:

1. Like first-century Christians, it's easy to think the world is spinning out of control. Announcing the corrective "God's in control" comes across trite. Yet, think of a time when you felt out of control—like the world was caving in.

   ‣ Where do you see God's fingerprints?

   ‣ Where do you see God's control that typically can only be seen when looking back? Be specific.

2. Often we focus on interpreting a text but forget to apply the text to our lives.

   ‣ Why is application so essential?

   ‣ What is the relationship between application and the context of the first-century Christian?

   ‣ Is there danger in focusing too much on application of the text?

> **THE TEXT:** The call of Christ (Rev 15:1–16:21). We are not saved by our works. But we have been saved for the purpose of doing good works. Watch this video (www.ivpress.com/wood-7b) and answer the following:

1. We often see our works as competition to Christ's salvific work on the cross, prompting many to say, "I'm not earning my salvation."

   ‣ How does this struggle damage our theology of work?

   ‣ Does Jesus seem concerned that we don't compete with his work by our works?

   ‣ How can the church change its language to match the New Testament view of works?

2. Revelation 15–16 emphasizes the importance of seeing things clearly. Think of an argument or debate that you were a part of or witnessed.

> Did either side see their counterpart clearly?

> If not, why?

> If so, how?

> What are keys to seeing each other and ourselves clearly, especially in times of tension?

THE TAKEAWAY: Thematic study. Revelation has various threads and/or themes interwoven throughout its imagery. What follows is an important principle of interpretation for Revelation and other books of the Bible. Here's how it works:

---

1. Trace *one* of the following themes from Revelation 15–16 throughout the entire book of Revelation:

> finances (e.g., wealth, luxury, poverty, money, cargo, etc.)

> numbers (e.g., seven, number of items in lists, etc.)

> colors (e.g., red, pale green, etc.)

> weather (e.g., thunder, lightning, clouds, etc.)

> senses (e.g., seeing, hearing, tasting, etc.)

2. Categorize your findings.

> The goal is to organize the material in a digestible manner to assist the analysis that follows.

3. Follow the prompts to assess your findings:

> Observations about your research (e.g., surprises, affirmations, contradictions, etc.)—what insights stick out to you as significant?

> Difficulties/ambiguities in your research—what aspects were difficult to categorize or understand?

> Conclusion to your research—what's the importance of this theme to your interpretation of Revelation 15–16?

8

THE BEGINNING OF EVIL'S END
(Revelation 17:1–19:10)

Violence, Infighting, and Parasites

In the beginning God created the heavens
and the earth. . . . And God saw that it was good.

GENESIS 1:1, 10

EVERYONE HAS A STORY. A narrative. A beginning that, if known, unearths actions and attitudes in the present otherwise misunderstood or misdiagnosed. Learning someone's story is sacred, because it unveils much. Which is probably why we gravitate toward biographies even as we bury our own.

I learned this pastoring students and pastors. I learned this walking through the city. I learned this talking with the houseless. I learned this in the Middle East.

The summer after the attacks on 9/11, I went to the Middle East to love on Muslims. It was the only way I knew how to respond. Loving them into moments of transformation with the gospel of grace. With Jesus.

Each morning, our team would meet in a small apartment to learn Arabic, worship, and receive our destination for the day. Which was quite a shock at first.

"Shane," the leader said, "today you and your team are going to Ibn Tulun. Jessica, your team . . ."

"Whoa, excuse me," I interrupted. "You didn't tell us how to get to Ibn Tulun."

This was before smartphones. Before GPS in your pocket. I was directionally challenged but willing to give it a try with a map or at least an address.

The leader smiled, "You're right," he said, nodding his head. "And I'm not gonna give you directions."

A long pause ensued. Terrifyingly long. I can't tell you how others were responding, because my head was spinning, my heart racing, my face contorting, my hands fidgeting.

"*Okay*," I said, sarcasm dripping from my lips. "Then how do we *get* there?"

"Ask the people."

Three words. Four syllables. Complete disbelief.

"The *people*," he emphasized. "The people *out there*, out in the streets. The people on the trains. Ask the *people* . . . and see what happens."

I couldn't believe it. I shook my head, trying to dispel the confusion to no avail. I looked back up into his eyes, hoping to see a smile or hear a "Just kidding." But nothing. He was resolute. Strangely confident. *Ask the people.*

"All right," he broke the tension. "Now go," creating new tension. Greater tension. An incomprehensible tension.

I looked at my team of two, mouths agape. We stood up. Gathered our things. Clumsily walked out the door. Looking for people.

I was incensed, or maybe just petrified. At nineteen, this was my first time out of the country. The first time I struggled with currency conversion, cultural confusion, and language barriers that at times seemed insurmountable. And yet, on the first day, I'm stumbling through the streets of a foreign land with no direction other than *ask the people*?

My team and I wandered in a stupor to the local train station. We searched the signs in vain. Finally, one of my teammates decided to *ask the people*, "Excuse me. How do we get to Ibn Tulun?"

Without hesitation, the first man replied, "I'll take you there."

And he did. He set aside his plans, his agenda, his morning to make sure we arrived at our cryptic destination. And on the way? We heard his story.

We talked about life, religion, love, and his kids. And when we arrived at Ibn Tulun? He invited us to dinner with his family in his home.

I didn't know what to say. I'd never encountered hospitality like this. A love like this. It was without question a first for me.

The firsts increased with each day. With each conversation. With every adventure. The first time I encountered soldiers fit with AK-47s in the airport and on the streets; the first time I met a Muslim-based believer converted by Jesus tenderly talking to him in a dream; the first time I saw on a T-shirt the plane hitting the Twin Towers; the first time I rode a felucca adrift in the Nile listening to Muslims hear about Jesus; the first time I wept with my friend Mohammed, sitting outside his family-owned bakery that one day he would take over, even though he wanted to be an artist—something his family would never approve; the first time I was robbed in the back alley of an ancient Middle Eastern market, trapped in a small room with a darkened door to my left, with a man standing ominously on the threshold, prompting the first time I thought I was about to die, saying my goodbyes in my mind to my parents and my loved ones while whispering to my Lord, "I'm ready."

Each step unveiled a new story. A new perspective. A new depth of love and appreciation for this beautiful land and people.

Shortly after returning to America, I remember watching a news report of more unrest in the Middle East when a family member tersely remarked, "We just need to bomb them back to the stone age."

I didn't say a word, but my face was flush with emotion as he left the room. "But that's Waseem," I muttered. "That's Sayeed. That's Mohammed. I *know* them. I love them."

I couldn't speak. I was confused. Conflicted. Paralyzed not by careless words. But by story.

Everyone has a story. A story filled with laughter and wounds, dreams and disappointments, passions and pain. To learn someone's story is to step into a sacred space where they are known. Seen. Experienced.

Stories can confront hate, cure prejudices, and even expose us to us. Stories are powerful guides. Especially stories of origin. Narratives of "in the beginning." For quite often, the beginning gives insight to the end.

THE DEMISE OF THE GREAT PROSTITUTE

In Revelation 17:1, an angel previously entrusted with one of the seven bowls is now entrusted to tell John a story. A story of betrayal and violence. A story of an empire's end, which mirrors its beginning.[1] "Come," the angel commands, "I will show you the judgment of the great prostitute, the one sitting by many waters" (Rev 17:1; cf. Rev 21:9).

The demise of the great prostitute (Rev 17:1–19:5) begins the rapid dismissal of all evil in the narrative. The two beasts are destroyed in Revelation 19:11-21, and the red dragon is disposed in Revelation 20:1-10, inverting the order in which the *un*holy trinity and its empire appeared. A chiasm that unveils a key insight:[2]

    A. The red dragon introduced (Rev 12)
      B. The two beasts introduced (Rev 13)
        C. Babylon introduced (Rev 14:8)
        C'. Babylon dismissed (Rev 17:1–19:5)
      B'. The two beasts dismissed (Rev 19:11-21)
    A'. The red dragon dismissed (Rev 20:1-10)

The unveiling of the *un*holy trinity unmasks the deception that everything seen is not all that's there, that the *true* enemy lingers in the background of a cosmic war. Nevertheless, it's Babylon, earth's evil empire, that stands in the center of the chiasm, the position of primacy in this ancient literary device.

---

[1]Commentators disagree about whether the prostitute in Rev 17 is Israel/Jerusalem or the Roman Empire/Rome. In favor of the Israel/Jerusalem position, (1) the Old Testament does associate faithless Israel with promiscuous language. See Hos 2:5; Is 1:21; Jer 5:7; etc.; J. Massyngberde Ford, *Revelation*, Anchor Bible 38 (New York: Doubleday, 1975), 283-85; and (2) In Rev 17:18 the prostitute's label "the great city" is the same title in Rev 11:8 for Jerusalem ("where their Lord was crucified"). See Edmondo F. Lupieri, *A Commentary on the Apocalypse of John*, trans. Maria Poggi Johnson and Adam Kamesar (Grand Rapids, MI: Eerdmans, 2006), 178-80, 280-81. In favor of the Roman Empire/Rome option, (1) the prostitute as "Babylon" (Rev 17:5) parallels Jewish literature following the destruction of the temple in 70 CE, where Rome is referred to as "Babylon" (e.g., 4 Ezra 3:1-2, 28-31; 2 Baruch 10:1-3; 11:1; 67:7; Sibylline Oracles 5.143, 159-160); and (2) Rev 17:9 depicts the woman sitting on "seven hills," an allusion to the "seven hills" of Rome. See David E. Aune, *Revelation*, WBC 52A-52C (Nashville: Thomas Nelson, 1997–1998), 3:915-61. In what follows, Rome will be assumed as the identity of the great prostitute for arguments included in this footnote as well as evidence surfaced in the chapter itself.

[2]Nils W. Lund, *Chiasmus in the New Testament: A Study in the Form and Function of Chiastic Structures*, (repr., Peabody, MA: Hendrickson, 1992), vii: "[A chiasm] refers to an inverted parallelism or sequence of words or ideas in a phrase, a sentence, or any larger literary unit . . . [that] involves fundamentally two elements: inversion and balance. Often this leads to a third basic feature: climactic centrality."

Not, though, because the empire is the most important figure in the narrative, but because the empire is the most visible evil to the churches of Asia Minor. The physical expression of the *un*holy trinity's satanic attacks. Pastorally, then, Revelation highlights the truth that the cosmic war isn't just fought beyond the veil but experienced by first-century Christians through the evils of Rome. A truth apparent also in the cross of Christ (Jn 18:28–19:24; 19:28-34). The church's origin story.

Ironically, to show John the demise of the great prostitute, the angel guides him to a "wilderness [ἔρημον]," a place of protection for the cosmic woman in Revelation 12 (Rev 12:6, 13). The great prostitute is astride a "scarlet" beast that, like the sea beast of Revelation 13, has "seven heads and ten horns" (Rev 17:3; cf. Rev 13:1).[3] Draped in luxury, the woman is drunk, clutching a "golden cup" (Rev 17:4) filled with "the blood of holy ones, the blood of the witnesses [μαρτύρων] of Jesus" (Rev 17:6). The brand on her forehead tells her story: "Babylon the great, the mother of prostitutes and the abominations of the earth" (Rev 17:5). Her abominations are many, rehearsed throughout Revelation 17–19 as a macabre introduction to the unblemished bride of the Lamb (Rev 19:6-8). Her moniker links her actions to Old Testament infamy and hints at her identity: Babylon, the great enemy of God's people, who destroyed Jerusalem's temple and carried away its cultic items to temples of its own (Dan 1:1-2; Ps 137). An unthinkable act in Israel's history shared also by the great prostitute: the Roman Empire.[4]

As the city of Rome, the great prostitute sits on "seven hills" (Rev 17:9). Seven hills that extend like fingers toward the Apennine Mountains, cupping the Campus Martius nestled in the elbow of the Tiber River.

Seven hills that adorned imperial coins and populated imperial poetry.[5] Seven hills that housed not just the city of Rome and its inhabitants but also the story of Rome. The foundational myth of Rome. The empire's "in the beginning" that starts with the death of a king and ends with the death of another.

---

[3]The word for "scarlet" (κόκκινον) is not the same word used to describe the "fiery red [πυρρός] dragon" (Rev 12:3). Nevertheless, the "scarlet" hue is included to reiterate the connection between the beast and the dragon. In fact, both words are used in the book of Revelation only in reference to agents of evil: κόκκινον—Rev 17:3-4; 18:12, 16; πυρρός—Rev 6:4; 12:3.

[4]Compare Dan 1:1-2 and Josephus, *J.W.* 7.161-162.

[5]Virgil, *Aeneid* 6.783; *Georgics* 2.534; Tibullus, *Elegies* 2.5.55.

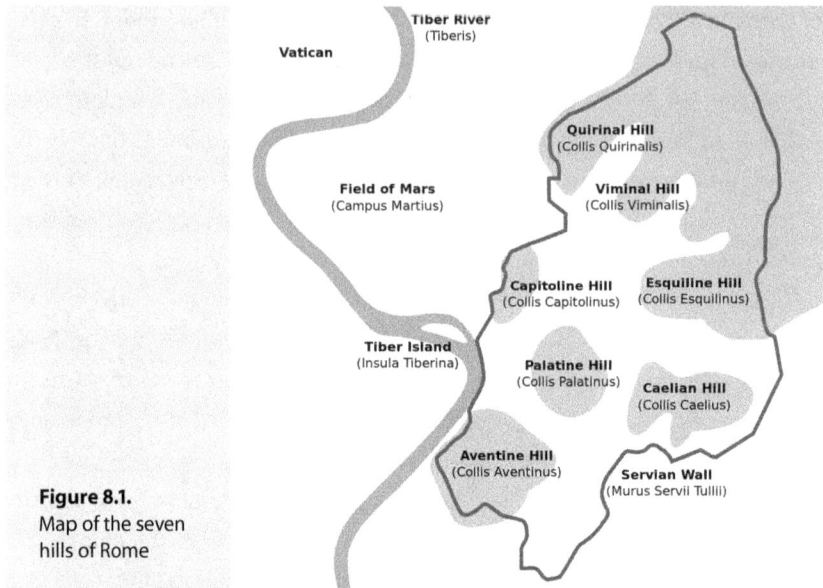

Figure 8.1.
Map of the seven
hills of Rome

Figure 8.2.
Vespasian: *RIC* 2.108 (71 CE).
Roma reclining on seven
hills, with Remus and
Romulus suckled
by the she-wolf

THE STORY OF ROME'S BEGINNING[6]

To recount an origin story—whether an individual's, an institution's, a couple's, or even a nation's—is to do more than retell a sequence of events. Beginnings trace the contours of character, the elements of laughter, the paradigms

---

[6]What follows is a reconstruction of various strands and traditions of the Roman foundational myth. There's significant debate over several elements in the story as well as the historicity of the story as a whole. Those important academic conversations, however, won't occupy the retelling below. The purpose of what follows isn't to argue for a particular version of the story but to demonstrate the contours of the Roman foundational myth as the underpinnings for the narrative of the great prostitute in Rev 17. For further exploration, see: Livy, *Hist. Rom.* 1.3.1–1.17.11; Ovid, *Fasti* 4.49-60; Dionysius of Halicarnassus, *Ant. rom.* 1.75.1–2.58.3; and T. P. Wiseman, *Remus: A Roman Myth* (Cambridge: Cambridge University Press, 1995).

of personality, the values one's willing to die for and at times kill for. In other words, to recount "in the beginning" is an unveiling of the end. Of the telos.

The story of Rome begins with two brothers, Numitor and Amulius. Their father, the king of Alba Longa, had just died, leaving Numitor as the rightful heir to the throne. However, as Livy recounts, "Violence proved more potent than a father's wishes or respect for seniority."[7] Amulius deposed Numitor and seized the throne for himself.

To secure his power, Amulius killed Numitor's sons and promoted his only daughter, Ilia, as a priestess of Vesta.[8] This "honor," though, was quite deceptive, for Vestals were perpetual virgins. Thus, the promotion was a political ploy to ensure no offspring could lay claim to the throne and avenge Amulius's wrongs. That is, until the gods intervened.

One day, Ilia was in the sacred grove of Mars retrieving water when the sky darkened and a large supernatural figure descended on the defenseless Vestal and ravished her. The perpetrator of the abominable act was the god Mars, the god of war. The assault left Ilia pregnant with his twin sons.

For a time, Ilia feigned illness to hide the divine violation. Eventually, despite her best efforts, Amulius discovered her pregnancy and immediately ordered Ilia's perpetual imprisonment and "the children committed to the river."[9] The twins were placed in a box, carried to the banks of the Tiber, and set in the waters, exposing them to the fate of the river's ebbs and flows.

Against all odds, the twin sons of Mars survived, coming to rest at the base of the Palatine hill, the first of the seven hills of Rome. Attracted by their cries, a she-wolf approached, licked the babies clean, and suckled them to health. So significant is this moment in the origin story of Rome that statues, coins, and altars celebrate the miracle with suckling images, commemorating the intervention of the gods through creation to rescue the twins thrust into peril.

---

[7] Livy, *Hist. Rom.* 1.3.10-11, in *History of Rome*, trans. B. O. Foster, 14 vols., LCL (Cambridge: Cambridge University Press, 1919–1959).

[8] There's confusion about whether Numitor had one son, named Lausus (Ovid, *Fasti* 4.53-56), or multiple sons (Livy, *Hist. Rom.* 1.3.11). Also, the name of Numitor's daughter is remembered as both Ilia (Ovid, *Fasti* 4.55) and Rhea Silvia (Livy, *Hist. Rom.* 1.3.11), with Dionysius of Halicarnassus listing both names (*Ant. rom.* 1.76.3).

[9] Livy, *Hist. Rom.* 1.4.3-4 (trans. Foster). Livy mentions only her imprisonment, whereas Dionysius of Halicarnassus records various accounts of Ilia's fate, including immediate death (*Ant. rom.* 1.78.5–79.3).

Figure 8.3.
The Capitoline Wolf statue

Figure 8.4.
Vespasian: *RIC* 2.961 (77/78 CE).
She-wolf suckling Remus
and Romulus

Nearby, a swine herdsmen named Faustulus witnessed the miraculous scene. His wife, Larentia, had just given birth to a stillborn child. He retrieved the twins from the she-wolf and returned home to raise the boys as his own, naming them Remus and Romulus.[10]

Growing up, the boys took after their adopted father as swine herdsmen, ironically tending the flocks of King Amulius. This occupation was quite contentious, for Numitor's herdsmen warred with the twins over pastureland between the Palatine and Aventine hills.

One day, when Romulus was out offering a sacrifice, Remus was ambushed and taken prisoner to Numitor.[11] Romulus, with a natural propensity to war, wanted to rescue his brother with a full-scale attack on Numitor and his men.

---

[10]Dionysius of Halicarnassus, *Ant. rom.* 1.79.10.

[11]Dionysius of Halicarnassus, *Ant. rom.* 1.79.12-14—although Dionysius (1.80.1-3) and Livy (*Hist. Rom.* 1.5.1-4) include an alternate option involving the festival of the Lupercalia. Both accounts, however, end with the same result.

To deter him, Faustulus unveiled to Romulus the entire story of his birth and origins. Moved "with compassion for his mother and with solicitude for Numitor,"[12] Romulus instead decided to free Numitor from Amulius's tyranny, restoring his ravaged family.

After a series of deceptions and double crosses, Romulus and Faustulus united forces with Remus and Numitor to storm the citadel.[13] With little resistance, Amulius was slain. Numitor was restored to his rightful throne.

Among his first acts as king, Numitor rewarded his grandsons by granting them permission to found a city. The twins returned to the site of the suckling she-wolf to seek the will of the gods to determine who would be the king of the city and on what hill the city would begin. A dispute, however, broke out between the twin sons of Mars about how to discern the will of the gods. In the end, the Palatine hill was determined to be the site of the city, with Romulus as its ruler. The fate of his brother, though, was far more grim. Remus was murdered, and some even say it was by the hand of his twin brother.[14]

THE STORY OF ROME'S TELOS

The story of Rome's "in the beginning" is filled with violence and treachery, deception and perfidy, war and murder, even of one's own. Greed rendered alliances tenuous at best. Bloodlines did little to provide unity or trust. As Rome was birthed by the god of war, might was the only measure of divine will, and conquest the only metric of morality.

The reign of Romulus (753 BCE–716 BCE) was remembered as a golden age, although it was riddled with endless war. Neighboring towns were ravaged to expand Rome's domain, treaties violated to assert Rome's interests. The reign of Romulus mirrored his beginning, and his end would follow suit.

Confusion and *controversy* are just a few words appropriate for the death of Romulus. Although conflicting reports shroud the event, one detail attained consensus: Romulus suddenly disappeared. *How* he disappeared is

---

[12]Dionysius of Halicarnassus, *Ant. rom.* 1.80.4.

[13]For a full account, see Livy, *Hist. Rom.* 1.5.6–1.6.2; Dionysius of Halicarnassus, *Ant. rom.* 1.81.1–1.83.3.

[14]Livy, *Hist. Rom.* 1.6.2-3. Dionysius of Halicarnassus suggests it wasn't Romulus who killed Remus but Celer, one of Romulus's men (*Ant. rom.* 1.87.4). Other accounts attribute Remus's death to a general quarrel that broke out between the two brothers and their men (Livy, *Hist. Rom.* 1.7.1-2; Dionysius of Halicarnassus, *Ant. rom.* 1.87.1-3), a war that Dionysius suggests killed Faustulus as well (1.87.2).

another matter. Some said he was gathered by the gods on high, never to be seen again.[15] Others said he was killed by the senate, torn limb from limb so that no portion of his body or clothing was ever found.[16] Either way, the sudden death of the first king of Rome left a vacuum of power that the senate was eager to fill.

Strife, however, saturated the senate ranks, with various factions attempting to seize the vacant sovereignty.[17] Nevertheless, the army and the people of Rome clamored for a king, and so, fearing violence, the senate devised a system to share power among them until a proper king arose. Over the entire year following the death of Romulus, the senate was divided into sets of *ten* men in a set rotation who exercised authority as *one*.[18]

Finally, the senate agreed to appoint Numa Pompilius (715–672 BCE) as the second king of Rome. But Numa wouldn't be the last. Beginning with Romulus, there were *seven* kings of Rome reigning almost 250 years, from the foundation of the city (753 BCE) to the rise of the republic (509 BCE), when the senate seized control and replaced the monarchy with a plurality of leadership, shifting from a single ruler to rule by the many.

The founding myth of Rome is filled with violence, betrayal, and tragedy. Founded by the twin sons of Mars, the god of war, the empire was birthed into quarrel and conflict, where, at times, Roman killed Roman, devouring their own to secure power, to perpetuate agendas divorced from compassion or grace for the other. From its inception and through each ebb and flow of power, the threads of greed and war were woven into a fate of selfishness and brutality. Something the seven churches of Revelation knew firsthand.

OUR STORY OF "IN THE BEGINNING"

Rehearsing Rome's history isn't an exercise in futility or a meaningless intellectual inquiry. It's an exploration of identity, an examination of present reality. For your beginning unveils your end; your origin reveals your telos.

---

[15]Livy, *Hist. Rom.* 1.16.1-8; Plutarch, *Romulus* 27.7–28.3; Dionysius of Halicarnassus, *Ant. rom.* 2.56.1-3.

[16]Livy, *Hist. Rom.* 1.16.4-5; Plutarch, *Romulus* 27.5-8; Dionysius of Halicarnassus, *Ant. rom.* 2.56.3-6. Dionysius finds this option most plausible (2.56.3).

[17]Livy, *Hist. Rom.* 1.17.1-4.

[18]The sets of ten were known as the *decuria* (Dionysius of Halicarnassus, *Ant. rom.* 2.57.2; Livy, *Hist. Rom.* 1.17.5-6). This year of no king was known as the interregnum (Livy, *Hist. Rom.* 1.17.6-7; Dionysius of Halicarnassus, *Ant. rom.* 2.57.1).

And the same is true for Christians.

"In the beginning" we don't detect violence or deception or betrayal; we find love and blessing and fidelity. We find God wooing creation into existence. Chaos tamed with his word. Darkness dispelled by his whisper. Light birthed at his call. As each day is clothed with evening and morning, God's blessing adorns his creation with the radiant appellation "good."

Seven times in the first chapter of our origin story, God calls his creation "good," even "very good" (Gen 1:31; see Gen 1:4, 10, 12, 18, 21, 25).[19] And he treated it as such, creatively curating the land and its fruit, the sky and its stars, the sea and its streams, and every creature of air, water, and land. With patient care, God tilled the ground of our beginning, tenderly plunging his hands into the earth, carefully crafting the virgin soil (Gen 2:5) into the form of humanity before gently breathing life into the vestal lungs (Gen 2:7). For we are God's workmanship, created in the beginning by grace—a movement of God as beautiful as it is mysterious.

Even as Eden was transformed by tragedy, the character of God did not wane. Pained that humanity would hide from him, God cried out in the cool of the day, "Where are you?" (Gen 3:9). Distraught by the stain of death on what God had deemed good, the Creator mournfully inquired, "Who told you that you were naked?" (Gen 3:11). Grace had given way to guilt, purity pushed aside by shame.

Yet in the beginning, God's mercy knew no end; his love sought no limits. To counter the serpent's deception, his affection clothed humanity with garments of skin (Gen 3:21), preparing them for the journey east of Eden. Beyond the flaming sword. Always with the goal to return what was good to the garden once again.

Our origin story is baptized in grace. Flowing with the waters of mercy. Even when Cain killed Abel (Gen 4:8), a fratricide of our own, cries of vengeance from the blood of the earth (Gen 4:10) were met with protection, a mark sealing Cain as the Lord's own (Gen 4:15). Indeed, even from the foundations of the earth, the Lamb was slain (Rev 13:8), providing grace upon grace, revealing a love truly intent on enduring forever (Ps 136).

---

[19]The LXX adds an eighth "good" in Gen 1:8.

Our beginning unveils our end. We were birthed in the grace of Eden, and to Eden one day we will return (Rev 22:1-5). Restored. Redeemed. Cherished and living in the light of God's love. For he is our origin, and to him we will once again belong.

In the meantime, though, we labor in the shadow of an empire birthed by violence, crafted in the image of the god of war who ravages his own, devours his own, and brings his own to an end much like the beginning.

RETURN TO MARS

In Revelation 17:1, the angel invites John to witness the end of Rome, the great prostitute "who sits by many waters" and on "seven hills" (Rev 17:9). The scene unfolds with undercurrents of Rome's foundational myth. Her end, unsurprisingly, sharing similar patterns with her beginning.

At the outset, the twin beasts from Revelation 13 are unexpectedly reduced to a single beast, albeit with hues of red reminiscent of the dragon (Rev 17:3) and the god Mars.[20] The prostitute is intimately connected to the twin beast (Rev 17:3, 7), whose seven heads are not just "seven hills" like Rome but also "seven kings" like Rome (Rev 17:9-10).

Even the presence of a prostitute elicits Rome's "in the beginning," albeit through a play on words and a scandalous rumor. The Latin word for prostitute (*lupa*) is the same Latin word for "she-wolf" (*lupa*). This ambiguity led some to suggest that "the one who nursed and suckled [Remus and Romulus] was not a she-wolf" at all, but Faustulus's wife Larentia, "who, having formerly prostituted her beauty, had received from the people living round the Palatine hill the nickname Lupa [prostitute]."[21]

The *lupa* of Revelation 17 isn't enshrined in statues like the suckling *lupa* of Rome's beginning. Instead, the great prostitute becomes a target of hatred

---

[20]Red was associated across various cultures and empires with blood and, by extension, war. Mars/Ares, the god of war, is identified as a "bloodstained stormer of cities" in Homer's *Iliad* 5.31 and a "blood-stained slayer of men" in a first-century BCE oracle. See H. W. Pleket and R. S. Stroud, *Supplementum Epigraphicum Graecum* (Leiden: Brill, 1994), 41.1411. Additionally, most ancient cultures associated the "red planet" with the name of their god of war, including the Babylonians, Greeks (*Hymn 8 to Ares*, from the Homeric Hymns), and Romans (Hyginus the Astronomer, *Astronomica* 2.42.3.1-8). On the Babylonians' association of Mars with the name of their god of war, see Tamysn Barton, *Ancient Astrology* (London: Routledge, 1994), 112.

[21]Dionysius of Halicarnassus, *Ant. rom.* 1.84.4. Cf. Livy, *Hist. Rom.* 1.4.7-8; Plutarch, *Romulus* 4.3; see also Tertullian, *Apology* 25.9.

and violence for the scarlet beast. In addition to the seven heads that are "seven kings" (Rev 17:9-10), the beast has "ten horns" that are "ten kings" (Rev 17:12), who rule as a senate-like group with "one purpose" (Rev 17:13) but for only "one hour" (Rev 17:12). This set of ten viciously attacks the prostitute, leaving her "naked" (γυμνὴν), burning and devouring her flesh (Rev 17:16), virtually tearing her limb from limb.

Her end mirrors her beginning—violence, betrayal, deception, and greedy grasps of power. As in the trumpets of Revelation 8–9, evil is unveiled as one who destroys its own. Abandons its own. Abuses and uses its own.

Evil knows not intimacy but only lust. Relationships are transactional and parasitic, like a courtesan and a client. Even in Revelation 18, at the funeral procession for the great prostitute, the "kings of the earth" (Rev 18:9-10), "the merchants of the earth" (Rev 18:11-17), and "all who earn their living from the sea" (Rev 18:17-19 NIV 2011) do not mourn the loss of her life but lament and worry that their power and profits, siphoned from her excess luxury, will now diminish or disappear. They "weep and mourn" not at the tragic loss of a beloved friend but "because no one buys their cargo any longer" (Rev 18:11). They lament as parasites who've lost their host.

The treatment of the woman in Revelation 17–18 is abhorrent. Grotesque and condemnable. But evil knows no other end. Evil knows no other grammar, no other ethic, no other way to process kings or cowards, friends or foes except through violence and greed, hatred and betrayal. Love is reduced to lust, intimacy to a sexual craving. In the end, the demise of the prostitute is actually a return to the beginning. A return to Mars, the god of war, who saw Ilia as nothing more than an object to satisfy his carnal cravings.

RETURN TO CHRIST

Everyone has a story. A sacred "in the beginning" that when unearthed unveils much. If, that is, we have eyes to see and ears to hear. For too often we try to outrun our origin, avoid our wounds, paper over the distant sadness that matures into explosions of anger or debilitating addictions. Yet our stories are relentless, untiring in their pursuit, entertaining our evasions, knowing that in the end our beginning will find us.

Revelation thins the veil to reveal that this is true of both evil and redemption, the foundation of Rome and the "in the beginning" of Genesis. For

there's a sacred story that stretches far before 753 BCE, far beyond the reach of the ancient serpent. A story of redemption woven into the foundations of the earth, where the seed of God's grace was placed in the virgin's womb so that the breath of God in the flesh of God could pave the way for the children of God to return to Eden. Back to God's sacred garden.

It's no mistake, then, that the demise of the great prostitute (Rev 17:1–19:5) bleeds into the wedding feast of the Lamb (Rev 19:6-8). Is the preamble to the presentation of the radiant bride of Christ clothed not in garments of skin but "fine linen, bright and clean" (Rev 19:8). A radiant bride whose tale twists and turns with the testimony of God's relentless grace. Whose gown glows brilliant and white because she's washed in the blood of the Lamb. No longer separated by sin or held hostage by death's constraint but returned to her lover's embrace. Restored to the innocence of Eden. Redeemed by the God of "new beginnings." "And [the angel] said to me, 'Write: Blessed are the ones invited into the wedding feast of the Lamb!' And he said to me, 'These are the true words of God'" (Rev 19:9).

GOING DEEPER

> **THE TOOL:** Context, part 3: What about the mark of the beast? (Rev 13:16-18). The mark of the beast has a long and storied history. Yet our interpretations of it often overlook a key question: What did the mark of the beast mean to the first-century audience of Revelation? Watch this video (www.ivpress.com/wood-8a) and wrestle with the following:

1. What was your reaction to the video's "simple" explanation of the number?

    › Did it provide relief? Confusion? Frustration?

    › Why?

    › What's at stake if the simple explanation of the mark of the beast is true?

2. Our theology must affect everything we do, otherwise it's absolutely worthless.

> Would someone know which side of the battle you were on simply by looking at how you live?

> Think about the last twenty-four hours: Do your actions reflect Christ or the enemy?

THE TEXT: Our end in Christ (Rev 17:1–19:10). The character of evil brings about betrayal and deception and destruction of one's own. But what about the character of Christ? Watch this video (www.ivpress.com /wood-8b) and answer the following:

---

1. Christ knows no arrogance. He's not self-serving or willing to forget even one.

   > How does this contrast with evil?

   > Think of a situation where you encountered severe narcissism. Without accusation, process the situation:

      > What were key characteristics of the person's actions?

      > How did this person view other people?

      > What would sacrifice mean for this person?

2. Regarding the prostitute, Revelation 18:23 laments, "Your merchants were the world's important people."

   > How do you process such a statement when in our world today businesswomen and businessmen hold our positions of prominence? Not just in society but in our churches.

   > How do you strike the balance between wealth as a blessing and wealth as a curse?

THE TAKEAWAY: Praying through God's imagery. Revelation is saturated with imagery. Some grotesque, some beautiful; some terrifying, some comforting. Each image in God's Word intends to affect the reader, calling them to transformation and action. What follows is an ancient Christian prayer practice called visio divina, which centers on the transforming power of an image from God's Word. Here's how it works:

First movement: Viewing the image

1. Go to the following address on your web browser: www.ivpress.com /wood-8c.

2. Sit in silence for one to two minutes, asking the Spirit to bring to your mind a word or phrase from the image.

3. Write down the word/phrase without any elaboration.

Second movement: Reflecting on the image

1. With the image still in view, sit in silence for two to three minutes, reflecting on this question: "How does this word/phrase intersect with my life today?"

2. Prayerfully write down your answer.

Third movement: Responding to God's Word through the image

1. With the image still in view, sit in silence for two to three minutes, reflecting on this question: "How is God calling me to respond?"

2. Prayerfully write down your answer.

Fourth movement: Resting in God

1. With the image still in view, sit in silence for two to three minutes, resting in God's Word communicated through this image.

2. Close your time with a spoken prayer thanking God for this encounter with the Holy Spirit.

9

GOD'S TRIUMPHAL PROCESSION
(Revelation 19:11–20:15)

Why Satan Must Be Released

And when the thousand years are completed,
Satan will be released from his prison.

REVELATION 20:7

SATAN IS MANY THINGS, but stupid isn't one of them. He's a master of deception, an expert at misdirection. He's rarely brazen, often restrains from open assault, although he's not above it. He's subtle. Strategic. He stokes tension. Breeds mistrust. Births miscommunication, resulting in passive-aggressive jousts over a perceived slight. He seduces our tendencies toward self-preservation, blurring family and foe, reason and reprimand, care and contempt. He stirs our inner critic, sifting our subconscious for censure and shame, relentlessly scolding, blaming, and berating in a voice indistinguishable from our own. He divides churches, divorces families, and isolates each of us behind walls of self-protection that over time imprison us.

Satan's serpentine schemes are hard to detect. He's cunning. Artful, even. Sinuous in his strategies, yet deadly in his intent. Even a carefully crafted question can alter our Eden. Even an oft-overlooked word can cause us to cower instead of advance. Retreat instead of charge. Argue instead of unite. A demonic strategy employed in Matthew 16:13-18.

Jesus' Galilean ministry is about to turn toward Jerusalem (Mt 16:21). Sensing the shift, he sets his attention on his disciples and asks, "Who do people say the Son of Man is?" (Mt 16:13). It's a question of identity born out of a question of legitimacy. In Matthew 16:1, the Pharisees and Sadducees demand "a sign from heaven" to validate Jesus' ministry. Never mind the two miraculous feedings in the past two chapters—five thousand in Matthew 14:13-21 and four thousand in Matthew 15:29-39—or the countless other miracles peppering his ministry since his baptism in Matthew 3, when a voice from heaven announced, "This is my Son" (Mt 3:17; see Mt 4:23-24; 8:1-17, 23-32; 9:6-7, 20-25, 27-30, 32-33, 35; 12:9-13, 15, 22). In the mind of the Jewish elite, the actions of Jesus don't match the presumed identity of Jesus. Especially his grace toward Gentiles (see Mt 5:43-48; 8:5-13; 12:38-42; 15:21-28; 28:18-20).[1] "But what about the crowds?" Jesus inquires. "Who do they say I am?"

The initial report is quite underwhelming. "Some say John the Baptist, but others say Elijah, and still others say Jeremiah or one of the prophets" (Mt 16:14). Yes, each answer is astonishing in its own right, and some of them nothing short of miraculous. Jeremiah and John the Baptist would necessitate a type of resurrection or reincarnation, whereas Elijah would require a divine descent after his miraculous ascent in a chariot of fire (2 Kings 2:1-12).[2] Even being accounted as "one of the prophets" is honorable—that is, unless you're the incarnate Son of God.

So, Jesus reroutes the question closer to those present. "But what about you? Who do you say I am?" (Mt 16:15). There's a lot at stake for anyone posed this question. Answers to "Who is Jesus?" can heal wounds, mend marriages, topple tyrants, transfer loyalties. For who Jesus is transforms the identity of whoever follows him and everything thereafter. Which is why it's unsurprising to find Satan lurking in the spaces between these red letters. Subtly so.

---

[1] The question for a "sign from heaven" in Mt 16:1 isn't due to lack of miraculous evidence but a result of Jesus' benevolence toward Gentiles in Mt 15:1-39. After declaring all foods clean (Mt 15:1-20) and healing the Canaanite woman's daughter (Mt 15:21-28), Jesus repeats the miracle of the feeding of the five thousand (Mt 14:13-21) with the miracle of the feeding of the four thousand (Mt 15:29-39). The difference is that the feeding of the four thousand was done in Gentile territory to, presumably, a Gentile audience. Such a shift from a singular focus on "the lost sheep of Israel" (Mt 15:24) to Gentiles merited explanation, or at least a "sign from heaven" (Mt 16:1), from the perspective of the Jewish leaders.

[2] John the Baptist was beheaded (Mt 14:1-12), and Jeremiah, according to tradition, was stoned to death in Egypt (Tertullian, *Scorpiace* 8; cf. *Lives of the Prophets* 2).

Simon Peter responds with confidence and uncommon insight. "You are the Christ, the son of the living God" (Mt 16:16). What exactly he envisions, though, is yet to be disclosed, for the boldness to pronounce Jesus as King also compels Simon Peter to rebuke his Christ just six verses later (Mt 16:22). Nevertheless, here in Matthew 16:16, Simon Peter's answer secures a blessing and a new name. "'Blessed are you, Simon son of Jonah,' Jesus responds, 'for this was not unveiled to you by flesh and blood, but by my Father in heaven. And also, I declare to you that you are Peter, and on this rock, I will build my church. And the gates of Hades will not overpower it" (Mt 16:17-18).

Over the centuries, Satan has done much to obscure this text. To distort its intent. To misdirect our attention. For centuries, Christians have quibbled over one word while ignoring a far more potent one. "Is the word *rock*," so the story goes, "referring to Peter or his confession?" The battle lines are drawn, with Catholics clinging to the former and Protestants cleaving to the latter, each with their points and counterpoints, concerns and accusations, arguments and carefully crafted criticisms. All the while, Satan sits unassailed, relishing in his devilish diversion. For as the Christian conversation centers on the word *rock*, Satan enjoys our neglect of the word *gates*.

In the ancient world, gates were a military weapon. A tool of war in the mold of a shield. The city gates hugged the city streets, encased the comings and goings of everyday life. In times of conflict, however, the gates were the last line of defense, a central feature of any secure stronghold. As the enemy laid siege, the prayers of the people ascended, hoping against hope that the gates would hold. That the gates would overcome the onslaught of their invaders. In Matthew 16:18, the gates belong to Hades. To the kingdom of Satan. To the devil.

Yet many Christians today live life in a posture of perpetual defense, cowering behind gates of our own instead of storming the gates of hell. Anxiety fills the pews with each presidential cycle, worried that if the wrong candidate prevails, all is lost. Hope is placed, then, in political pundits espousing propaganda for their political party while selling "the truth, the whole truth, and nothing but the truth" along with a strong dose of fear. Fear of the other. Fear of the foreigner. Fear of anyone and anything that disagrees with slogans and slants that form the rock on which we stand. "Fight for the rock," the serpent

implores, hoping against hope that Christians will overlook the mission contained in the word *gates*.

Revelation 19:11–20:15, however, thins the veil. Exposes the satanic diversion. Uncovers the demonic deception. Reveals that the serpent isn't alive and well but bound and languishing; the battle isn't *un*decided and *un*determined but secured and resolved on Calvary. For as the nations gather for war, Jesus graces the scene with his robes already dipped in blood.

THE NO-BATTLE MOTIF

In Revelation 19, "the beast and the kings of the earth" transfer their assault from the great prostitute to Jesus and his followers (Rev 19:19; see Rev 19:11-14). Assembling their armies, evil "gathered together to wage war [συνηγμένα ποιῆσαι τὸν πόλεμον]" (Rev 19:19). Yet there is no war. There is no battle. In the very next verse, the beast is captured, along with the "false prophet" (i.e., the beast from the earth), and unceremoniously cast into "the lake of fire, the one being burned in sulfur" (Rev 19:20).

No battle. No war. Just an execution.

This isn't the first time in Revelation a gathering for battle ends without war. And it won't be the last. In fact, including Revelation 19, this no-battle motif occurs three times in Revelation.

Just before the seventh bowl in Revelation 16, "demonic spirits" advance on the kings of the earth "to gather them for war [συναγαγεῖν αὐτοὺς εἰς τὸν πόλεμον] on the great day of God Almighty" (Rev 16:14). But there is no war. There is no battle. There is no Armageddon (Rev 16:16). The seventh bowl begins in the very next verse with "a loud voice from the throne" emphatically declaring, "It is done!" (Rev 16:17).

The same pattern unfolds in Revelation 20:7-9, where Satan himself advances on "the nations" in order to "gather them together for war [συναγαγεῖν αὐτοὺς εἰς τὸν πόλεμον]" (Rev 20:8). Yet, once again, there is no battle. For in the very next verse, fire comes down from heaven and devours them (Rev 20:9). As unceremonious and uneventful as the previous two gatherings for war, the battle with the "ancient serpent called the devil and Satan" (Rev 20:2) ends without fanfare or warfare. Just a sacrifice. An offering of the enemy as the end.

In all three scenes where the evil army is "gathered" (συνάγω) to make war (Rev 16:14, 16; 19:17, 19; 20:8), there is no battle, just an anticlimactic end. But this isn't an oversight or simply a strategy to save space in the scroll. Like the multiple ends of the world or the three sets of seven, this no-battle motif carries a message. Clarifies the call. Unveils a truth often forgotten but essential to the Revelation of Jesus Christ: there is no war because the battle was already won on the cross. The battle was won by the slain Lamb.

Yes, in Revelation 12:7-9, a battle *is* actually fought. A "war [πόλεμος] unleashed in heaven" between "Michael and his angels" and "the dragon and his angels" (Rev 12:7), where the "ancient serpent called the devil and Satan" (Rev 12:9) is cast out of heaven, igniting a hymn with an interpretive key:

> Now have come the salvation and the power and the kingdom of our God, and the authority of his Christ.
>
> For the accuser of our brothers and sisters, the one accusing them before our God day and night, has been cast out.
>
> And they conquered [the dragon] by the blood of the Lamb and by the word of their testimony [μαρτυρίας], for they did not covet their lives in the face of death. (Rev 12:10-11)

The birth of Christ to begin the chapter (Rev 12:1-6) climaxes with the death of Christ in the middle of the chapter (Rev 12:11) to remind the reader at the end of the chapter that when the dragon begins "to wage war [πόλεμον]" against "the ones keeping God's commands and holding fast to the testimony [μαρτυρίαν] of Jesus" (Rev 12:17), we do not need to cower behind our city gates or bow to the menacing face of fear. Regardless of what our eyes may see or the enemy may say, the battle is secure. Jesus has already won the war.

Indeed, an oft-overlooked detail in Revelation 19:11-21 signals this same truth. This scene, which gathers the threads and themes from the entire Revelation, begins with "heaven standing open" unveiling a white horse, "whose rider is called Faithful and True" (Rev 19:11; cf. Rev 3:14), whose name is "the Word of God" (Rev 19:13). His eyes are flickering like a "fiery flame" (Rev 19:12), with a "sharp sword" protruding from his mouth (Rev 19:15), the same eyes and mouth John encountered in the cosmic Christ at the outset of this unveiling (Rev 1:14, 16). This rider is sovereign over all, ruling the nations "with an iron scepter" (Rev 19:15; cf. Rev 12:5), the one worthy to wield justice and

"wage war [πολεμεῖ]" (Rev 19:11), the one worthy of the title "King of kings and Lord of lords" (Rev 19:16; cf. Rev 1:5; 17:14), the one worthy to tread the "winepress of the wine of the fury and the wrath of God Almighty" (Rev 19:15; cf. Rev 14:17-20), the one followed by the "armies of heaven" who are, like the bride (Rev 19:8), "clothed in fine linen, white and clean" (Rev 19:14). Yet, strangely, even before the evil army "gathered together to wage war" (Rev 19:19), the robe of Jesus, the rider on the white horse, is already "dipped in blood" (Rev 19:13). Not the blood of the enemy, mind you, but the blood that secured the victory over the *true* enemy: the blood of the slain Lamb shed on Calvary.

There is no battle, because the battle has already been won. The victory already attained. On the cross. Through Christ. For us.

WHY MUST SATAN BE RELEASED?

When Jesus offered himself as the sacrificial Lamb, he secured not only our resurrection and his, but victory in the cosmic battle with the *un*holy trinity—that is, for those with eyes to see and ears to hear. Yes, Satan rages in fury, deceiving any who will listen, gathering any willing to "wage war" against God's people, but "he knows that his time is short" (Rev 12:12). He's fully aware of his defeat. The no-battle motif, then, reiterates the same message stretched throughout the entire book of Revelation: the battle has already been won on the cross (Rev 1:17-18; 5:6, 9-10, 12). Yet, this no-battle motif *also* positions the reader to answer an age-old question confounding commentators and prophecy experts alike: Why *must* Satan be released (Rev 20:3, 7)?

In Revelation 20:1, an angel descends from heaven with two objects: a key and a great chain. The image of the key (κλείς) is used four times in Revelation, the first of which (Rev 1:18) characterizes the other three (Rev 3:7; 9:1; 20:1). In Revelation 1, at the sight of the cosmic Christ, John fell at his feet "as though dead" (Rev 1:17). Tenderly, Jesus reached out and touched John, commanding him, "Do not fear" (Rev 1:17). Such assurance is anchored in Jesus' identity and action: "I am the First and the Last. The Living One. I was dead, but look! I am alive—for ever and ever!" (Rev 1:17-18). The sovereignty of Christ unveiled in the death and resurrection of Christ. In this context of the Christ-event, Jesus adds, "And I possess the keys [κλεῖς] of Death and of Hades" (Rev 1:18).

In the ancient world, as today, a key was a symbol of sovereignty, ownership, or authority. House keys are possessed by the person(s) who owns the house or has been granted authority to enter the house. So, in Revelation 3:7, Jesus explains to the church of Philadelphia that, as the one "who possesses the key [κλεῖν] of David," they can rest assured that "what he opens, no one will close, and what he closes, no one opens." Sovereignty, ownership, authority. Revelation 1:18 specifies that the "keys" Christ possesses are for the doors "of Death and of Hades."

In Revelation 9:1, at the sound of the fifth trumpet, the star that fell "from the sky to the earth" (cf. Rev 12:9-12) is given "the key [κλεὶς] to the shaft of the abyss" (Rev 9:1). The same "key [κλεῖν] to the abyss" mentioned in Revelation 20:1. The same key acquired by Christ on Calvary (Rev 1:17-18).

Revelation 20:1 therefore invokes the death and resurrection of Jesus as the means through which the descending angel "seized the dragon" and "bound him for a thousand years" (Rev 20:2). The imagery compounds in Revelation 20:3, as the angel casts Satan "into the abyss, and closed and sealed it over him."[3] The defeat depicted is definitive; supreme sovereignty at the cross employed to bind and imprison the ancient serpent. To that end, the reader is stunned by the declaration concluding Revelation 20:3, "After [the thousand years], [the dragon] must [δεῖ] be set free for a short time."

Why? Why must Satan be released? This is not a fleeting detail or a slip of the quill, for the word "must" (δεῖ) is a verb that connotes divine necessity or by divine mandate. Oddly, then, Satan's release isn't a jailbreak or an accidental escape. No, his release is as divinely willed as his capture. But why? Why would God ever will the release of the enemy who tortures his own (Rev 9:1-19; 17:16)? Why would God ever necessitate the release of the evil one who maliciously pursues the holy ones with murderous intent (Rev 12:17; 13:7-10)?

Unfortunately, the Old Testament offers little help in disentangling this divine mandate. Nowhere in the sacred texts is there anything parallel to such a scene. Yet, as in the demise of the great prostitute (Rev 17:1–19:10), Revelation's imagery reaches clarity through Roman history.

---

[3]The word *sealed* (ἐσφράγισεν) in Rev 20:3 is the same word used in Mt 27:66 in reference to Jesus' tomb after he was crucified: "So they went and made the tomb secure by putting a seal [σφραγίσαντες] on the stone and posting the guard." Ironically, though, both seals are broken: Jesus' through victory and Satan's through defeat.

THE ROMAN TRIUMPHAL PROCESSION

Rome was an empire bent on conquest. Birthed from the god of war, Rome was a warring people, and as such they were baptized in a context of violence, from gladiatorial games, to public crucifixions, to grotesque imagery adorning public arches and imperial coinage. Violence was celebrated as the means by which the empire was sustained and expanded. Thus military heroes were at times awarded unique honors, privileges to exalt the culture of conquest. Chief among the tributes was a Roman triumphal procession.

Throughout history, many battles are fought and forgotten, but certain victories were deemed worthy of collective memory, emblazoned into the hearts and minds of onlookers through architecture, altars, and elaborate parades such as a Roman triumph. Roman triumphal processions (or triumphs) were the pinnacle of honor for the victor and the zenith of humiliation for the vanquished. They could be dayslong affairs, sparing no expense or restraint, celebrating a remarkable military victory that uniquely expanded the empire.

A Roman triumphal procession contained predictable elements and repeated features all accentuating the magnificent military victory. Citizens would line the streets, dressed in white robes of victory, trying to catch a glimpse of the spoils of war paraded with increasing luxury.[4] Foreign weaponry and exotic armor were interspersed with strange animals and alien flora; luxurious treasure and royal furniture were punctuated with placards lauding statistics of deaths in battle and the names of towns and territories now reduced to a state of *pax*; victorious soldiery intermingled with the subjugated enemy, who were forced to march in bondage fully dressed in their "native costumes."[5] The more exotic and elaborate the plunder, the greater the honor.

---

[4]Plutarch, *Aem.* 32.2; Ovid, *Ep. Pont.* 2.1.

[5]Appian, *Mith.* 116, in *Roman History*, trans. Horace White, LCL (Cambridge, MA: Harvard University Press, 1912–1913). See also Florus, *Epitome of Roman History* 1.37.5; Ovid, *Ep. Pont.* 2.1; Ovid, *Tristia* 4.2. Josephus also specifies that generals sought the "tallest and most beautiful" captive soldiers for the triumph to accentuate the honor in the victory (*J.W.* 6.417). On exotic armor, see Appian, *Mith.* 116; Livy, *Hist. Rom.* 34.52; Plutarch, *Titus Flamininus* 14.1; Plutarch, *Aem.* 32.5-7. On the plants, see Pliny the Elder, *Nat.* 12.9; Velleius Paterculus, *Hist. Rom.* 56.2. On the animals, see Pliny the Elder, *Nat.* 7.45; 8.2; Appian, *Pun.* 66; Josephus, *J.W.* 7.136. On luxurious treasure, see Velleius Paterculus, *Hist. Rom.* 56.2; Appian, *Pun.* 66; Plutarch, *Titus Flamininus* 14.1-2; Plutarch, *Aem.* 32.8-9; Plutarch, *Lucullus* 36.7; Josephus, *J.W.* 7.134; Suetonius, *Divus Augustus* 41.1; Dio Cassius, *Hist. Rom.* 51.21.7; Tacitus, *Ann.* 2.41. See also Dio Cassius, *Hist. Rom.* 67.7.4. On royal furniture, see Appian, *Mith.* 116;

The goal of the Roman triumph, though, was more than mere celebration of a battlefield victory. Triumphs transferred the onlooker from an
observer to a participant, from the streets of Rome to the field of battle.[6]
Throughout the procession, float-like constructions depicted key moments
of the celebrated victory. Elaborate expressions of armies storming city
walls or fire engulfing temples were reenacted with striking detail, at times
even executing the enemy army during the parade in full view of the citizens as a type of sacrifice to the gods.[7] The spoils of war, therefore, included not just material possessions but the sovereign narrative of Rome,
the message of the empire's mastery over the whole world, enacted with
such elaborate detail it was "as if [the onlookers] had been [at the battle]
really present."[8]

Roman triumphal processions were so significant that the empire converted the moment of the parade into lasting impressions emblazoned on
stone and metal, architecture and coins.

Figure 9.1.
The Arch of Titus (front)

Josephus, *J.W.* 7.148-150. On placards lauding statistics of deaths in battle, see Appian, *Mith.* 117;
Plutarch, *Pompeius* 45.1-3. On the names of towns and territories now reduced to a state of *pax*, see
Pliny the Elder, *Nat.* 5.36-37; Livy, *Hist. Rom.* 37.59.3; Plutarch, *Pompeius* 45.2. See also Tacitus,
Ann. 2.41; Propertius, *Elegies* 3.4.16; Dio Cassius, *Hist. Rom.* 68.29.2.

[6]Appian, *Mith.* 117; Appian, *Pun.* 66; Tacitus, *Ann.* 2.41; Josephus, *J.W.* 7.139-144.

[7]Josephus, *J.W.* 6.418; 7.96, 142-147; Velleius Paterculus, *Hist. Rom.* 56.1.

[8]Josephus, *J.W.* 7.146. See also 7.143-144; Ovid, *Ep. Pont.* 2.1.

The Arch of Titus, for instance, erected in the shadow of the Coliseum, cemented the legacy of the Jewish subjugation into the Roman public memory (fig. 9.1). On its inner panel, the arch depicts the Flavian triumphal procession in 71 CE, where artifacts from the temple in Jerusalem, including the seven-armed menorah and the table of showbread, are paraded by the victors as spoils of war (fig. 9.2).

Figure 9.2.
The Arch of Titus (inner panel: procession of menorah)

The panel its opposite, however, celebrates the climactic moment of every triumph, where at the end of the parade the victorious general would emerge in a quadriga, a chariot pulled by four white horses (fig. 9.3).[9]

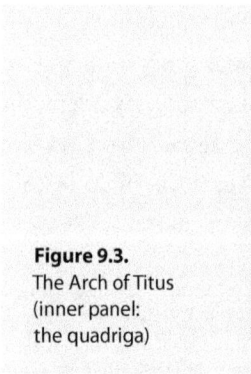

Figure 9.3.
The Arch of Titus (inner panel: the quadriga)

---

[9]The *quadriga* was at times used as a metonymy for the entire triumphal procession. So, Augustus: *RIC* 1.96-101, 107a-b, 108a-b, 109-112, 113a-b, 131-33, 134a-b, 135-37, 144-45, 221-24, 258-59, 263, 303, 399, 508-10. Tiberius: *RIC* 1.1-4. Caligula: *RIC* 1.36. Claudius: *RIC* 1.122. Nero: *RIC* 1.4-6 (elephant), 7 (elephants), 143-50, 498, 500. Galba: *RIC* 1.33, 134. Vespasian: *RIC* 1.44, 54, 68, 159, 163, 206-7, 273, 294, 364, 368, 451, 524, 536, 546, 612, 629a-b, 638, 645, 658, 688, 700. Titus: *RIC* 1.6, 12, 18, 60-61, 102, 143-44. Domitian: *RIC* 1.128, 165, 185, 185a, 204, 207, 222, 261 (elephants), 391 (elephants), 416 (elephants). See also Augustus, *Res gest.* 35.

The quadriga was an unmistakable reference to Jupiter, the chief god of Rome, and a patent reminder of the favor of the gods that secured this extraordinary military victory (figs. 9.4, 9.5).[10]

Figure 9.4.
Trajan:
RIC 2.777 (112–114 CE).
Jupiter and a quadriga

Figure 9.5.
Vespasian:
RIC 2.1127 (ca. 70–71 CE).
Quadriga in a triumphal procession

With such elaborate displays, the Roman triumphal procession was regarded as not just a parade but the consummation of a battle considered incomplete until this moment of celebration. A battle already won yet not properly resolved.[11] Not entirely complete, that is, until one final feature marched in the parade: the chief enemy leader bound in chains.[12]

---

[10]Livy says the emperor was "decked with the robes of Jupiter" (*Hist. Rom.* 10.7.10 [trans. Foster]), and some scholars suggest the face of the emperor was painted with red to parallel Jupiter (based on Pliny, *Nat.* 33.1-2). These symbols (along with others) suggest the emperor was intentionally portrayed as both god and king. See H. S. Versnel, *Triumphus: An Inquiry into the Origin, Development and Meaning of the Roman Triumph* (Leiden: Brill, 1970), 84-93; David Andrew Thomas, *Revelation 19 in Historical and Mythological Context* (New York: Peter Lang, 2008), 42-58. For a complete discussion, see Mary Beard, *The Roman Triumph* (Cambridge, MA: Harvard University Press, 2007), 219-56.

[11]Tacitus, *Ann.* 2.41.

[12]Ovid, *Ars amatoria* 1.2.30; *Tristia* 4.2; Horace, *Carmina* 2.1; Cicero, *Verr.* 2.5.66; Florus, *Epitome of Roman History* 1.36.17.

Exceeding the illustrious plunder and the elaborate battlefield depictions was the procession of the chief enemy leader manacled and marched directly in front of the quadriga.[13] The significance of this element can hardly be overstated. Victors went to great lengths *not* to kill the chief enemy leader but to secure and preserve them for the triumphal procession. "Reports do not relate," Velleius Paterculus recounts, "how the most eminent leaders of the enemy were slain in battle, but rather how the triumph displayed them, in chains."[14]

For example, after the Battle of Actium and the death of Marc Antony, Augustus feverishly pursued Cleopatra "to seize her alive and to carry her back for his triumph." Even after her successful suicide, Augustus desperately attempted to revive her. When all attempts failed, Caesar "excessively grieved on his own account, as if he had been deprived of all the glory of his victory."[15] To celebrate a triumph in all its glory was to parade the chief enemy leader in chains, which is why some captive leaders were even bound and imprisoned for years after the battle.[16]

As a "splendid fruit of victory," the chief enemy leader was sought by spectator and conqueror alike, a key feature in the parade even engraved on coins and open-air altars, such as the one here from the city of Ephesus.[17]

The front panel is adorned with an array of plunder, ranging from treasure to armor to weaponry. As the bounty unfolds in erratic formation, the onlooker's eye is drawn to two figures at the center of the altar (left quadrant; fig. 9.8). One figure stands with a mallet raised over his head as the second figure sits with hands bound behind his back, dressed in the garb of a foreign

---

[13]Beard, *Roman Triumph*, 124-25. See also Dio Cassius, *Hist. Rom.* 51.21.9; Livy, *Hist. Rom.* 6.4.

[14]Velleius Paterculus, *Hist. Rom.* 2.121.3, in *Velleius Paterculus and Res Gestae Divi Augusti*, trans. Frederick W. Shipley, LCL (Cambridge, MA: Harvard University Press, 1924). See also Dio Cassius, *Hist. Rom.* 61.32.4a, where Mithridates begs Claudius for a hearing so that "he might not be summarily executed or led in the triumphal procession." Cf. Tacitus, *Ann.* 12.21, 36.

[15]Dio Cassius, *Hist. Rom.* 51.14.3, 6. See 51.10.9 for Antony's death. To salvage this essential feature of his triumphal procession, Augustus has "an effigy of the dead Cleopatra upon a couch" carried in the parade, "so that in a way she . . . was a part of the spectacle and a trophy in the procession" (Dio Cassius, *Hist. Rom.* 51.21.8). See also 61.32.4a; Tacitus, *Ann.* 12.21, 36; Velleius Paterculus, *Hist. Rom.* 2.121.3).

[16]Cicero, *Verr.* 2.5.66. Unless otherwise noted, translations of *In Verrem* follow *The Orations of Marcus Tullius Cicero*, trans. C. D. Yonge (London: George Bell & Sons, 1903).

[17]Cicero, *Verr.* 2.5.77. Augustus: *RIC* 1.6; Claudius: *RIC* 1.69-70; Vitellius: *RIC* 1.151; Vespasian: *RIC* 1.16, 114-15, 201, 208, 287, 289, 294, 424-26; Titus: *RIC* 1.1-2, 5, 11, 17, 17a, 21a-b; Domitian: *RIC* 1.252, 255, 266, 278-79, 285, 312, 318. Cf. Galba: *RIC* 1.77-84.

Figure 9.6.
Open-air altar
from the Temple
of Domitian in Ephesus
(side panel)

Figure 9.7.
Open-air altar
from the Temple
of Domitian in Ephesus
(front right panel)

Figure 9.8.
Open-air altar
from the Temple
of Domitian in Ephesus
(center panel)

leader. As an altar, then, the sacrifices commingle with the narrative invoked by the iconography, the climactic moment of the Roman triumphal procession when the chief enemy leader, bound in chains, is executed in honor of the gods.

The final destination of the Roman triumph was the steps of Jupiter's temple.[18] The clamor of the parade would die down as the audience waited in silence for the commencement of the pinnacle moment.[19] "At the climax of the pageant," Scott Hafemann writes, "those prisoners and royalty who had been led in triumph and were not destined to be sold into slavery were executed in honor to the victor as the ultimate sign of his conquest and in homage to Rome's deity."[20]

For subjects and sovereigns of the empire, the Roman triumphal procession showcased the sovereign narrative of Rome in unparalleled fashion. Emblazoned in memories, stone, and metal, the military victory, now consummated in the procession, proclaimed Rome as the ruler of the kings of the earth due to the favor of the gods. The *pax* following the parade is the bounty bestowed by the deities worshiped amid the revelry and honored by the spilled blood. Especially the blood of the chief enemy leader bound in chains and marched across the breadth of the city as a living sacrifice, an insight from Roman history that provides clarity to the imagery of Revelation 19:11–20:10.

GOD'S TRIUMPHAL PROCESSION

In Revelation 19:11-21, Jesus processes from heaven on a white horse adorned with regal imagery, wearing "many crowns" (Rev 19:12) and heralded as "King of kings and Lord of lords" (Rev 19:16). Following close by, the "armies of heaven" also appear, riding "on white horses" (Rev 19:14), but they're not dressed in military garb essential for battle. The army is "clothed in fine linen, white and clean" (Rev 19:14), like onlookers of a Roman triumph.

Jesus himself doesn't approach the alleged battle with garments of war but with "a robe dipped in blood" (Rev 19:13), a garment in celebration of the war

---

[18]For the triumphal procession route, see Beard, *Roman Triumph*, 335.

[19]Josephus, *J.W.* 7.153.

[20]Scott J. Hafemann, "Roman Triumph," in *Dictionary of New Testament Background*, ed. C. Evans and S. Porter (Downers Grove, IL: InterVarsity Press, 2000), 1005. See Cicero, *Verr.* 2.5.77; Plutarch, *Aem.* 33.3–34.2; 36.6; *Antonius* 84.2-4; Appian, *Mith.* 117; Josephus, *J.W.* 6.433-434; 7.153. See Beard, *Roman Triumph*, 14, 128-32.

already won. Just like a triumphal procession. As preeminent Roman scholar Mary Beard observes, "Though a military ceremony in many respects, there is no sign that the general ever appeared in military garbs [in a Roman triumph]. Quite the reverse: his war was over."[21] The battle had been won; the parade consummates a war already fought. Yes, the armies of evil "gather to make war" in Revelation 19:19-21, but there is no war. Only an annihilation. A sacrifice of sorts. An elaborate depiction of the battle already fought but only in service of the execution of the enemy. Just like a Roman triumph.[22]

Yet there's one key element missing from Revelation 19:11-21. An element essential to all Roman triumphal processions. An element generals pursued and onlookers anticipated. An element not at the beginning of the parade but the "splendid fruit" saved for the end: the march of the chief enemy leader bound in chains.

In Revelation 20:1-3, the angel from heaven wields the sovereignty of Christ and descends on Satan with two key actions: (1) binding Satan with a great chain (Rev 20:2) and (2) imprisoning Satan in the abyss (Rev 20:3). Two distinct actions that, although linked, contribute two separate elements to the imagery. Satan is manacled *and* imprisoned.

Revelation 20:3 forecasts God's divine will for the demonic prisoner. "After [the thousand years], [the dragon] *must* be set free for a short time." A divine mandate that, after a time of imprisonment, commissions the captive's release. A divine *must* realized in Revelation 20:7—to an extent. "And when the thousand years are completed, Satan will be released from his prison" (Rev 20:7). The actions of Revelation 20:1-3, then, are only partially reversed in Rev 20:7. The text specifically states that Satan is "released from his prison," but it never states that he's released from his chains.

This omission offers a striking portrayal often overlooked but essential for answering the question, Why *must* Satan be released? Satan is released from

---

[21] Beard, *Roman Triumph*, 225.

[22] Building on the suggestion of David Aune, David Andrew Thomas argues persuasively for the Roman triumph as the driving imagery behind key symbols in Rev 19:11-21. See Aune, *Revelation*, WBC 52A-52C (Nashville: Thomas Nelson, 1997–1998), 3:1050-52; Thomas, *Revelation 19*, 21-89. For the argument that follows, see Shane J. Wood, "God's Triumphal Procession: Re-examining the Release of Satan in the Light of Roman Imperial Imagery (Revelation 20:7-10)," in *Currents in British Research on the Apocalypse*, ed. Garrick Allen, Ian Paul, and Simon Woodman (Tübingen: Mohr Siebeck, 2015), 209-23.

prison to march across the "breadth of the earth" (Rev 20:9) bound in chains. Just like the chief enemy leader in a Roman triumph.

The scene unfolds, therefore, as a reenactment of his defeat, a retelling of the battle, a recapitulation of the war already won by the slain Lamb and his followers. So, in Revelation 20:8, Satan coerces the nations to "gather for war," but as in Revelation 16:16 and Revelation 19:19, there is no battle. Only an execution. With the names "Gog and Magog" hovering in the syntax like a placard at a parade, Satan's vast army marches in formation to lay siege to the people of God (Rev 20:9), the offspring of the cosmic woman (Rev 12:16-17), the ones who follow the Lamb wherever he goes (Rev 14:4).[23]

Yet, like Elijah's sacrifice on the altar at Mount Carmel (1 Kings 18:38-40), Satan and his soldiers are devoured by fire from heaven (Rev 20:9), with the devil "cast into the lake of fire and sulfur, where also the beast and the false prophet had been thrown" (Rev 20:10). As before, there's no battle at all. Why? Because the battle has already been won. The "ancient serpent" already defeated (Rev 20:2; cf. Rev 12:9). The dragon already conquered "by the blood of the Lamb" (Rev 12:11).

As in a triumphal procession, Satan is released from prison still bound in chains, marched as a spectacle on full display. As the chief enemy leader, Satan is manacled and paraded just before the emergence of the one on the "great white throne" (Rev 20:11). Like the elaborate floats in a triumph, the devil performs an elaborate depiction of the battle, the key moment of his defeat at the cross of Calvary, where the war reached its pinnacle, and the parade reaches its climax: the chief enemy leader is executed.

Taken together, the answer to our question becomes quite clear. Why *must* Satan be released? To march in God's triumphal procession.

DON'T BE DECEIVED

The Revelation of Jesus Christ thins the veil. Uncovers our eyes. Allows us to see beyond what blinds us. To see through the affliction and deception and assaults of the evil one to "the suffering and kingdom and patient endurance

---

[23]The phrase "Gog and Magog" alludes to Ezek 38–39, where Gog, from the land of Magog, is envisioned as the evil ruler hellbent on destroying the people of Israel. Though he travels with his armies from distant lands to siege God's people, Gog and his forces are dismantled by God with ease, demonstrating God's power and holiness. The aftermath is overwhelming in its scale and breadth, for Ezek 39:12 says it will take seven months for the Israelites to bury all the dead soldiers from Gog's forces.

in Jesus" (Rev 1:9). Thinning the veil corrects our wayward assumptions and clarifies the truth about the chief enemy leader. The battle is over, the dragon defeated, the *un*holy trinity conquered by the blood of the Lamb and the testimony of the holy ones willing to die as Christ did.

So, don't be deceived. In Christ we are "more than conquerors" (Rom 8:37). We are "a kingdom and priests" (Rev 1:6; 5:10). We're the bride of Christ (Rev 19:8), the 144,000 "following the Lamb wherever he might go" (Rev 14:4). We do not cower in fear. We do not shrink from death. We don't question the outcome. We storm the gates of hell with confidence in our mission to love our enemies into moments of transformation, come what may, for we are not uncertain about the war. We know the battle has already been won. The dragon already conquered. The ancient serpent already bound and imprisoned by the life, death, resurrection, and ascension of Jesus Christ.

So we don't wait in the meantime as those with no hope or those unsure of whether Satan is alive and well. We wait as victors in a battle awaiting its consummation. Awaiting Eden's arrival and evil's denouement. Awaiting God's triumphal procession.

GOING DEEPER

> **THE TOOL:** Context, part 4: What about the rapture? (Rev 4:1). If you take the Bible out of context, you can make it say whatever you want. When it comes to Revelation, assumptions guide our questions, which at times hijack the original context for our own purposes. The rapture is a case in point. Watch this video (www.ivpress.com/wood-9a) and wrestle with the following:

1. Interpretation takes great humility, which is why I always remind my students, "You're allowed to disagree with me and get an A."

   ➤ If the video on the rapture is true, what would be lost?

   ➤ What would be gained?

   ➤ What's at stake?

2. Sometimes we can take issues of opinion and transform them into litmus tests for whether someone is a Christian.

> Should the rapture be held with such intensity?

> Is there room for disagreement on this issue even within the church?

THE TEXT: Victory in Jesus (Rev 19:11–20:15). It's easy to assume Satan is winning. But the message of Revelation 19:11–20:15 sings a different melody: Christ won the battle on the cross; we're just awaiting God's triumphal procession. Watch the following video (www.ivpress.com /wood-9b) and answer the following:

---

1. If you truly believed Jesus was victorious on the cross and Satan was bound, what would change in your life?

   > How would this victory affect your fear or anxiety?

   > How would it affect your boldness?

   > How would it transform your compassion toward your greatest enemies?

2. Satan is a master of deception. Lies are his native tongue.

   > Why would Satan want to distort whether Jesus was truly victorious on the cross?

   > What would Satan gain by this deception?

   > What does he lose if truth exposes this lie?

THE TAKEAWAY: Praying with the Word of God. The Word of God is living and moving, searching our hearts and minds for areas where sin distorts and the enemy's lies reign. Combining the Word of God with our prayer practices, then, proffers a powerful combination for transformation in the Word itself. What follows is an ancient Christian prayer practice called lectio divina, which centers on the transforming power of God's Word in prayer. Here's how it works:

First movement: Reading the text

1. Read Revelation 19:11-16 aloud two times slowly and distinctly with pauses.

2. Sit in silence for one to two minutes, asking the Spirit to bring to mind a word or phrase from the text.

3. Write down the word/phrase from the Spirit without any elaboration.

Second movement: Reflecting on God's Word

1. Read Revelation 19:11-16 aloud for a third time.

2. Sit in silence for two to three minutes, reflecting on this question: "How does this word/phrase intersect with my life today?"

3. Write down how this word/phrase is affecting you in this moment.

Third movement: Responding to God's Word

1. Read Revelation 19:11-16 aloud for the fourth time.

2. Sit in silence for two to three minutes, reflecting on this question: "How is God calling me to respond?"

3. Prayerfully write down your response to God's call.

Fourth movement: Resting in God

1. Read Revelation 19:11-16 aloud for the last time.

2. Sit in silence for two to three minutes, merely resting in God's Word.

3. Close your time with a verbalized prayer thanking God for this encounter with his Spirit.

10

FROM GARDEN TO GARDEN
(Revelation 21:1–22:21)

Pursuing the God of Pursuit

On each side of the river stood the tree of life. . . .
And the leaves of the tree are for the healing
of the nations. No longer will there be any curse.

REVELATION 22:2-3 NIV

WHAT MAKES GOD GIDDY? What makes his pitch heighten and his words quicken? What makes him stutter and stammer with delight? Or makes his legs quake with anticipation? What excites God? What ignites God? What does God desire? At his core, throughout all of Scripture. What's the thread of God's pursuit that holds together each narrative from Genesis 1 to Exodus 3 to 1 Samuel 8 to Isaiah 1 to Matthew 4 to Acts 2 to Hebrews 10 to Revelation 21–22? What makes God giddy?

I always know when my kids are giddy with excitement. Their body trembles as their voice hurries; they overemphasize certain words with facial expressions that light up the room. They betray the object of their delight by repeating a key word or phrase over and over and over again.

Years ago, my youngest came home from his new school. Curious, I asked how it went. His response was delightfully explosive.

"Oh, Dad!" he howled. "The playground is a-ma-zing!" He jumped up, unable to contain his joy. "In the middle, there's this enormous slide," he

beamed. "I couldn't believe it! I went down the slide, then back up the slide, then my friends and I took turns going down the slide together, then we tried to climb up the slide, going the wrong way, but the slide was so big we slipped and went back down the slide!"

"So," I smiled wryly, "it sounds like you liked the slide?"

He smiled back, almost out of breath, shaking his head, "Oh yeah . . . the slide was awesome!"

In Revelation 21:1-7, God is giddy. Childlike. Overflowing with excitement. Unveiled at the outset is a "new heaven and a new earth" void of "any sea" (Rev 21:1), free from any evil and all chaos. The "holy city, the new Jerusalem," descending "out of heaven," free from any threat and all sin, radiant in glory as a "bride beautifully adorned for her husband" (Rev 21:2). And the one on the throne simply can't contain himself. He delightfully howls: "Look ['Ιδού]! The dwelling place of God is now *with* humankind, and he will dwell *with* them. They will be *his* people, and God himself will be *with* them and will *be their God.* . . . Those who conquer will inherit *all* of these things, and I will be *their* God and they will be *my* children" (Rev 21:3, 7). You can hear his smile, sense his delight, feel his joy, see his desire. To be *with* us. Among us. As it was in the beginning. Dwelling beside us without a veil. Without separation. Without sin or death threatening to divide us from the one who longs to put an end to pain, to sunset all mourning, to wipe every tear from our eyes (Rev 21:4) and satiate all cravings "as a gift" (Rev 21:6).

At the end of the Bible, God is giddy. As excited as he was at the beginning of Scripture. As elated as he was when he decreed, "Let there be light" (Gen 1:3). As ecstatic as he was when he decided, "Let us make humankind in our image" (Gen 1:26). As delighted as he was when he placed his beloved creation in a garden, free from suffering and shame, centered on the tree of life and life with him (Gen 2:8-9). Their Creator. Their King. Their God.

A lot has happened since "in the beginning." Death's detour and deception disturbed our vision of God and his hope. Yet here, at the end of Revelation, with the final words of Scripture, the veil separating heaven and earth evaporates; humanity is once again in a garden, and God is seen. *Fully* seen. His overflowing delight is on full display. Illuminating not only our future but how he beholds us in the present.

A PLACE OR A PERSON?

The invitation at the end of Revelation is obvious: "Come." The Spirit cries, "Come"; the bride says, "Come"; and anyone "who hears" the revelation is commanded to shout the same, "Come" (Rev 22:17). Three times Jesus states with excitement, "I am *coming* soon!" (Rev 22:7, 12, 20), to the last of which John adds, "Amen. *Come*, Lord Jesus" (Rev 22:20). "Come" punctuates the end of Revelation with invitations and declarations, all emphasizing a movement toward, a union with, a gathering of, a coming together. Not for battle, though, for all threats are gone (Rev 21:8, 27); no need to even shut the city gates (Rev 21:25). No, the last words of Revelation are reserved for a convergence, a blending of heaven and earth, an intermingling of humanity and divinity, an interpenetration of what is seen and what is beyond the veil. A celebration of Christ's accomplishments *for* us and *to* us.

In Revelation 21:9, as in Revelation 17:1, an angel from the seven bowls gathers John's attention with the word "Come [Δεῦρο]," followed by an invitation to show the Seer a woman. Not a prostitute but a bride. Not to describe her demise but to describe her beauty, her glory, her purity, her victory. "Come," says the angel, "I will show you the bride, the wife of the Lamb" (Rev 21:9).[1]

Yet, as the angel whisks John away, once again, "in the Spirit" (Rev 21:10; cf. Rev 1:10; 4:2; 17:3), he isn't shown a bride at all. Instead the angel shows John a city. Not Babylon, as before (Rev 17:5), but "the holy city, Jerusalem, coming down out of heaven from God" (Rev 21:10). A city radiant "with the glory of God" (Rev 21:11), affixed with walls and gates cementing God's redemptive story into each stone: twelve gates engraved with "the names of the twelve tribes of the sons of Israel" (Rev 21:12) and twelve foundations inscribed with "the names of the twelve apostles of the Lamb" (Rev 21:14).

Like God himself, the city is brilliant, shining like jasper (Rev 21:11, 18-19; cf. Rev 4:3), and organized in a perfect cube (Rev 21:16), reminiscent of the

---

[1] Parallels between Rev 17:1-3 and Rev 21:9-10 demonstrate an intentional juxtaposition of the great prostitute and the bride of the Lamb. (1) Both visions are delivered by one of the seven angels from the seven bowl plagues; (2) both times the angel invites John to "Come!"; (3) in both cases, John is carried away "in the Spirit" (Rev 17:3; 21:10). (4) Also, the Greek for each passage begins the same: Καὶ ἦλθεν εἷς ἐκ τῶν ἑπτὰ ἀγγέλων τῶν ἐχόντων τὰς ἑπτὰ φιάλας . . . καὶ ἐλάλησεν μετ' ἐμοῦ λέγων δεῦρο, δείξω σοι.

holy of holies itself (1 Kings 6:20).[2] The city is interwoven with divine intimacy, streets paved with not just gold (Rev 21:21) but the story of redemption, where God confronts every boundary, every barrier, to once again draw close to his creation as it was in the beginning.

Unlike Jerusalem of old, in this city God's presence is not confined to a space; it's the space itself. For the place is a person. The city a bride. God is all and is in all (Col 3:11). Thus the new Jerusalem (Rev 21:2, 10) has no temple to house the presence of God, for "the Lord God Almighty and the Lamb are its temple" (Rev 21:22). The holy city has no sun or celestial bodies, "for the glory of God illuminated it, and its lamp is the Lamb" (Rev 21:23; cf. Rev 22:5). Even the "river of the water of life" has God as its source, "flowing from the throne of God and of the Lamb" (Rev 22:1), sustaining life in the heavenly city.

At each point, in every stone, the presence of God interpenetrates the holy city. For the community enjoyed by the Trinity throughout eternity is now present to all humanity. Humanity no longer blinded by Eden's curse (Rev 22:3); divinity no longer shrouded by Death's veil. For in this place, God's servants "see his face, and his name will be on their foreheads" (Rev 22:4). In this place, as in Eden before evil, intimacy knows no limits.

THE TRIAL OF HEAVEN

Sometimes I wonder whether we've forgotten our *true* end. Whether Christians have forgotten our *ultimate* destination. Whether we've exchanged the subject of our worship for something far less. From both the pulpit and my prayer closet, I've inquired: As Christians, are we worshiping a person or a place? Do we yearn for heaven or for intimacy with God? Or to state it differently: If there were no promise of heaven, would we still pursue God with the same intensity with which he pursues us?

This isn't a criticism of theology or a knavish play on words to elicit false conviction or something more akin to coercion. This isn't a denial of heaven or the restoration of earth when God makes all things new (Rev 21:5). This is

---

[2]Revelation 21:16 measures the cube's length, width, and height as 12,000 stadia (or $12 \times 10 \times 10 \times 10$). Twelve is a number of completion usually attached to the people of God, while ten is a number of completion usually attached to a time period of suffering or persecution through which God proves to be faithful. Thus, the 12,000 stadia of the new Jerusalem stand for the complete number of God's people who endured suffering through which God proved to be faithful. For more on numbers in Revelation, see "Appendix: Interpreting Numbers in Revelation" below.

a question of our end, of intimacy, of the purpose and meaning of the Revelation of Jesus Christ. This is an inquiry into community and communion with the Holy Trinity.

Relationships that last are never transactional. They're never based on what the other offers or what the other can provide. Enduring relationships are centered on mutual self-sacrifice, the complete offering of self for the other. Otherwise they wither. Devolve from delight into devastation. Destruction. Devouring each other to serve the purposes of self. Something more akin to a parasite and its host, a prostitute and her beast, evil and its own. But nothing like the love between Christ and his bride.

Over the years I've performed countless weddings. Some inside, some out; some with tension, others without; yet for each, my message is the same. Sure, I tailor each sermon to match the couple, but my homily always centers on the same aim from the same passage in Mark 10:35-45.

After James and John, the sons of thunder, ask Jesus for the seats of glory, for positions of power and prominence (Mk 10:35-37), Jesus confronts their definition of power. Of authority. How to wield it, discern it, recognize it, acquire it. "You know," Jesus explains, "that the ones who seem to rule the nations lord it *over* them" (Mk 10:42), use their power to tyrannize, to dominate, to subjugate, "their 'great' ones exercise authority *over* them" (Mk 10:42). Emphatically Christ contrasts, "But not so with you. Whoever desires to become great among you must be your servant, and whoever desires among you to be first must be slave of all" (Mk 10:43-44). The definitions of power and authority couldn't be more different between the kingdom of earth and the kingdom of Christ. The former defines power and *pax* with the sword and threats of violence, while the latter sees sovereignty as service, the sacrifice of self for the other. Something Jesus embodied: "For even the Son of Man came not to be served, but to serve, and to give his life as a ransom in the place of many" (Mk 10:45).

It's at this point in the ceremony where I look directly into the eyes of the bride and the groom and say, "How much more with us? If the Son of Man, the King of kings, the Creator of the universe, didn't come to be served but to serve, then how much more with me? How much more with you? If you're coming to this marriage—either one of you—with the expectation of being served, then regardless of how beautiful the ceremony, your life together is

destined for strife and struggle over power and authority. Your arguments will be laced with self-protection and distrust, your daily life shrouded with plots and ploys to seize what *you* deserve even if it disrupts or destroys the other. A relationship based on selfishness cannot last. But Christ reveals on the cross that a relationship based on self-sacrifice thrives. Dreams are realized, disagreements minimized, and love unfolds deeper each day with the mutual commitment 'not to be served, but to serve.'"

Love is never transactional, never fights for self, never withholds, resists every temptation to measure and record any and all wrongs. Love offers all without expectation, sacrifices all without worry of return on investment. Love lingers long enough to be detected but refuses our trivial definitions. Indeed, Jesus revealed all we know and understand about love, for "this is how we know what love is: Jesus Christ laid down his life for us" (1 Jn 3:16 NIV).

Yet, at times in our relationship with God, we cling more to the idea of getting out of hell than the feet of the resurrected King. More to a location than to love itself. In concert with the imagery of Revelation 21–22, though, John 17:3 discloses, "And this is eternal life: that they might know you, the only true God, and Jesus Christ, whom you sent."

But is that enough? Can that answer satisfy our soul? Is the bride really in love with the groom, or is she just after his money? In it for what she gets? Are we in love with a person or merely obsessed with a place?

In Revelation 21–22, heaven is indeed real. The earth is indeed renewed and ready for life to resume as it was in the beginning. But without question, heaven is more than a place tucked away in the sky by and by. Heaven is an invitation. An unmistakable "Come." An Edenic scene centered on love, fidelity, inseparability, and unimaginable intimacy. Intimacy that pervades the person and the place. Divine presence that saturates the soul and the land like dew in the cool of the morning. A union of the human and the divine. A coming together of God and his people, a divine mystery as ineffable as the incarnation itself, where "the two become one" (Gen 2:24 LXX) in a union beyond what the physical can comprehend or solve. A mystery, Paul says, that is "profound," for the union of Genesis 2:24 stretches far beyond a married couple, extending to the nuptials of the Lamb and his bride, for as Paul shocks,

"I am talking about Christ and the church" (Eph 5:32 NIV). In Christ and through Christ, the two become one (Jn 15:4-14).[3]

Union is at the center of Revelation 21–22. Heaven becomes one with earth; the abode of God unites with the abode of humankind (Rev 21:1-3). Death no longer separates or distorts (Rev 21:4); the curse no longer divides or deceives (Rev 22:3). The veil has been torn, Eden restored, the tree of life once again made accessible, providing healing for the nations (Rev 22:2) and avenues of intimacy for all creation and their Creator (Rev 22:4).

More than just a place, Revelation 21–22 envisions intimacy unencumbered by selfishness, unhindered by sin, unfettered and freed by love and self-sacrifice. Two coming together as one. An economy only understood through the revelation of Jesus Christ, through the revelation of the Holy Trinity, where one + one + one = one. Three persons, one being. Divine intimacy and eternal unity. The new heavens and the new earth, then, celebrate not mere streets of gold but the coming together of two. Not to war with the other but to unite through mutual commitments of "not to be served but to serve."

Yes, Revelation 21–22 is a depiction of heaven, a real place accessible to everyone in Christ. But its emphasis is decidedly not on a location but on a relationship. Not on a place but on a people. Not on a destination but a culmination of intimate promises between God and his own, between Christ and his bride, between the Spirit and the church.

GOD'S TENDER PURSUIT

Like first words, last words matter. A parent's last words are as cherished as a child's first. For last words, like first words, define what we value. Bring clarity to who we are and, by God's grace, who we can become.

In Revelation 21–22, we hear God's last words. The last words of his revelation. The last words of a narrative stretching back to Eden that now, at its end, returns to a garden. A garden void of the curse. A garden teeming with life. A garden without a veil. A garden that invites a depth of intimacy between God and his own unseen since "in the beginning." Last words that

---

[3]For more on the significance of Eph 5:31-32 and "union with Christ" in Paul, see Shane J. Wood, "Interpenetration Logic: Pauline Spirituality and Union with Christ," *Religions* 13, no. 8 (2022): 680, https://doi.org/10.3390/rel13080680.

unveil a God unhindered by our rebellion, effusive in his delight. Last words that celebrate a God of pursuit. A God who throughout all sixty-six books of the canon stopped at nothing to set the wrongs right, to undo sin's curse, to draw near to his beloved. Last words that reveal God's tender pursuit of his fallen creation, which culminates in intimacy, not tragedy.

At the end, the Revelation of Jesus Christ proudly proclaims that God's pursuit never ends. Regardless of the adversity or the perceived catastrophe, God's pursuit doesn't wane or admit a single defeat. The Bible's last words unveil that "Let there be light" wasn't undone when darkness entered creation at the taste of forbidden fruit; death's victory in Cain and Abel didn't undo all of life east of Eden. God greets each movement of sinful humanity with a resilient tenderness. A passionate pursuit. A love as deep as it is reckless. An invitation as soothing as the Spirit's simple call to "Come."

The Revelation of Jesus Christ unveils God's tender pursuit. An insight odd for some who understand Revelation as justification for unbridled violence, imagery that authorizes lust for one's enemy to be tortured in at least the sixth circle of Dante's inferno. But the text is resolute, firmly rooted in God's tenderness that welcomes even "the Gentiles" and "the kings of earth" into the new Jerusalem (Rev 21:24). Revelation's end is persistent in portraying God's patient presence. His tender pursuit of all humanity. Including you. Including me.

Revelation 21–22 confronts us with compassion and kindness beyond comprehension. God's body-warming smile seems to hold space for all my flaws and beauty in this new Jerusalem. His grace, in the end, reminds me of his mercy in the beginning, when, in my own story and in Revelation 1:17-18, he made the first move. He reached across the chasm, unafraid of my disease of deadness, and touched me. Gently. Whispering words I still war against in my soul: "Shane, do not be afraid."

I'm painfully aware that he knows my struggles yet still smiles. Probes my wandering heart yet still nods in approval. He knows me yet still loves me. Pursues me. Is tender with me.

What kind of King is this? A King who lets me place my fingers in the holes of his hands as we walk side by side up the mountain. What kind of God is this? Who spots me cowering in the corner of the feast, feeling unworthy, yet, at John's request, insists I lay my head on his chest. What kind of Spirit is this?

Who knows the depths of my union with death yet pierces the veil of my heart with a mother's delight, not disdain; with acceptance, not accusation; with joy, not disgust.

"But you know my story!" I protest.

Yet the three-in-one sings in unison, "And that's why we love you."

What type of tenderness is this? That confronts all barriers and boundaries between us with intense ferocity. What kind of power is this? That spans all struggles and suffering with silence that soothes my soul, reminding me of who I am. Whose I am. What I'm here for. Whom I'm here for. Where I belong, where I'm going, to whom I'm returning.

What type of love is this? That refuses to let me stay the same even as it accepts me as I am. A love that comforts me yet challenges me to obey. Teaches me to unfold. Guides me to the leaves of healing in the tree of life. Invites me to begin anew. Calls me to live and love once again.

What kind of grace is this? That collapses cosmology to remind me that I am his and he is mine. He is my love, and I'm his beloved.

God's last words strike me dumb. I grow mute with each thought of his tender pursuit. Maybe a blank page would say more than any of this ink spilled in search of how to apprehend this divine mystery. This cosmic intimacy. Perhaps silence is more equipped to explore the depths of God. Yet his tenderness invites me to come. To speak. To witness. To testify that in the end, all is grace. In the end, all is God.

A LOVER'S PURSUIT

I want to know him. Desperately. Yes, I want to be known by him, but intimacy is a reciprocal relationship: being fully known and fully knowing another. I want to know him as deeply as he knows me.

I want to know the sound of his laughter in a crowded room. I want to know what he's thinking at the slightest upturn of his mouth. I want to know what gifts make his heart smile and what memories cross his mind when he gazes at a sunset. I want to know what makes him giddy and what grieves his soul. I want to know his favorite fruit, his most prized possession, his proudest moment. I want to know the smell of his tears and the pattern of his wrinkles that web the corner of his eyes with each smile. I want to recognize the sound of his sigh, the cadence of his steps, and the tone and timbre of his mellifluous

voice. I want to know whether he chews with his mouth open or bites his nails or has a double cowlick on the crown of his head.

I want to know him.

Not just get gifts from him. Not just one day live in proximity to him, for proximity doesn't always result in intimacy. Many a neighbor live side by side without truly knowing the other. No, I want to know him. Intimately. I want to hear him finish my sentences as I try to finish his Word. I want to catch his passing scent and know he's nearby. I want to watch him play with the little children in the meadow, throw his head back in laughter, and nod to me as a tender reminder that he sees me, loves me, and longs to be with me.

I want to know him, and incredibly, he wants to know me. To be with me. To shower me with love, gifts, time, and pursuit. He wants me to see myself the way he sees me, as his beloved. As one worthy of love. As someone you get excited about when you're told, "They're almost here!" As someone you promise to protect, sometimes even from yourself. God knows me and wants to know me, sees me and longs for me to see myself through his eyes.

"Shane," he tenderly whispers, "you are my beloved." Words that collide with my own self-criticism. Words that woo me away from the siren call of self-hatred.

"Listen to me, my beloved: you are beautiful, flaws and all."

I shake my head in disbelief, daring to challenge the tender words of my King. Yet he sings a song of hope that drowns out the sound of my doubt.

"I see you, my son. All of you. Who you were. Who you are becoming. Your sin. My image. All of you. And I know, Shane, together we can break through to a new day."

In the end, the Revelation of Jesus Christ doesn't settle for a place or mere prediction. Its target is far more grand. Far more elaborate. Its target is you. Is me. The transformation of the reader through intimacy with the God who calls you by name. Even by a new name. With a voice only you recognize, for you know the Good Shepherd and choose to trust his calls for rest and his warnings that danger is near and it's time to move on from here. From this place of self-hatred, from this space of self-service, from this world of sin and shame, guilt and despair.

As you journey, he reminds you of times gone by when you couldn't distinguish his voice from your own. When you used to long for his love even

as you were lured away by lovers far less wild. He chuckles at how often you worried about tomorrow, forgetting the gift of today. He sighs when you recall yet another sin he's already forgiven, taken, removed. He shakes his head with delight when you retell the gospel story, remembering his time in flesh. In garments of skin. After a time, he holds you because he knows you're tired. Allowing your head to rest on his chest, listening to the heart of a father whose every beat reminds you that you're safe. That you're loved. That he is yours. And you are his. And you're together.

IN THE END

God's last words remove the veil between heaven and earth, clarifying the depths of grace, the ineffable movements of God toward us. Grace that beckons us to respond with a pursuit of our own. A pursuit of God that violates the world's logic (1 Cor 1:18), redefines victory in the shape of the cross, and joins the choir of saints shouting, "Amen! Come, Lord Jesus!" (Rev 22:20). A pursuit that prompts us to look deeper into ourselves, our friends, our enemies, and all of creation for the fingerprints of God that don't just reveal his pursuit but remind us of his presence. Remind us that, even on this side of eternity, the veil between heaven and earth isn't as thick as we assume.

In Revelation 21–22, God is giddy. Teeming in anticipation for what is now emerging: union with his people. Presence with his people, where he will be their God and they will be his people (Rev 21:3), where he will be with them and they will be with him (Rev 21:7). United for eternity in an intimacy that only faintly remembers loneliness as what was but now is not. For now, in this moment of union, nothing separates the Lover from his beloved (Rev 21:4). Not sin or fig leaves or even a cherubim with a flaming sword (Rev 22:3). Eden is restored in the shape of and through the power of the cross.

Gazing into his eyes, it's easy to forget to look forward to a place (heaven), because I'm simply captivated by the person (God). Lack of pain isn't what compels me forward. But the belief that one day I will come face to face with *him*, and he will reach out and wipe away the tears streaming down my cheeks. Healing me with a touch. Soothing me as I sob. Reminding me that the old order of things has passed away, and from now on I will rest beside him. Beside the still waters of his Spirit that rests as clear as crystal, without a ripple disturbed by evil or angst.

He pulls me close and whispers, "It's okay. I'm here."

I feel him crying too. Not the same tears as my own but the tears of a tender Father proud of what his son has just accomplished, overcome by what his child has been through, overwhelmed by his love that seems to grow with each exhale in this tender embrace.

His squeeze lessens. I gently pull away. He stoops down, close to my ear, and turns me around with the tender command, "Look."

As far as I can see, hills are peppered with laughter. Creation playing with creation. Toddlers atop lions, grasping their manes as they gallop. Children piling on top of big brothers. Mothers smiling as they wipe dirt from the face of the young. Joyous cries as another teenager launches from the rope into the water that doesn't understand the word *drown*, for its only desire is to love and support those brave enough to plunge into its depths.

The trees sway and sigh, offering shade and leaves of healing to all who pass by and sit in silence and gratitude that, once again, humanity and creation are one. Are at peace. Not warring for attention or clinging to precious metals, not quarrelling under the bondage of decay. Truly in harmony, a trinitarian union, where one serves the other in a continuous cycle of love and self-sacrifice.

The grass groans with delight, with each step of God's beloved pressing down the petals, not doing damage but mutually coming together so that one moves the other. The clouds peruse the Edenic land in search of the parched, longing to water the weary and satiate the thirsty. The sun doesn't scorch but wraps every element of creation with the warmth of God's love. All creation in concert and in love with all creation. All creation mirroring the God of love who stopped at nothing to serve his own.

I long to know him. Not because of the place but so that when I enter heaven it doesn't feel foreign but feels more like home than the world whence I came. I want no surprises in heaven, for heaven is merely a reflection of its Creator, and I know him. All of him. By his design. For his glory. Through the cross of Calvary. Through the Revelation of Jesus Christ. God, fully unveiled. Fully known. Intimately so.

GOING DEEPER

> **THE TOOL:** Heaven. Our understanding of heaven is often divorced from our understanding of God. Yes, heaven is a place, but it's created by a person. Imbued with the divine will and love of God. Watch this video (www.ivpress.com/wood-10a) and wrestle with the following:

1. Heaven must transform our lives today.

   › How does heaven change the way you see today?

   › How does heaven change the way you live today?

   › How does heaven challenge the way you talk to your loved ones, your neighbor, or even your enemies?

2. If heaven is properly understood as "setting the wrongs right," what actions should we engage to bring heaven to earth today?

3. When you reflect on heaven, what characteristics of God surface?

> **THE TEXT:** The pursuit of God in Christ (Rev 21:1–22:21). Revelation 21–22 unveils our God as a God of pursuit. In creation, God pursues; in our rebellion, God pursues; in the incarnation and the procession of the Spirit, God pursues. Watch this video (www.ivpress.com/wood-10b) and answer the following:

1. Where have you seen God's pursuit in your own life?

2. If we become who we worship, how does pursuit play into the life of the disciple? Give examples.

3. Children love games of pursuit: hide and seek, freeze tag, and so on.

   › What insights do children offer us into the character of God?

   › What can we learn from children that will transform how we live today?

> **THE TAKEAWAY:** Writing prayers to God. Understood appropriately, Revelation is a written prayer. An experience of "in the Spirit" that John penned and God preserved for Christians to encounter. What follows is a challenge to emulate John by writing words to God. Here's how it works:

1. *Preparing to receive*

   ‣ Sit down with a pen and paper (or a computer).

   ‣ Offer a prayer of invocation, inviting God's presence to fill this space.

2. *Writing prayers*

   ‣ Set a timer for thirty minutes.

   ‣ Press start and write without stopping. Don't edit. Don't correct. Don't stop. Just keep writing.

3. *Vulnerability*

   ‣ Allow the Spirit to surface whatever God wants to unearth in your life.

   ‣ Explore the diamond as a precious gift.

4. *Thanksgiving*

   ‣ After the timer goes off, offer a prayer of thanksgiving to God for meeting you in this sacred space.

   ‣ If you're willing, share what God unearthed in you with a trusted friend or loved one.

APPENDIX

Interpreting Numbers in Revelation

NUMBERS PERVADE REVELATION: seven lampstands in Revelation 1, four heads of the beast in Revelation 13, twelve gates of the new Jerusalem in Revelation 21, and countless other examples. The sheer volume can be overwhelming, the interpretations bewildering. Yet there's a discernible strategy in John's use of numbers, predictable patterns understood by his audience. First, in Revelation, numbers aren't measured; they're weighed. They carry symbolic weight derived from the Old Testament. What follows are interpretations of key numbers in Revelation, along with their Old Testament referents.

THE NUMBER: FOUR

Definition

> Four is a number of completion usually attached to the earth.

> *Completion* indicates that the entirety of something is being addressed.

> For example, the "four corners of the earth" means "the *whole* earth."

Old Testament referent

> Ezekiel 7:2—"four corners of the land"

Numerical use in Revelation

> Revelation 7:1—"I saw four angels standing at the four corners of the earth"

Rhetorical use in Revelation

> Revelation 7:9—"a great multitude . . . from every nation, tribe, people and language"

THE NUMBER: SEVEN

Definition

> Seven is a number of completion usually attached to creation or the creative act.

> "Creation" isn't limited to past events but includes what's being created now or in the future.

Old Testament referent

> Genesis 1—God's creative act producing all of creation in seven days

Numerical use in Revelation

> Revelation 6:1–8:5—The seven seals binding the scroll

> As the slain Lamb opens each seal, God's new creation unfolds on the earth.

Rhetorical use in Revelation

> Revelation 1:3; 14:13; 16:15; 19:9; 20:6; 22:7, 14—Seven "beatitudes" ("Blessed is the one . . .")

> Each beatitude promises the holy ones unique participation in God's re-creation of the earth.

THE NUMBER: TEN

Definition

> Ten is a number of completion usually attached to a time period of suffering or persecution through which God proves to be faithful.

Old Testament referent

> Daniel 1:11-17—Daniel and his companions are tested for ten days by Babylonian officials, through which God demonstrates his faithfulness

Numerical use in Revelation

> Revelation 2:10—To the church of Smyrna, Christ reveals an impending ten-day persecution through which God will prove to be faithful

Rhetorical use in Revelation

> Revelation 20:4—The holy ones reign with Christ for one thousand years

> > The number one thousand is a trinity of tens: $10 \times 10 \times 10$.

> > Thus, the number one thousand is a number of completion indicating a period of suffering or persecution through which God's reign is realized.

THE NUMBER: TWELVE

Definition

> Twelve is a number of completion usually attached to God's people.

Old Testament referent

> Genesis 49:1-28—The origin and God's blessing of the twelve tribes of Israel

Numerical use in Revelation

> Revelation 21:12, 14—The new Jerusalem has twelve gates engraved with the names of the twelve tribes of Israel and twelve foundations inscribed with the names of the twelve apostles

Rhetorical use in Revelation

> See "144,000" below

THE NUMBER: 144,000

Definition

> 144,000 is the complete number of God's people who endure a period of suffering or persecution through which God proves to be faithful.

Old Testament referent

> There's no clear Old Testament parallel to this number.

Numerical use in Revelation

- ➤ Revelation 7:4; 14:1-3—Those sealed by God who worship the Lamb in the new creation
  - ➤ 144,000 is $12 \times 12 \times 10 \times 10 \times 10$
    - ➤ The number twelve is a number of completion usually attached to God's people.
    - ➤ The number ten is a number of completion usually attached to a period of suffering or persecution through which God proves to be faithful.
  - ➤ The dyad of twelves and the trinity of tens intensifies the symbolic weight for each number.

BIBLIOGRAPHY

Altink, Willem. "Theological Motives for the Use of 1 Chronicles 16:8-36 as Background for Revelation 14:6-7." *AUSS* 24, no. 3 (Autumn 1986): 211-21.

Amorth, Gabriele. *Padre Pio: Stories and Memories of My Mentor and Friend.* San Francisco: Ignatius, 2016.

Appian. *Roman History.* Translated by Horace White. 4 vols. LCL. Cambridge, MA: Harvard University Press, 1912-1913.

Aune, David E. *Revelation.* WBC 52A-52C. Nashville: Thomas Nelson, 1997-1998.

Barton, Tamsyn. *Ancient Astrology.* London: Routledge, 1994.

Bates, Matthew W. *The Birth of the Trinity: Jesus, God, and Spirit in New Testament and Early Christian Interpretation of the Old Testament.* Oxford: Oxford University Press, 2015.

Beale, G. K. *The Book of Revelation.* NIGTC. Grand Rapids, MI: Eerdmans, 1999.

Beard, Mary. *The Roman Triumph.* Cambridge, MA: Harvard University Press, 2007.

Beasley-Murray, G. R. *The Book of Revelation.* New Century Bible. Grand Rapids, MI: Eerdmans, 1974.

Behr, John. *John the Theologian and His Paschal Gospel: A Prologue to Theology.* Oxford: Oxford University Press, 2019.

Bousset, Wilhelm. *Die Offenbarung Johannis.* 5th ed. Göttingen: Vandenhoeck & Ruprecht, 1906.

Caird, G. B. *The Revelation of Saint John.* Black's New Testament Commentaries. Reprint, Peabody, MA: Hendrickson, 1999.

Charles, R. H. *A Critical and Exegetical Commentary on the Revelation of St. John.* Vol. 1. International Critical Commentary. Edinburgh: T&T Clark, 1920.

Church, Alfred John, and William Jackson Brodribb, trans. *The Agricola and Germania of Tacitus.* London: Macmillan, 1877.

Cicero. *The Orations of Marcus Tullius Cicero.* Translated by C. D. Yonge. London: George Bell & Sons, 1903.

Collins, Adela Yarbro. *The Combat Myth in the Book of Revelation.* Reprint, Eugene, OR: Wipf & Stock, 2001.

———. *Crisis and Catharsis: The Power of the Apocalypse.* Philadelphia: Westminster, 1984.

Daltrop, Georg, Ulrich Hausmann, and Max Wegner. *Die Flavier: Vespasian, Titus, Domitian, Nerva, Julia Titi, Domitilla, Domitia*. Berlin: Mann, 1966.

Dio Cassius. *Roman History*. Translated by Earnest Cary. 9 vols. LCL. Cambridge, MA: Harvard University Press, 1914–1927.

Dionysius of Halicarnassus. *Roman Antiquities*. Translated by Earnest Cary. 7 vols. LCL. Cambridge, MA: Harvard University Press, 1937–1950.

Ford, J. Massyngberde. *Revelation*. Anchor Bible 38. New York: Doubleday, 1975.

Friesen, Steven J. *Imperial Cults and the Apocalypse of John: Reading Revelation in the Ruins*. Oxford: Oxford University Press, 2001.

———. *Twice Neokoros: Ephesus, Asia and the Cult of the Flavian Imperial Family*. Religions in the Graeco-Roman World 116. Leiden: Brill, 1993.

Gunkel, Hermann. *Schöpfung und Chaos in Urzeit and Endzeit*. Göttingen: Vandenhoeck & Ruprecht, 1895.

Hafemann, Scott J. "Roman Triumph." In *Dictionary of New Testament Background*, edited by Craig A. Evans and Stanley E. Porter, 1004-1008. Downers Grove, IL: InterVarsity Press, 2000.

Hemer, Colin. *The Letters to the Seven Churches of Asia in Their Local Setting*. Reprint, Grand Rapids, MI: Eerdmans, 2001.

Hendriksen, William. *More than Conquerors: An Interpretation of the Book of Revelation*. Reprint, Grand Rapids, MI: Baker Books, 1982.

Hurtado, Larry. *Lord Jesus Christ: Devotion to Jesus in Earliest Christianity*. Grand Rapids, MI: Eerdmans, 2003.

John of the Cross. *Selected Writings*. Edited by Kieran Kavanaugh. New York: Paulist Press, 1987.

Korfmacher, William Charles. "Vergil, Spokesman for the Augustan Reforms." *Classical Journal* 51, no. 7 (1956): 329-34.

Livy. *History of Rome*. Translated by B. O. Foster. 14 vols. LCL. Cambridge: Cambridge University Press, 1919–1959.

Louw, Johannes P., and Eugene A. Nida, eds. *Greek-English Lexicon of the New Testament: Based on Semantic Domains*. 2nd ed. New York: United Bible Societies, 1996.

Lund, Nils W. *Chiasmus in the New Testament: A Study in the Form and Function of Chiastic Structures*. Reprint, Peabody, MA: Hendrickson, 1992.

Lupieri, Edmondo F. *A Commentary on the Apocalypse of John*. Translated by Maria Poggi Johnson and Adam Kamesar. Grand Rapids, MI: Eerdmans, 2006.

Maximus the Confessor. "On the Lord's Prayer." In *The Philokalia: The Complete Text Compiled by St Nikodimos of the Holy Mountain and St Makarios of Corinth*, compiled by St. Nikodimos of the Holy Mountain and St. Makarios of Corinth, translated by G. E. H. Palmer, Philip Sherrard, and Kallistos Ware, 2:285-305. London: Faber & Faber, 1981.

Middleton, Paul. "Revelation." In *T&T Clark Social Identity Commentary on the New Testament*, edited by J. Brian Tucker and Aaron Kuecker, 585-620. New York: T&T Clark, 2020.

Moffatt, James. "The Revelation of St. John the Divine." In *The Expositor's Greek Testament*, 5:279-494. Grand Rapids, MI: Eerdmans, 1951.

Ogilvie, R. M. *The Romans and Their Gods in the Age of Augustus*. London: W. W. Norton, 1969.

Osborne, Grant R. *Revelation*. Baker Exegetical Commentary on the New Testament. Grand Rapids, MI: Baker Books, 2002.

Pasquale, Gianluigi, ed. *Padre Pio's Spiritual Direction for Every Day*. Translated by Marsha Daigle-Williamson. Cincinnati, OH: Franciscan Media, 2011.

Paul, Ian. *Revelation*. Tyndale New Testament Commentaries. Downers Grove, IL: InterVarsity Press, 2018.

Philo. *The Works of Philo*. Translated by C. D. Yonge. Peabody, MA: Hendrickson, 1995.

Pleket, H. W., and R. S. Stroud. *Supplementum Epigraphicum Graecum*. Vol. 41. Leiden: Brill, 1994.

Rolfe, J. C., trans. *Suetonius*. 2 vols. LCL. Cambridge, MA: Harvard University Press, 1913.

Rowland, Christopher C. "The Book of Revelation: Introduction, Commentary, and Reflections." In *The New Interpreter's Bible*, 12:501-736. Nashville: Abingdon, 1998.

———. *The Open Heaven: A Study of Apocalyptic in Judaism and Early Christianity*. New York: Crossroad, 1982.

Sandy, D. Brent. *Ploughshares and Pruning Hooks: Rethinking the Language of Biblical Prophecy and Apocalyptic*. Downers Grove, IL: InterVarsity Press, 2002.

Schüssler Fiorenza, Elisabeth. *The Book of Revelation: Justice and Judgment*. Philadelphia: Fortress, 1985.

———. *Revelation: Vision of a Just World*. Minneapolis: Fortress, 1991.

Shea, William H. "The Covenantal Form of the Letters to the Seven Churches." *AUSS* 21, no. 1 (Spring 1983): 71-84.

Stanley Spaeth, Barbette. "The Goddess Ceres in the Ara Pacis Augustae and the Carthage Relief." *American Journal of Archaeology* 98, no. 1 (January 1994): 65-100.

Strack, Hermann, and Paul Billerbeck. *Commentary on the New Testament from the Talmud and Midrash*. Edited by Jacob N. Cerone. Translated by Joseph Longarino. Vol. 3. Bellingham, WA: Lexham, 2021.

Strand, Kenneth A. "A Further Note on the Covenantal Form in the Book of Revelation." *AUSS* 21, no. 3 (Autumn 1983): 251-64.

Tacitus. *The Agricola and Germania of Tacitus*. Translated by Alfred John Church and William Jackson Brodribb. London: Macmillan, 1877.

Teresa, Mother. *Come Be My Light: The Private Writings of the "Saint of Calcutta."* Edited by Brian Kolodiejchuk. New York: Doubleday, 2007.

Thomas, David Andrew. *Revelation 19 in Historical and Mythological Context*. New York: Peter Lang, 2008.

Thompson, Leonard. *The Book of Revelation: Apocalypse and Empire*. Oxford: Oxford University Press, 1990.

Velleius Paterculus. *Velleius Paterculus and Res Gestae Divi Augusti*. Translated by Frederick W. Shipley. LCL. Cambridge, MA: Harvard University Press, 1924.

Versnel, H. S. *Triumphus: An Inquiry into the Origin, Development and Meaning of the Roman Triumph*. Leiden: Brill, 1970.

Virgil. *Ecologues, Georgics, Aeneid*. Translated by H. R. Fairclough. 2 vols. LCL. Cambridge, MA: Harvard University Press, 1916.

Walvoord, John F. *The Revelation of Jesus Christ: A Commentary*. Chicago: Moody, 1966.

Wiseman, T. P. *Remus: A Roman Myth*. Cambridge: Cambridge University Press, 1995.

Wood, Shane J. *The Alter-Imperial Paradigm: Empire Studies and the Book of Revelation*. Leiden: Brill, 2016.

———. *Between Two Trees: Our Transformation from Death to Life*. Abilene, TX: Leafwood, 2019.

———. "God's Triumphal Procession: Re-examining the Release of Satan in the Light of Roman Imperial Imagery (Revelation 20:7-10)." In *Currents in British Research on the Apocalypse*, edited by Garrick Allen, Ian Paul, and Simon Woodman, 209-23. Tübingen: Mohr Siebeck, 2015.

———. "Interpenetration Logic: Pauline Spirituality and Union with Christ." *Religions* 13, no. 8 (2022): 680. https://doi.org/10.3390/rel13080680.

ILLUSTRATION CREDITS

2.1. Two out of the thirty-five to forty Attic deities atop the Temple of Domitian in Ephesus. *Image by Shane J. Wood.*

2.2. Statue of Domitian from the Temple of Domitian in Ephesus. *Image by Shane J. Wood.*

2.3. Open-air altar from the Temple of Domitian in Ephesus. *Image by Shane J. Wood.*

2.4. Vespasian: *RIC* 2.1 (69/70 CE). In celebration of Jewish subjugation. *Image is Public Domain (PDM 1.0).*

3.1. Family photo of Shane J. Wood preaching at age three. *Image by Shane J. Wood.*

4.1. Galba: *RIC* 1.60 (68 CE). Roma stands on a globe in victory. *Image used with permission of Classical Numismatic Group (www.cngcoins.com).*

4.2. Vitellius: *RIC* 1.16 (69 CE). Winged Victory stands on globe triumphantly. *Image used with permission of Numismatica Ars Classica.*

4.3. Titus: *RIC* 2.162 (79-81 CE). Vespasian hands Titus a globe. *Image used with permission of Classical Numismatic Group (www.cngcoins.com).*

4.4. The Ara Pacis Augustae altar (front). *Image by Shane J. Wood.*

4.5. The Ara Pacis Augustae altar (upper register: front left). Remus and Romulus. *Image used with permission from Rabax63 (Wikipedia Commons), under the CC BY-SA 4.0 license.*

4.6. The Ara Pacis Augustae altar (upper register: front right). Aeneas. *Image used with permission from Carole Raddato (Wikipedia Commons), under the CC BY-SA 2.0 license.*

4.7. The Ara Pacis Augustae altar (upper register: back right). Roma seated on pile of weapons. *Image by Shane J. Wood.*

4.8. The Ara Pacis Augustae altar (upper register: back left). The goddess Pax enthroned. *Image by Shane J. Wood.*

4.9. The Ara Pacis Augustae altar (lower register). Floral scroll. *Image used with permission from Carole Raddato (Wikipedia Commons), under the CC BY-SA 2.0 license.*

6.1. Family photo of Shane J. Wood's family nativity scene with a red dragon. *Image by Shane J. Wood.*

6.2. Diagram of the two trinities: holy and *unholy*. *Image by Shane J. Wood.*

6.3. Diagram of the two trinities and their respective followers. *Image by Shane J. Wood.*

8.1. Map of the seven hills of Rome. *Image used with permission from Reneta3 (Wikipedia Commons), under the CC BY-SA 4.0 license.*

8.2. Vespasian: *RIC* 2.108 (71 CE). Roma reclining on seven hills, with Remus and Romulus suckled by the she-wolf. *Image used with permission of Classical Numismatic Group (www.cngcoins.com).*

8.3. The Capitoline Wolf statue. *Image by Shane J. Wood.*

8.4. Vespasian: *RIC* 2.961 (77/78 CE). She-wolf suckling Remus and Romulus. *Image is Public Domain (PDM 1.0).*

9.1. The Arch of Titus (front). *Image used with permission from ThePhotografer (Wikipedia Commons), under the CC BY-SA 4.0 license.*

9.2. The Arch of Titus (inner panel: procession of menorah). *Image used with permission from Carole Raddato (Wikipedia Commons), under the CC BY-SA 2.0 license.*

9.3. The Arch of Titus (inner panel: the quadriga). *Image used with permission from Carole Raddato (Wikipedia Commons), under the CC BY-SA 2.0 license.*

9.4. Trajan: *RIC* 2.777 (112–114 CE). Jupiter and a quadriga. *Image is Public Domain (PDM 1.0).*

9.5. Vespasian: *RIC* 2.1127 (ca. 70–71 CE). Quadriga in a triumphal procession. *Image used with permission of Classical Numismatic Group (www.cngcoins.com).*

9.6. Open-air altar from the Temple of Domitian in Ephesus (side panel). *Image by Shane J. Wood.*

9.7. Open-air altar from the Temple of Domitian in Ephesus (front right panel). *Image by Shane J. Wood.*

9.8. Open-air altar from the Temple of Domitian in Ephesus (center panel). *Image by Shane J. Wood.*

SUBJECT INDEX

SCRIPTURE INDEX